A█████ █ARSH was born in Essex, and worked as a typesetter, an advertising person and an internet expert before moving to Norfolk as a househusband and self-employed writer. It was here that he unexpectedly found himself a minor internet celebrity with privatesecretdiary.com, described by the *Independent on Sunday* as the work of 'a post-modern Mr Pooter'. Having already once hit the musical big-time, with a support slot for the Sultans of Ping at the Pink Toothbrush club in Rayleigh, he hopes to repeat this success both on the rock stage and on the bowling green. He is 39.

ALEX MARSH

Sex and Bowls and Rock and Roll

FRIDAY
BOOKS

The Friday Project
An imprint of HarperCollins*Publishers*
77–85 Fulham Palace Road
Hammersmith
London W6 8JB

www.thefridayproject.co.uk
www.harpercollins.co.uk

This edition published by The Friday Project 2010

1

A catalogue record for this book
is available from the British Library

ISBN 978-0-00-735547-1

Set in Minion by Palimpsest Book Production Limited,
Grangemouth, Stirlingshire

Printed and bound in Great Britain by Clays Ltd, St Ives plc

For R, with thanks for putting up with me.

It was a new day yesterday, but it's an old one now

'Are you sure that we're meant to be here?' I scuffed my feet over the shingle, not willing to let this go. 'It doesn't matter that we're not members?'

'I'm a member,' reassured Big Andy, pulling his bag out of the boot. I was already intimidated by its professionally battered look, as if it had been passed down through generations of top-level bowls players. Big Andy had always struck me as somebody who would be good at any sport – he is just one of those people. Personally, I have always suspected people who are good at sport – I certainly never thought that I'd end up being friends with one. Perhaps his likeability was just a ruse, in order to lull me into a false sense of security before he chucked me in the showers and stole my dinner money.

'Yes, but we're not,' I insisted, jerking my head towards Short Tony who had jumped down from the back seat. At least he would be as culpable as me. Big Andy didn't answer this, clearly not appreciating my genuine concerns.

I did not even have the right shoes.

The green itself was sheltered behind a low wooden fence that shielded from public view a raised concrete path and two weather-beaten benches. Big Andy placed his gear on one of these; Short Tony followed suit with me lagging behind, surveying the scene with narrow, wary eyes, Clint Eastwood in *A Fistful of Bowls*.

'What if a man comes and shouts at us?' I wondered aloud.

I have never been a particularly confident type – at least, not without a guitar in my hand. All the key memories from my early life are scary, nerve-inducing ones: accidentally wandering into a fierce lady's garden in order to pick acorns from her oak tree. Discovering that the hand that I'd reached up to grip tightly for reassurance wasn't actually my grandmother's, but belonged to a random stranger who happened to be getting off the same bus. Getting the phone number wrong on a big press advert for the Royal Philharmonic Orchestra and thus ensuring that a Barnet pensioner was telephoned at ten-minute intervals by people seeking tickets for a grand Tchaikovsky gala at the Royal Albert Hall.

There are two types of people in Britain – people with the confidence to take risks with social etiquette, and people who spend their lives concerned that a man will come and shout at them.

'Who'd shout at us?' asked Big Andy.

I considered this.

'The groundsman.'

'Naaah. He's fine.'

My nervousness did not abate. I didn't know any of the other club members and I did not want to start our relationship off on the wrong foot – certainly not as a shoutee.

'Some other important club official?'

'Earlier this year, we came up here on our own a lot,' he insisted. 'It's practice. And practice is always encouraged.'

'Are you sure?'

'How will you know whether you want to play,' he demanded, 'if you don't know whether you're any good or not?'

Short Tony, who was looking upon the experiment as the start of a potentially interesting new hobby, similarly did not have proper bowls shoes. But they were at least brown, and from a distance they looked like proper bowls shoes. Mine looked like non-proper non-bowls trainers. I studied the terrain carefully. There was some long grass at the far end, where the green ended and met the farmland beyond. If a man came and shouted at us for playing without permission then I would attempt to quickly step into the long grass, thus camouflaging my footwear and ensuring that he would not be able to follow up his 'Trespasser!' shout with: '*Plus you have not got proper bowls shoes on!*'

I tried to make myself relax. It didn't help that I was probably going to be rubbish at this, and thus make myself look like an idiot. I took a deep breath. There was no man in sight. Instead there was the weak but encouraging-looking sun of an autumnal, early lunchtime casting dewy shadows on an English bowling green.

'Pint, anyone?' offered Short Tony, motioning his head towards the big pub that stood looking over us like a comforting older brother appearing with a towel after the rough beating-up kids have been dispersed.

This seemed like a good idea, but I was cautious.

'Are we allowed?' I asked. 'To take drinks onto the green, I mean.'

Short Tony disappeared off to buy beer.

The grass was soft and earthy, with well-worn patches from a season's play. I padded around guiltily in my clandestine trainers. Big Andy handed me two of his woods; I tossed them down carelessly and they made small indentations in the surface. I drew breath sharply, but no shout came. He then disappeared into the small shed that adjoined the green, re-emerging seconds later with a white ball. Disappearing into a shed! Some people have all the self-confidence. If illegal walking on a bowling green wearing incorrect shoes merited a shout, I was sure that shed-disappearing would warrant at least something cruel and unusual.

The bowls police failed to leap out from behind a hedge and charge us with electric batons.

I picked up a single wood. It was wet from the grass, but felt comfortable in my hand, warm and smooth, not the wood of a guitar body, but a pleasing object nonetheless. I have nice dainty, nimble hands and I suspected that it might be slightly too large a size for them, and perhaps a little heavy for me to be totally sure of control. But I did not say anything for fear of bowls ridicule.

Big Andy, my tutor, lobbed the cott ahead to the other side – it bumped and bobbed on the grass. He then knelt and expertly pitched his wood, which rested intimidatingly close to the target. I watched Short Tony reappear from the pub, ambling up the short hillock and across the gravel car park with a tray of beers the colour of bowls shoes.

And then it was my turn. It is always good to give new things a try. But I couldn't honestly see it being my sort of thing.

ONE

New towels for the old ceremony

'Excuse me?'

There is a voice. I turn, surprised, from the post box to locate its source.

A man is ambling over from a small four-by-four thing. He is demonstrably from a town somewhere – it is one of those designer jobs that no genuine country-dweller from round here would dream of possessing. The engine chugs over, chug chug chug chug chug. He is clearly the source of the 'Excuse me.' I allow my letter to fall from my hand into the post box's receptive womb, easing my wrist from its slot and giving my new acquaintance my full attention.

Silver-haired, he is wearing immaculate cream pressed slacks, which reveal that he is comfortably off and retired, and probably has a wife named Pat.

'I don't suppose you know where these agents are based?' He gesticulates towards the 'For Sale' sign on the bungalow over the road.

A number of houses around mine are for sale – I do not know whether to take this personally or not. This particular one right opposite has been on the market since about Wednesday, 14th March at 11.32 a.m., and I am excited that I might be meeting a

5

potential new neighbour. New people! I study his face closely. I will need to remember, so that I can report the details back to everybody at the village pub.

I give him the information he requires, waving my hand in the general direction of the coast. He asks me what living in the village is like, and I offer him long examples of how we all know what each other is doing and just pop into each other's houses to say hello at any time of day or night, sometimes when we have been drinking heavily. It is a neighbourly community like that. He looks a bit less enthusiastic after this, and glances over his shoulder several times as he retreats to his car before accelerating off at some speed, doubtless to catch the estate agents before the shops close for the evening.

He did seem like a pleasant chap, and I am determined to stick by my parting words to him: that I would be quite happy to give him a hand with carrying all his stuff from the van when he eventually moves in.

Before he disappears around the corner, I make sure to take the number of his car. He is not from round here, after all, and he could have been looking at houses for sale with a view to committing some crime. I remember it all the way across the road, all up the path and into the kitchen, where I scribble it on the corner of some newspaper, along with 'Old bloke. Silver hair. McJeep.'

There is no more excitement, but it will be good to have something extra-interesting to tell the LTLP when she gets home. Time is getting on – I need a bath and something to eat before I go.

*   *   *

I can't remember exactly when I gave up.

It was probably on a platform at Harringay Station. Perhaps and probably it was raining. Harringay Station in the rain, fighting with hundreds of others for a modicum of shelter under the narrow footbridge, the loudspeaker broadcasting crackling messages of doom from a British Rail announcer based hundreds of miles away in a secret bunker buried deep beneath the Cairngorm mountains.

'We apologise for the delay to the seven forty-four service to London Moorgate. This service is running approximately fifty-two minutes late. The first train to arrive will be the eight fourteen service, also to London Moorgate. Due to a short train, this service will consist of half a coach only, which will be of convertible open-top design, have no seats, and will be powered by passenger-manned oars. We apologise for any inconvenience that this might possibly cause you. To cheer you up, here is some music by the Stereophonics.'

When I say 'a platform', that implies a multitude of the things. In fact, there are but two platforms at Harringay Station. Standing, boxed in, elbow to arse with frustrated Key Account Executives and Change Implementation Managers and Human Resource Officers. Waiting, worrying if the tingly electricness of the rain is a genuine cause for concern as it drips from the overhead power lines onto your face. Pacing, irresistibly tempted to bolt for that footbridge, to leap aboard one of the frequent empty and invariably on-time trains returning north from the City, and head for the overwhelming excitement and vibrancy of Enfield Chase, New Southgate or, at a pinch, even Potter's Bar. But of course you don't. The train arrives and you fight for any form of nook, stuffing yourself frantically up against your fellow passengers like a veal calf undergoing sardine-replacement therapy.

Yes, it must have been then that I gave up. Then.

I've never given up on the music, however.

OK, I'm a bit older now. But Debbie Harry was already thirty when Blondie was formed; she was thirty-five when they released 'Atomic', which would have made her almost as old as I am. And yet she was famous and successful the world over at this late age, becoming an icon and achieving sales in the millions of millions, with men becoming physically sexually aroused – literally *sexually aroused* – whenever she sang or appeared on *Top of the Pops*. I've almost got there once, having supported the Sultans of Ping on one key date of their seminal 1992 UK tour. But Debbie Harry is one hell of an inspiration, and a lesson to anybody who thinks that exciting popular music can only be made by teenagers. Given just one small lucky break, there really is no reason whatsoever why I should not be the next Debbie Harry, but with women.

I call her 'the LTLP' for the purposes of the narrative.

I don't want to upset her by using her real name. The WAGs are generally lower-key than their football equivalents; more down-to-earth and less publicity-hungry. She is my life-partner and has been for a long time; one of the very few people who have been both WAG and rock-chick wife. Every bowls player needs their Yoko Ono figure. She gives me an airy wave as I leave the house.

The canvas bag is weighty, betraying my relative novice status with its clean newness. It contains my four bowls (or 'woods', as we bowls people know them), an old beer towel for wiping purposes and some deeply, deeply unfashionable shoes. You have to have four woods, even though you only ever use two, as otherwise the other bowlers will laugh at you and think that you are some sort of idiot amateur without all the proper equipment. I lug it down the drive, across the road, and then sprint to Big Andy's as fast as an unfit fat bloke carrying a rigid square bag of heavy bowls implements can sprint. He is jangling car keys impatiently; Mrs Big Andy stands hands-on-hips in their doorway, shaking her head and making 'have a good evening, if this is *really* the way you want to spend your Friday night' noises. I leap into the passenger seat and we are away in a haze of dust and sporting expectation.

In my pocket: house keys, some small change, a mobile phone. A mobile phone! Why do I bother with a mobile phone these days?

I do not have important people to call any more; there is no reason why anybody would need to get hold of me. I get the odd text message from Short Tony that simply reads 'pub?', but seeing that he lives in the cottage next door you cannot really count the mobile connection as a vital communications lifeline. My mum and dad have a mobile phone but do not know how to use it; the LTLP knows where I'll be all day. My friend Unlucky John, the only other person in the world whom I speak to, tends to prefer mobile to landline. But he's in London, where such status is important.

It is a comfort thing, however. I will have it to hand should there be an emergency at bowls. The LTLP's employers have given her a BlackBerry, which means that half the emails that pop up in my inbox with a cheerful 'bing!', causing such excitement and anticipation, turn out to be mundane and uninteresting things like 'get the dinner on and don't burn it this time you idiot'. So I took her old phone when my one finally gave up the ghost. It is a bright lurid pink Motorola, small and dainty, and adorned with girlish graphics.

But who cares? Once, this pink phone would have been a shameful accessory for me, as I wandered amidst the Neanderthal plains of people in chequered suits and wanky black-rimmed spectacles, of braying rah rah me me me idiots, of money-and-status-obsessed bottled-beer-drinking, testosteroned pre-Dibley clowns. That's one of the big advantages of living in a tiny village in Norfolk. Nobody is particularly bothered about the superficial. Just one more stupid unnecessary mental weight that disappears when you leave the world of commuter trains and Strategic HR Initiatives.

It's an easy-going game; none of the other bowlers really mind if you leave your phone on through the evening. Aside from that one time when it escalated a bit, and people ended up shouting 'Well fuck you then! Fuck you!' at each other, across the green. That was an exception.

Personally, I have a system. I keep my mobile phone switched on just in case there *is* an emergency or somebody important does call – but I make sure that I leave it in the pocket of my anorak which hangs in the clubhouse. That way nobody will hear it ringing and be disturbed during a crucial end. It seems a reasonable compromise.

* * *

Yes, my name is Alex Marsh and I play bowls.

I am thirty-thing years old, and I play bowls. Bowls is what I play. I am not ashamed of it; I do not seek to apologise or be defensive. I play bowls. It is not as if I am Mrs Karen Matthews, or have been exposed having sex with livestock on YouTube, or wrote and produced 'There's No One Quite Like Grandma'. I play my bowls with pride. I would shout it from the rooftops, but I am afraid of heights.

My name is Alex Marsh and I play bowls. And so does Eddie, and Nigel, and Big Andy, and even John Twonil's been persuaded to give it a try. We are the exciting new faces of the sport. It sits oddly with the guitar hero status, I know. But there have been stranger combinations. Rock and roll, bowls; bowls, rock and roll. There's nothing mutually exclusive – it does not need to be an either/or. One does not preclude the other. It is perfectly possible to both jack, and to Fleetwood Mac.

Barry Hearn knows.

Barry Hearn is the legendary sporting Svengali who does the snooker, and boxing, and darts. The man who made Steve Davis. The Don King of Romford. The Billy Graham of the baize. What Barry Hearn doesn't know about marketing sport isn't worth knowing. And he thinks bowls is going to be the next thing – which is why he has put it on Sky TV, during peak morning viewing. So scoff at the beautiful sport at your peril.

I suppose I have mixed feelings about this. It is like when you discover a new band – you want them to be your own special band all to yourself. You do not want them to become popular and mainstream and put on by consensus as background music at dinner parties. And whilst wishing your special band all the goodwill in the world, you would rather that they starved in the gutter than enjoyed any form of commercial success, as this would spoil it for you.

Something a bit like that happened to my own band. However, more of that later.

Will bowls as we know it survive the Sky TV experience? Will it retain its unique nature, or will it sell out to the forces of Evil Marketing? Will the money grow and nurture it, or will it corrupt it? Will it retain the nobility of sport, or will it descend into a new WWF pantomime?

The television camera itself is a great distortion pedal, a two-dimensional screen that loses the subtleties and many of the unsubtleties also. When you watch cricket, it's impossible to judge how fast the bowler's letting the ball go – you have to work it out from where the wicket keeper's standing. Football is robbed of the intense physical aspect, horse racing is sterile without the flying hooves and mud; long pots on the snooker table appear easy and unmissable. I would not want the casual Sky TV viewer to see what I do every week and to dismiss it casually as some gentle meandering pastime. That would be crushing. But I think Barry Hearn and I are on the same wavelength.

Barry Hearn knows that it's the new rock and roll.

'Here you go.'

Nigel strides like a parade sergeant before the row of benches, where we are sitting changing into our deeply, deeply unfashionable shoes. He stops at each player and hands out new kit from a plastic bag – a brand-new, pristine, never-been-used, soft and lovely Stella Artois beer towel.

'Thanks!' I say in surprise.

'I got them from work,' he explains, moving on to Glen. 'Given to me.'

Along the line, people take their towels and beam in gratitude, holding them up to look closer. Matching beer towels! The whole thing looks bloody professional, in tune with the new image of bowls, a co-ordinated wave of red that will raise pride and morale in the team, aside from providing more efficient wiping.

That's us. The village bowls team. Sponsored by Wifebeater Lager.

It's just a roll-up tonight. No opposition – merely a friendly opportunity to get together and to have a bit of practice before the league starts in earnest. But there is still a buzz of excitement in the air. The dawn of a new season – the first date on my headlining UK tour. The bowling green is my raised stage; the woods are my guitar, and the mat represents my effects pedals. I have not actually ever been on a headlining UK tour, but the parallel is there. The scoreboard is my set list; the beer towel is my guitar lead. Nigel, skipper of our block, is my bass player; Big Andy is my drummer. We don't have a screaming hysterical audience of teenage girls – our most loyal and regular supporter has been unable to turn out to spectate since he got his foot amputated – although Eileen is here, and she sometimes likes to sit and watch, chucking in the odd heckle, in lieu of playing. But the parallel is definitely there.

I am pleased with my analogy. Songwriting is all about analogies – good songwriting is all about unexpected, hidden ones. 'There She Goes' by the La's is about heroin, not a lady who is going. Really, playing bowls is just like being in a successful rock band. I can't really see many differences.

Big Andy, Nigel and I do play like a well-drilled trio. We are comfortable in each other's presence; there is a telepathy between the three of us, like Cream (featuring Eric Clapton). We don't feel under pressure in front of each other; we barrack and praise each other in equal measure, and we go to the village pub afterwards. That's the difference between a 'side' and a 'team', although just to be confusing, in bowls it is called a 'block'. We are settled together this year – I have high hopes that our near-telepathic under-standing will give us a big advantage. There is mutual respect and support there.

There are moments in making music when it all comes together. When you're rehearsing a new song, the band hits a new chord change, someone drops in a phrase, hits a particular note and it's just – right. You catch the eye of the bass player, of the drummer, and you know. That's a magic moment. The tension resolved; the song opens out into perfection.

It's the same when the skip bowls and you can see the wood coming towards the pack – slowing and arcing for the gap you pointed out, running out its weight perfectly, nudging past the short woods, skipping the bare patch, squeezing through the narrowest of spaces and finally falling to a halt touching the cott itself. It's magic, it's perfect. It's like the big piano chord at the end of 'A Day in the Life'.

It's time to start playing again.

TWO

Last night a Strategic HR Initiative saved my life

Past the church gates, past the old Methodist chapel, up through the Tofts and out between the fields of beet. Past the small shed in the woods that acts as the hub of BT's broadband activities in the area; down the hill through the woods to the junction with the main road that will take me into town.

I've lived in three places in Britain: Essex, with my mum and dad; London, in a flat underneath a man with an enormous toilet; and here, in this small and friendly corner of Norfolk. It's here that I truly feel at home, in this place that's impossible not to love, in countryside and a community where I truly belong. Where I have my friendly neighbours (Big Andy, Short Tony, etc.), my close family (the LTLP) and – perhaps for the first time in my life – true and unconditional membership of a youth tribe (bowls). DJ Ken Bruce asks a question on the radio, the answer to which is clearly 'Norman Greenbaum'.

Past the gates of the old airfield, up the gentle hill towards the old service station. The sunshine washes across the fields and hedgerows and the music fills the car. I'd say that it was the sort of morning that made it impossible to have a worry or a care in the world about life, if I weren't so worried and full of cares about life and – specifically – the morning ahead itself.

I park the car and slowly walk up the street towards my appointment. It's a nice day, but let's not get complacent. It's at just these sorts of moments when life has a habit of hitting you in the face with a hammer.

I am hit in the face with a hammer.

I recoil from the shock and surprise. Not being complacent is one thing, but it is fair to say that I was not expecting anything quite so unpleasantly *literal*. The man hits me in the face again. Boff.

It is not a nice feeling, not a nice feeling at all, and improves not one jot when he repeats his assault twice more.

At some point, I tell myself, I should say something. He does seem pretty competent, and I get on with the chap reasonably well (although perhaps less so now, seeing that he is hitting me in the face with a hammer), but truth be told it is an unpleasant experience and I would like him to stop.

'Diss crown is priddy impossible to shift,' he explains, in a South African accent. 'I hev tried wiggling it with dee pliers. Now I am hitting it with diss hemmer.' He bashes my tooth with his hammer once more, to emphasise the point. Boff.

Randy Newman wails from my MP3 player. Unfortunately, I have absent-mindedly selected the wrong 'genre' in my haste for musical distraction, and instead of uplifting and rousing cheerful pop music, my head is filled with mournful minor-key reflections on losers and low-life tragedies in the medium of the blues, whilst I am being hit in the face with a hammer.

The anaesthetic seems to have made my face swell up, as if somebody has pushed a marble into my mouth and under my top lip. They may well have done. Or perhaps it is a snooker ball. It certainly feels the *size* of a snooker ball. It could be a penis, for all I know. I have my eyes firmly shut. I do not wish to open them as the hammer is unpleasant enough as it is without watching its descent. I can't believe that it is a snooker ball – what dental purpose would that serve? I also do not think it is a penis, as he would not be hammering it so hard if so.

The only really good thing about a dentist putting his penis in your mouth and starting to hit it wildly with a hammer whilst you are under local anaesthetic and have your eyes firmly shut and are listening to mournful Randy Newman songs is at least you know that you will get offered some mouthwash afterwards.

'It's coming,' he explains, not entirely reassuringly.

The sterilising machine in the corner of the dental surgery starts up with a big 'whooooosh'. It makes me jump, but diverts me momentarily from the hammering, and from Randy Newman, who has just finished singing a verse about a girl who stole his car and went on to cause a traffic accident, running over a man named 'Juan'. Randy Newman sounds particularly extra doleful about this; he has no car, and undoubtedly his insurance will be affected. The 'whooooosh' is presumably steam, but sounds remarkably like an enormous toilet being flushed.

* * *

Adam's enormous toilet was, due to a quirk in the architecture of the London flat conversions, situated directly above my face.

This is what it had sounded like anyway when I lay sleeplessly in bed, my stare fixed on the ornate ceiling, marvelling at the noises that could be made by a simple item of plumbing. Whooosh! it went. Rushhhh! Sloshhh! It is virtually impossible to describe to somebody who has never lived in a converted Victorian house just how loud the noise of a man weeing in the flat upstairs can possibly be. Cities are never quiet, but the background noise will fall to a dead silence when set against the watery rumble of half a pint of urine hitting the base of an enormous toilet bowl over one's head. The roar of the main stream, the sonically perfect echo of each single salty droplet as it splashed back against the rim.

Sloshhh! Slosssssshhhhhh!

I had been on friendly terms with Adam. He was an amiable man who tended to keep himself to himself, but would always be up for a cheery 'hello!' as we passed on the stairs. Living on his own, his habit was to go to the pub each evening, returning at around midnight to start weeing.

I would lay in bed listening to the performance, work anxieties surging around my head. Beside me, the LTLP would snore gently in her anxiety-free woman's world. As the weeing tailed off, the noises of the city would gradually fade back in: some drunks shouting, the clatter of freight on the East Coast line, perhaps somebody trying to steal my car. And then forty minutes or an hour later, the weeing cycle would begin once more.

Sloshhhhh! Slosssssshhhhhhh!

Boff. Boff.

Another couple of bashes with the hammer brings me back to the present day.

*   *   *

The music fills my head to bursting point. Piano, bass, slidey guitar. As each chord hits home, I concentrate hard on trying to envisage myself playing it; the shape of my left hand across the strings, or the sensuous womanly caress of a minor seventh on the ivories. It is not enough to dismiss the hammering stuff, no matter how I want it to. Boff. I blink to myself. Why am I here? Why the bloody hell am I here? The hammer pauses for the gap between songs and then starts up again in earnest.

Why am I here?

Boff boff boff boff.

Why the bloody hell am I here?

Boff the boffy-boff boff boff boff.

Why the . . . and more to the point, how is this man hacking into my own personal inner monologue in order that he can hammer in perfect time with it? I give him an angry look from behind my protective goggles.

Why am I here?

Boff boff boff boff.

* * *

Why *am* I here? Here in Norfolk, pressed rigidly down into a dentist's chair, being hit in the face with a hammer.

Lots of reasons.

The little picture reason is that I have a toothache; an abominably bad toothache that crept up on the roots of my incisors; a toothache that has lingered like a man in my area who has come round to give me a free consultation and a no-obligation quote.

The medium picture was the Harringay Station Herd, and the fact that my life seemed to consist of: wake up, fight my way to work, work, come home, listen to man weeing.

But the big picture was all to do with Strategic HR Initiatives.

* * *

Strategic HR Initiatives. The foundation stones of modern business. The management engines that are so vitally important to ensure that the companies of UK plc can innovate, thrive and come out clear winners in the global war for talent. There is nothing as pathetic as a moribund stuck-in-the-past company, doomed to hostile takeover, bankruptcy or a slow slide into sales oblivion because of the absence of great – or the implementation of poorly thought-out – Strategic HR Initiatives. That is why we must have them. And just as these initiatives invariably transform the fortunes of the smallest partnership to the most major conglomerate, so they have profound effects on individual employees.

This is what happened to me. Admittedly not *quite* in the way that was intended, but there you go.

I guess you would say that I had been quite successful in business alongside the musical accomplishments. Admittedly I hadn't actually *started* any businesses, or employed any people myself, nor had I spotted an idea that had become really really big and had led to my share capital becoming millions of pounds overnight. However, I had managed to get paid every month without killing anybody or provoking employment tribunals or bringing the company to its knees by confusing 'Press F1 for Help' with 'Press F8 to Delete Exchange Server' on the IT system.

I just wasn't entirely happy.

Modern, bland, large, rectangular. I was in a meeting room dominated by an impressive glass boardroom table – an artefact that had been hand-picked by somebody who knew the vital importance in business of impressive glass boardroom tables. I loitered at the back, nervously crushing and reforming my plastic tea beaker, thinking that perhaps I should be taking a more visible position with the other management types.

Dusty windows watched out across the City of London towards the bowling green at Finsbury Square – this was no glamour view, however, but the rooftops of low-rise rented office accommodation: fire escapes and heat extraction systems. Occasionally during a meeting I would identify the pipework of a particularly interesting heat extraction system and follow it around as far as my eye would go. It was a bit like examining the fantastic exhausts of a spaceship in the year 2508. The air shimmered above it, like on Venus.

Inside, we had no heat extraction system. The space was close and humid; there were too many people present. The lift was broken again – a succession of bodies staggered in, loosening ties with the sweat of a six-floor climb.

A succession of board-level speakers had lined up to intone to the room. This happened every week, as a way of motivating people for the days ahead. Words and phrases lumbered through the thick air towards and past me; some clung exhaustedly to the wall behind, some expired and slumped in defeat to the nylon carpet. It was, to all intents and purposes, a perfectly normal Monday morning.

And then, out of the blue, I had started to catch some of these words. And the interminable speaker of the moment drawling in a monotone as turgid as the very turge itself:

'La la la la la la la know that we are all genuinely excited about this new Strategic HR Initiative that we've been working on.'

I gaped at the man. The words churned round my head as I tried to grip hold of them. And as the phrase settled down inside me I looked around the room and, to my horror, saw a sea of nods of interest and concentration and enthusiasm and thoughtful assent. Left, right, left again. Nods – genuine nods. And the fear gripped me, with the icy fingers of a creeping Gantt chart. These people were not pretending; this was no sham for personal corporate advancement, no calculated sucking-up to the powers-that-be.

I was in a room with people who were genuinely excited about a new Strategic HR Initiative that was being worked upon.

It was alarming. My eyes darted round the room looking for exits. I was too far away from the door. They would catch me and wrestle me to the ground and beat me and inject me with the Strategic HR Initiative serum that the others had been given. Catch me! Catch me and inject me! Tape an institutional hub across my eyes and force delivery outcomes into my anus. Brandishing photographs of Harringay Station and massive tubes of Toilet Duck.

That's why I'm here.

Randy moves on a track.

If that's why, what's how?

How did this major change happen? What coup did I pull off, what stroke of daring, what gamble did I take with my life, risking it all on the throw of one die for the sake of a new horizon? Like a frontiersman of the early days of the American nation, what was in my mind as I grimly stowed a rifle and provisions in the wagon, pulled my woman close to me and explained that – for all the dangers, the unknowns, the immense hardships – sometimes a man has to strike out and face these, in order to carve a new life from the dust and rock?

'I'll expect dinner when I get in every night,' said the LTLP. 'A proper one.'

Sexual equality has come a long way in a very short space of time. For thousands of years there were very clearly defined roles for the genders: the men would do the fighting and hunting and making the decisions etc., whereas the women would do the stuff at home and have babies. Then, from the sixties onwards, society entered a period of hypocrisy. This was when women were ostensibly given the same opportunities as men, but thwarted at every turn with casual sexism. Meanwhile, blokes still would not get involved with domestic chores.

It is impossible to say why the final sea-change occurred: perhaps it was the sudden nineties surge in the average male's confidence about their sexuality, perhaps it was the advent of *The Vicar of Dibley* on BBC1. But we are happily out of the sexist Neanderthal period, and it is not unusual at all now for men to do women's jobs like housework or cooking. Twenty years before, options simply wouldn't have been available to me, and I would have been forced to remain a stressed, insomniac, on-a-downward-spiral putting-a-brave-face-on male provider. But with a flash of fortune, I was the beneficiary of a second sexual revolution.

I became a househusband, and I'm not ashamed.

('Househusband' is not quite the right word, as it is a bit effeminate. But it will do as a short-term description.)

So that was it. I shed the trappings of Neanderthalism and stepped bravely into my own corner of twenty-first-century post-Dibley Britain. The LTLP took her massive and important new job in the east of England, and I took my huge leap of faith. I packed up, I handed in my resignation. We said goodbye to friends, goodbye to Harringay Station, goodbye to meeting rooms and motivational addresses, goodbye to Adam in the flat upstairs with his enormous toilet.

And, gobsmackingly, I said goodbye to the band.

Taking my last few big gulps of choking, Strategic-HR-Initiative-polluted London air, I had felt joyful for the first time in a decade. A stressed businessman, with all the trappings of success but with no time or energy to make the most of them, I was downshifting to the countryside to enjoy a better quality of life. Truly, it was a unique step that I was about to take – a pioneering move that I couldn't believe that anybody else had ever thought of, ever.

* * *

'You won't know it . . . I'll be right behind you . . . don't try and run away . . .' There should be an emergency Randy Newman button on MP3 players for just this situation. You would press it and it would immediately leap to something cheerful by S Club Seven or the Proclaimers. 'Little girl . . . wherever you go . . .'

The dentist now has my tooth by the pliers, gripping the crown and pulling and wiggling hard. It is like a surreal silent movie. I half expect him to put a boot up against my chest to aid leverage, or to use the pliers to pull my head back and forth exaggeratedly, bashing it alternately against the mouthwash basin and the head-rest. I would laugh, except he is pulling my tooth out with pliers having hit it repeatedly with a hammer.

A few more yanks and my old artificial tooth thing is no more; I have a huge gap in my mouth that is dripping pus and blood along with an unidentified fragment of metal that appears to have been left in there by a previous dentist. We take a two-minute break before he starts to clean out the abscess – but it could be two hours for all I know, such is my state of stunned distress. Randy croons dolefully in my ears.

When I was a small child, I fell off my bike quite spectacularly, via the simple mistake of trying to emulate not just US daredevil Evel Knievel and his stunt bike, but the plastic US daredevil Evel Knievel that you could wind up and send soaring over a dozen Matchbox lorries, as featured on Channel 4's *I Love the 50 Top Toys That You Should Not Try to Emulate.* I required an immense amount of dental surgery as a result, but I cannot remember those particular times being as bad as this. I suspect my teeth have become more sensitive as I've got older. The session finished, I take my jacket with shaking hands and stumble from the surgery in a dull state of shock.

The road outside is noisy; market town traffic passing each way, a brewery lorry unloading. But I hear nothing. I just walk, my eyes fixed on some random point in the far distance, my mind blanker than it has ever been. I take out my mobile phone to ring the LTLP, but a passer-by looks at me very oddly and as I do not feel like talking anyway, I shove it back into my trouser pocket.

I feel utterly alone. With shock I realise that I am already sinking into negative thoughts so early in my brave battle against tooth abscess. I should do something positive. If I write to the *Observer* demonstrating that I can face tooth abscess with wit, good-humour and poignant humanity then they will probably give me a column in their magazine, 'Tooth Abscess and Me'. Being the person who brings the 'TA' word out of the darkness of taboo and into an environment where people are not afraid to talk might be my crowning achievement in life.

'Crowning'!

Even in my lowest hour, I can still laugh at my own very funny jokes. I rejoice in the smile that spreads across my war-torn face as I traverse the mini-roundabouts and head towards the centre of town and the pharmacy.

THREE

Return of the grievous bowls players

Past the shop, past the village pub and south, where the cottages peter out and there dwell just deer, pigs and pheasants. Across the Peddars Way, the ancient thoroughfare that brought the Romans from Suffolk to their holiday villas on the north Norfolk coast; down through the fields and woodlands of the Royal estate to the main road. Popular Radio 2 DJ Chris Evans spurs us on, playing 'Can You Feel It' by the Jackson 5. If there was ever a record to pump you up for a bowls match then it is 'Can You Feel It' by the Jackson 5.

Game one. Game on.

Unusually, we have a passenger. Karen has joined us this year, from another club. It is her very first game for us, and she will probably be intimidated and nervous. Big Andy and I put her at her ease in between funking along to the music.

'Canyoufeeeeelit!' I sing, indicating right.

'It's quite a nice green tonight, although you wouldn't expect it right in the middle of town,' says Big Andy.

'And it's directly behind the pub,' I add. 'Although to be frank it was a bit lively in there when we went last year. 'Bahbahbahhhh-bahhbahbahcanyoufeeeeelit.'

'Wasn't there a fight or something?' he asks.

'I don't think it was exactly a fight,' I recall. 'I think it was just a bit lively. There was lots of shouting and stuff. Certainly I remember the barmaid running in and hiding behind the door. But then it was almost . . . six o'clock on a Friday night.' I slow down as we approach a roundabout. 'Baahbahbahhhbahhhbahhhbahhh-canyoufeeeelit!' I add.

'Hopefully we'll be there with a bit of time to spare,' says Big Andy. 'Get a quick pint before we start.'

'Right,' says Karen.

It is good to have a bit of new blood in the team. We struggled for players last year, after the club suffered green-uncertainty, and we had almost considered dropping out of the Thursday night league altogether. But a strong showing in the tables and our reputation for being a good-natured bunch of people have held us in good stead.

'You might find that we take it a bit less seriously than some of your old lot,' I call over my shoulder, as the Jackson 5 make way for the traffic report. 'We've got some good players, but everybody's there to have fun. There's a – there's a good atmosphere about it, is the best I can say.'

We will indeed be in good time. Park the car, go for a quick pint, get into the Zone. When you play bowls, it is very important to get into the Zone. Mental and spiritual preparation is everything.

'A good atmosphere,' confirms Big Andy, as we pull to a halt.

'No we are not fucking all right,' snarl Ron and Vicky, stepping out of their car and responding to my cheerful greeting quite alarmingly angrily. 'He hasn't picked us, has he? Years we've played for this club! Well he's a fucking arsehole so we've turned up here anyway to fucking tell him so, and he can stick his fucking bowls club where it belongs.'

The Zone announces a temporary suspension and apologises for the inconvenience.

'Right . . . um,' I reply.

'No offence to you lot, and we wish you well, but it's time he had a piece of my mind, and I shall fucking give it to him when he arrives and it won't be pleasant, I can tell you,' says Vicky.

'We've got the trophies from last year – he can fucking take those as well,' adds Ron.

'Um – perhaps we'll go for a quick pint and leave you to it,' suggests Big Andy.

'Best not to interfere,' I agree.

I see a car approaching out of the corner of my eye.

'Here he is now,' says Ron.

As the car pulls up, we realise that it is not Howard the club captain, but Nigel. I make frantic 'we are going to the pub, quick quick stop the car and leap out and join us as fast as you can as there is going to be an angry scene in the car park' gestures. But he just blinks at us in incomprehension, so we sportingly abandon him.

'Just a little disagreement,' explains Big Andy as we hasten away.

'Right,' says Karen.

I can see both sides of the quarrel. Doing the Human Resources for a small club is not a job that I would personally volunteer to do, even if I wasn't so busy at the moment what with the stuff at home and the sorting out the band and things. It is a thankless and tiring task, and you are always likely to upset someone in the act of doing it. But I have always got on well with Ron and Vicky, having played in their block many a time. I hope it will sort itself out, somewhere else, where I won't be involved with people shouting 'fuck' at other people. Big Andy clearly feels the same. We will hide bravely in the pub until the scene is over. It has always been a nice pub.

The pub is closed.

An aroma of angry dispute drifts on the air from behind us. 'It can't be closed!' I moan, pulling once more at the door, ignoring the scrunch of broken glass beneath my feet.

'It's definitely closed,' confirms Big Andy, stepping back from the tightly drawn blinds, the empty bottles discarded on the step, the sign on the door saying 'This Pub is Closed'.

There are more raised voices. We stand awkwardly on the concrete slabs, thinking that perhaps a cheerful and very slightly out-of-breath publican might suddenly arrive with a key. I wander round the corner to the other side of the pub. That side of the pub is closed as well.

'I guess we could just walk the streets for fifteen minutes?' I wonder.

There is a small huddle of players clustered by the gate to the green as we nervously walk back with a view to sprinting around the edge of the car park and thus not getting involved in shouting and finger-poking. It transpires that the gate is locked, so we join the huddle, like refugees from the Gaza Strip. We examine our shoes as the argument approaches. They really are very interesting shoes. You can stare at them for ages without getting bored. The stitching runs all the way round, from the heel, round the toes, back to the heel again. And they keep your feet warm. Warm. And dry.

'I'm sorry about that little scene,' the club captain says help-lessly, as his antagonists disappear in a cloud of petrol.

A greenkeeper arrives to unlock the gate. We traipse in slowly, in single file, still fixated on our shoes. The Zone hangs up a small sign: 'This Zone is closed'.

* * *

The rules of bowls are simple.

Of course, I mean the local rules: the rules that we play by every Friday night before we go to the village pub; rules that are probably written down somewhere but that may as well be unwritten, that have been passed down by generations of Norfolk bowlers. I am sure that there are variations in different counties, in different leagues, or when you go overseas to any of the other great bowls-playing nations. But as far as I am aware, there is no Sepp Blatter of bowls; no white-capped Juan Antonio Samaranch figure passing resolutions and presiding over standardisation. I guess there is Howard, who goes to the league meetings and picks the team. Howard, or Barry Hearn.

In any case, there aren't many rules in the big scheme of things. Not compared with cricket, or American football, or just living in general. If we assume that everybody knows the object of the game – to get as close to the cott – the little white ball – as possible, then we can dispense with that and get on to the important bits. And the most important bit comes at the very beginning of each match, before a mat has been laid or a wood tossed.

The first, undisputed law of bowls is to shake your opponent's hand and wish him a good game.

'Have a good game.'

'Have a good game.'

'And you – have a good game.'

'Have a good game.'

'Have a good game.'

If you are playing triples – three on each block – as is normal on Fridays, then that equates to eighteen announcements of 'have a good game'. That is, I wish each of the three people on the opposing block a good game, and each of those three wishes one back – six 'have a good game's. This is repeated by the two colleagues on my side, making eighteen declarations in total before you even acknowledge your own side. That is not all, however. A 'block' is merely one-third of a bowls team – we play nine-a-side, three blocks playing their separate games side-by-side on different parts of the green ('rinks'), their individual results being added together to decide the outcome of the match. That is fifty-four 'have a good game's resounding around the green, drifting amidst the trees and the mats and the scoreboards and echoing off the hedgerow. Often it is dark before we have finished wishing each other a good game.

And 'have a good game' it must be – that is the wording that is acceptable. There is no 'good luck'; no 'have a nice one'; no simple 'cheers' or 'all the best'. 'Have a good game' is the phrase that is said, and has been, and always will be.

'Have a good game.'

Cricket was my first sporting love.

Travelling with my dad to watch him play, my own small child's kit stashed hopefully in the boot, in the wishful anticipation of one of the men suffering a horrible injury and being unable to continue. Watching my dad intently as he stood crouched like a panther in the gully; ambling around the boundary together as he waited for his turn to bat. And then – oh joy! – somebody would be too slow to move and would be hit in the nuts at silly point, and I would be called upon to substitute. And then cakes at tea, and being given cider in the pub afterwards. What could be a better way of spending a Saturday afternoon for a boy?

Then making it into the team, and running around, and batting and bowling, and buying cider in the pub afterwards. And playing with your dad, and discovering rock music, and skipping the odd game because of band practice, and leaving before the cider to go drinking with your new friends, and not having so much time on Saturdays to do stuff with your dad, and . . .

I think I am a bit fat to play cricket these days. I did give it a go again a couple of years back, but I was really only still good at the cider bit, and after a while I became aware of small boys lurking around the ground, regarding me as a dead-cert nuts casualty. It was fun, but I don't miss it. That was then and this is now.

Football was never my thing. I did play at a reasonably high level, for the 3rd Billericay cub troop. My position was left back, which, as my dad explained to me, was probably the most important position on the field. Unfortunately, none of the other cubs realised this, and they used to shout things like 'Haha – left back in the changing room, more like! Left back! Left back in the changing room!' I didn't move on to another club when I left the cubs. My fellow players eventually went on to become people in the City with aggressive suits and wanky spectacles and too much testosterone. They were happy times.

Tennis half-killed me, and I was never built for rugby, so now it's just a bit of snooker, with John Twonil, Mick and Short Tony and the gang – and the bowls. I wonder what would have happened had I discovered bowls at a very early age? There are probably hundreds of thousands of small boys who have never had a chance to play; never seen a bowling green. It is a shame, and the reason why Barry Hearn must succeed.

* * *

Triples – three on a block. Each has a specific role: the 'skip', the 'lead', who bowls first, and the one who bowls second/in the middle, who does not have a particularly satisfactory title.

The first thing that you'll not appreciate on Barry Hearn's television coverage is this: when you step forward to bowl, you can't really see what's happening at the other end – the 'head' of woods that collect around the cott. It is too far away, and difficult to judge distances between the woods. This is the role of the skipper – to stand by the head, making judgements about the position of each wood and letting you know what's going on via a combination of words and gestures. These will include his recommendation on what would be the best shot to try in the circumstances. Sometimes this is a gentle suggestion, sometimes a barked order followed up with 'Oh well – do it your own fucking way then.' Skips have different styles.

Each player has two woods to bowl. The home and away skippers bowl theirs last, their responsibility being to tie everything up – not merely hoping to gain points for the team, but perhaps to knock an opponent's wood out from a scoring position, or to block things off in front in order to protect an advantage.

If you're the one in the middle, then you have a dual role to play. First, you will be looking to build up a good strategic position within the head, to make the skipper's life easier when he comes to claim the points. Second, you will sometimes be called upon to merely get as close to the cott as possible, if the lead bowler has failed to trouble the surrounding grass with his efforts.

The lead has a simple job – a very simple one. The lead must bowl two woods that come to rest right next to the cott, thus putting the opposition on the back foot from the word 'have a good game'. It is a big responsibility, and it takes a certain type of person to make a good lead. Paradoxically, as your two colleagues are yet to bowl, there is the opportunity of rescue, and thus the lead position is also a good place to hide somebody if they are shit.

I usually bowl lead.

Unlike many sports there are no white line markings, behind which you must stand. Instead, as you bowl, part of your body needs to be in contact with the mat. It's a black mat, but the colour isn't particularly important. Clubs can get hold of mats from specialist bowls providers, who can supply a range with a combination of grips and surfaces to suit wet or dry weather conditions, indoor or outdoor surfaces, or with their own logo embossed in the rubber. Ours are reassuringly bog standard.

Placing the mat is the responsibility of the lead bowler. It is a responsibility that brings much pressure. The exact position of the mat is defined in the rules – but the rules tend to be different for each league, and are complicated, involving distances. In general, you can split bowlers into two groups – those who know exactly where the mat should go, and those who haven't a clue. Being in the latter camp, and as a lead bowler, I have a particular mat-placing strategy that seems to work in all scenarios. I chuck it on the ground where I think it might go nicely, and if anybody shouts at me then I move it to where they say. It's the same for both sides. If you get excited about poor mat-positioning then you are very likely an arse, and should be formulating Strategic HR Initiatives rather than wasting your time playing bowls.

'Oh dear,' I mutter, as I land about ten feet away from my target. We are rusty; I am rusty. No matter how many rehearsals you go through, nothing will prepare you for leaping up on stage in front of an audience of thousands. Likewise, the roll-up has blown away a few cobwebs but that is all. It doesn't prepare you for the pressure of a match situation. I concentrate very hard for my second wood. I need to take quite a bit of pace off it, and give it a wider angle.

'Oh dear,' I repeat.

Some people would call the little white ball a 'jack' – in fact, this is probably the more commonly recognised term worldwide. A 'cott' or 'the dolly' are stubbornly local designations – I've never heard anybody use the J-word. If you referred to it as a 'jack' around here, people would immediately spot you for a tourist. It would be like walking through Edinburgh wearing a kilt and eating shortbread.

So the skips stand at the other end of the green, giving you instructions based on their reading of the game. But when the lead and second have bowled their two, then it's their turn. Everybody swaps places. We walk up to the head of woods; the skips return to the mat.

The halfway pass is a key moment. Normally, it is the cue for a whispered 'Well done!' or a muttered apology, or a snarl of contempt. Sometimes you might stop to discuss a tactic or two; sometimes you might fit in some constructive feedback.

'Put in a long cott. They haven't worked out the slope.'

'You're bouncing them slightly. Try to get closer to the ground as you release.'

'That was, without doubt, the biggest load of dog shit bowling that I have *ever* seen in my life.'

And suddenly, as you approach the cluster, the woods open out to reveal exactly what is going on in there. Invariably, your shot that you thought was really good turns out to be rubbish, whereas your shot that you thought was rubbish is still rubbish. Under normal circumstances it would be mine and Big Andy's turn to shout at Nigel. We enjoy this. We usually shout things like 'I'd go this way if I were you. Or that way.' Big Andy tends to offer lots of advice, I am often less vocal. Nigel listens and then does what he was planning to do anyway, which is usually for the best.

Bowls is scored very simply – the closest team to the cott gets the points. So if you have the two closest woods, and your opponent has the third closest, you get two points and he gets nothing. Even if that third closest is still very close indeed.

'Can't play next week – I'm going to Lord's,' Nigel mutters as we cross.

We stare at him; so much for well-drilled trios and mutual respect and support. 'Lord's,' I repeat.

'See the West Indies,' he explains.

No shots are counted until the end is finished. Tonight, Big Andy is getting one or two close, I am getting one or two close . . . but then their skipper is stepping up and rolling one closer. He is very good, demoralisingly so. Despite the initial Zone fiasco, we'd be winning by miles if it were just Big Andy and me against their support act. As it is, the game balances evenly – swinging this way and that, with one side never more than a couple of points ahead.

We go into the final end one point down. Then something odd happens – their skipper misses his shot twice. He's been playing like a bowls god all evening, but the pressure has got to him. We shrug in surprise as his second wood pulls up two feet short and wide. A missed drop shot, a saved penalty, Lewis Hamilton going through on the inside – who needs the likes of the West Indies when bowls can produce its moments of high drama such as this?

Final score: our block wins by one. The other blocks are yet to finish; the overall outcome will depend on their results, but Jason is a few shots behind and we are not going to make up that margin. A few minutes later and it is confirmed – but we have had a good game several times over. The mats and scoreboards are collected; the captains sign the cards. A big piano chord descends over the green.

We pass the closed pub sadly on our way out of the car park. Bowls is not a game to be played dry.

* * *

The village pub is austere and slightly intimidating from the outside, sitting haughtily in its prime position at the head of the little settlement. The whitewashed brick is always pristine; the metal tables dotted around outside polished and gleaming; the menu neatly typed in its menu box beside the front doors. Inside, modernity intrudes – some odd modern art prints and the remaining nine-tenths of the chandelier that Big Andy's raised fist had connected with after Liverpool scored in the Champions League. The left turn into the main bar reveals a smaller than expected room – the presence of an enormous chimney breast carving the area into an awkward 'L' shape that would make it very difficult to accommodate a band and PA equipment. I've thought about this a lot, and the only practical solution I can think of would be to move all the chairs and tables and set up at the very apex of the 'L'. There would still be very little room for the sort of audience that I would envisage, but they could overspill into the corridor, from where we could sell T-shirts and souvenir programmes.

There are more modern art prints, and a wooden floor that catches the light from the huge old mullioned windows that look back out across the road. There is a lot of history behind the building, I would expect, but really the main point of interest about the place is that it sells beer, will sell it to me, and I don't need to pay for it immediately due to my bar tab arrangement.

Here dwell the people with whom I spend my life: the staff – principally the Well-Spoken and Chipper Barman; Mike, Ben and Lottie – and the regulars, who stand clustered in the usual area, adjacent to the Mini Cheddars. Short Tony from next door; Len the Fish, who knows all there is to know about fishing and fish; John Twonil who drives the bus for the old folk; Eddie with his soft Cambridgeshire burr. I chuck my stuff on the side of the bar and throw my coat on the back of a stool, where it's gazed upon suspiciously by Len the Fish's dog – a rustic and uncomplicated countryside dog, the epitome of uncomplicated countryside dogginess in this epitome of uncomplicated countryside.

'Is that your phone?' gasps Short Tony incredulously.

I explain the phone situation, matter-of-factly. It would be foolish to spend money on a new flashy Londoner's phone when I hardly make any calls at all, and when the LTLP has a perfectly good one that I can use. Everybody laughs at the thought.

The Chipper Barman is a placid character. I am sure this placidity disguises some deeply hidden threat; his slightly short and swarthy appearance conceals a robust frame beneath. In fact, he is a double black belt in something from the Far East and despite being a steady and thoughtful chap, he could probably steadily and thoughtfully break your neck. I am always careful to compliment him on his barrel-tapping.

With the momentary rush at the bar easing off, he acknowledges us with a nod, wandering slowly over to the corner where we live.

'Show him your phone!' someone prompts.

The Chipper Barman's face lights up. 'Girl's phone! It's a girl's phone! Hahahaha!'

There is a bit more laughter, which I am starting to think might be at my expense rather than the ludicrous fashion-victimness of city types. It is good-natured, and I smile it off, but I am surprised by the 'pink is for girls' sexist implications, to be quite honest. It is as if *The Vicar of Dibley* never happened. I am not particularly affected by it – it is just boring and predictable. If people want to spend hundreds of pounds on the latest gadget when there is one in perfect working order that they can get for free then they are the idiots, not me.

John Twonil returns from the toilet.

'Mppphhhhhffrggghahahahaha!' he chortles, bringing up the phone thing again. He is bloody immature for somebody his age. Short Tony and Big Andy join in once more. So are they. Even Mrs Short Tony, who you think would have some sort of gender solidarity.

'You are wasting your breath,' I inform them. 'Water off a duck's back.'

Honestly, they are all living in the dinosaur age. It is the post-sexist twenty-first century now, and if I want to carry round a pink phone then I am perfectly at liberty to do so. The world has moved on, and I am proud to say that I have moved with it. There is a bit more laughter at my expense. I smile it off and place my order. The banter of the locker room is part and parcel of sport, and bowls is no exception; to be teased and wound up (albeit immaturely and unfunnily) means that you have genuinely arrived.

FOUR

There were three fine English boys

I go for a run.

Run, run, run!

Across the road, right at the tiny bus shelter, past the secluded bungalow that neither the silver-haired man nor Pat, his wife, have ever returned to. He was probably a time-waster, bored, with nothing else to do during the day. Across the lane that leads up to the church and towards the village shop and the back lanes.

Many people who knew me of old might find this unlikely. I was never a particularly fitness-conscious person, and even now I wonder whether I am doing the right thing or whether I am just encouraging myself to drop dead. Against other males of my age, my height and weight do place me comfortably into the norm group; unfortunately it is the 'Norm from *Cheers*' group, and I have been advised quite forcibly that I should do something about this.

That is the LTLP and her all-encompassing medical knowledge for you. But I have to concede her point. I'm not a natural dieter. And whilst bowls and snooker are sociable pastimes, you cannot really count snooker as exercise. If a further honing of my athletic physique makes the love between us ever stronger then the odd run is a price well worth paying.

Psychologically, running is nothing like bowls. With bowls, once you get into the Zone, your focus is entirely on the pack of woods ahead – the game, and what you must do. But I have come to find that running sets your mind free once you have got your legs and lungs working. It's great quality time to reflect and to lose yourself in the world.

* * *

I love music. I love music really a lot, much more so even than John Miles in the song 'Music', where he takes pains to emphasise that was his first love and will be his last. For as long as I remember it has enthralled me, apart from a few years in the 1980s when Miner Willy on the ZX Spectrum said more about the anxieties and aspirations of teenage life than Limahl.

'Highway Star', 'Autobahn', 'There She Goes, My Beautiful World'. Things that touch me in the way that other art has never been able to. Film, paintings, mime – they are all very nice as media, but are as ping pong and horse dressage are to bowls: you'd watch them if they were on the telly, but could never become truly emotionally involved. Whereas there is nothing like a good song.

The first ever song that truly spoke to me was 'We Are the Champions' by Queen. I had heard pop songs before, of course, Bob Dylan's and Steeleye Span's and Leonard Cohen's – but they were my mum and dad's music. 'We Are the Champions' was mine. It came on the radio and it was the most brilliant thing that I had ever heard. When you are a six-year-old boy, it is extremely cool to be a Champion. It is the best. For a six-year-old boy, the song says everything about what you want your life to be: it is noisy, it is rousing, it involves punching the air a lot and it involves being better than everybody else, who are all losers compared to you. 'We Are the Champions' is the 'Teenage Kicks' of being six. Verse, chorus, verse, chorus, then a final chorus with mindbogglingly aspirational lead guitar soaring high above it, to end on that oddly and yet brilliantly unresolved bass note.

I do not listen to 'We Are the Champions' any more. I have immense respect for Freddie and Brian still, but I have a policy of not listening to music that might ever conceivably be played over the tannoy at any sports arena on the occasion of a goal or point being scored. This discounts much of Queen's later reper-toire, as well as 'Simply the Best' and the woman that constantly and repeatedly sings that she is Ready to Go. I find this policy protects you from much pain, and if it has meant that 'We Are the Champions' has disappeared from my personal playlist then that is sad from a personal history point of view, but a price well worth paying.

Listening is one thing, playing is another. I love playing music. I love the butterflies beforehand; I love the embarrassed blink when you realise that it is about time to start. I love the looks on people's faces as you hit the first couple of chords and they realise that you are going to be brilliant; I love seeing drunks dancing as they lose any awareness of your presence as a musician and just start getting into the groove. I love the power of being behind a mic stand and holding an excruciatingly amplified guitar that sings and hums and squeals even though you're muting all the strings because it's so powerful. I just love the noise that playing music makes. I love it.

I cannot imagine a time when I will not be playing music. Apart from the present day, when I don't have a band or anywhere to play.

* * *

Speak to any musician and they are likely to tell you that they started small. My personal musical journey began like so many others – in a garage band. Dave's dad's garage.

Teenage bands are the most important thing in the development of popular music. Everybody should be in a band when they are a teenager, whether they want to be a successful musician or just a nicely well-rounded character. It doesn't even have to be a very good band, although I like to think that ours was better than most. It teaches you discipline and interpersonal skills, unlocks the man or woman within and provides a way in to understanding and exploring the fundamentals of intellectual creativity, arts and literature.

This, I think, is what we were attempting when we formed Wildebeeste.

I had a cheap white Hohner electric guitar and a small practice amplifier. Dave played the bass, four strings of utter cool through one single enormous bigger-than-Adam's-toilet speaker. The low notes resounded around the concrete and breeze-block like earthquakes. His younger friend Iain was a drummer, with all his own gear: drums, cymbals, sticks. Even back then I knew that this would be the start of something big.

Wildebeeste had a limited repertoire, solely performing works by Pink Floyd. This was the single band that each of us knew some songs by. There was a limited audience locally for a teenage band that solely performed works by Pink Floyd, and – what's more – one that solely performed them without a keyboard player to include the bits that might make them sound a bit like Pink Floyd. But Dave had a birthday party planned for his eighteenth, so we were able to gain our one and only public booking, from his mum.

When we were not getting bookings from his mum, we stuck to practising hard in our garage studio, which we had customised by taping an eiderdown against the door to create a modern noise-free rehearsal facility.

Growing in confidence, we incorporated 'Walking on the Moon', a song that didn't need a keyboard player but that retained the slow tempo required to let us consider which chord to play well in advance. Meanwhile we were starting to write and eventually added two original songs. One was by Dave the Bass Player himself and was a simple straight-from-the-heart statement that he didn't like motor racing. It was called 'I Don't Like Motor Racing'.

The chorus went like this:

> The best thing about it is the theme tune
> The best thing about it is the theme tune
> The best thing about it is the theme tune
> The best thing about it is the theme tune.

As a chorus it was pure gold – direct, hard-hitting, to-the-point. After the second time round, we would stop and play a bit of the Fleetwood Mac motor racing theme, before hitting the final verse, which resolved with a reconciliation between the lyricist and the sport of motor racing.

To my mind, it is a song that still has the power to shock today.

The other original number in our set was mine, and I was mighty proud of it. It was called 'Aliens' and was weightier all round, having more chords and being concerned with the implications to society of prospective extraterrestrial contact. The chorus to this one was more imaginative than a simplistic motorsport-related chant and stemmed from my early philosophical conviction that the human race cannot possibly be alone in this universe of unimaginable vastness. It went:

> We are the aliens. We come from the planet Og.
> We look like a cross between a monkey and a dog.

*   *   *

Run, run, run! Over the crossroads that might provide a sneaky short-cut home via Big John's unnaturally elongated cottage, and up the brief but steep hill where the village starts to peter out into non-village. The grass is growing long here, and I keep my eyes firmly fixed on the ground, in case of dog shit. Then it is a hard left and I am back on the ill-maintained tarmac. The MP3 player moves on a track. It is Echobelly! This spurs me on more – it is good to keep up with what the kids of today are into. The immense opening guitar riff crashes into my ears.

I have a particular criterion for running music – it needs to be stuff that I can imagine myself standing on a stage and playing. That helps me concentrate and switch off from the agonising pain of the actual running. I am not just 'listening to music' with each step, I am experiencing it, examining the guitar, keyboard and drum parts, hitting the guitar solos, stepping up to the mic for the lead or backing vocals. To a non-musician this might appear odd. But it enables me to immerse myself in my world of perform-ance. I do not close my eyes, in case of dog shit, but my brain and being is there, adrenaline pumping as I belt out the MP3 tracks.

I don't have any tracks of Wildebeeste – just a battered cassette tape in a drawer somewhere. It is a shame. We deserved a bit more than that.

* * *

A three-piece band puts huge pressure on the guitarist. We weren't quite Cream (featuring Eric Clapton), but we approached the rapport of the Alex/Big Andy/Nigel bowls power trio. Dave was the larger-than-life character – the charisma of the band – the guy who would go on to do all the band's media interviews, as he was funny and could do a more-than-passable Richie Benaud imper-sonation. Iain was a quiet lad, who preferred his hi-hats to toms, which is unusual in a teenage drummer. I brought everything together like glue and, as you have seen, was already developing as a promising songwriter.

When you are in a band as a kid, you suddenly become cool.

I am used to being cool now, and being looked up to even by the likes of Eddie and Short Tony and the guys on the bowls circuit, but it is a shock when you are seventeen and have a friend-of-your-mum's haircut.

'I'm sorry – I can't hang around outside Budgens today. I have band practice. I have to go and get my guitar. The electric one. Because I need to go to band practice. With my band.'

That's what rock and roll is about.

We were so cool that other people did not realise how cool we were, because we were so cool. I guess our main problem was getting noticed by the musical establishment. If you are in a garage band today, you have a million outlets for your music. YouTube, MySpace and the internet in general – idiots from London can even download your songs as text messages to use as the sound for when their mobile phone rings. Like the Beatles, Queen, Cream (featuring Eric Clapton) and Pink Floyd before us, Wïldebeeste did not have this advantage of technology. And whilst those bands got their lucky breaks, we were stuck in our Essex commuter town, perfecting our sound in Dave's dad's garage. We just practised. We practised and practised. Waiting for our own big break that we knew was just around the corner.

* * *

Just around the corner is the last stretch of my usual circuit – a barely perceptible upslope that takes me from Colin's farm up to the church gates. In fact, my entire run appears to be a barely perceptible upslope, apart from the upslopes that I very easily perceive. It is like one of those impossible Escher paintings. I am trapped in it, like a Kafkaesque Steve Cram, a Sisyphean Dick Beardsley, for ever destined to run uphill around a village.

Beside me on the road, a car slows to a crawl. A head pokes out of the driver's window. I know what is about to happen.

Mixed feelings go through my head. Helping people with

directions is the best thing ever, as it proves that I am as local as local can be. But we runners do not like stopping mid-run. It makes the breathing and stuff go all funny.

The car is an old Fiesta. It has been sprayed luminous yellow, given an outsized spoiler and some wheels that have been taken from a more powerful and striking vehicle, perhaps a Ford Focus or a Vauxhall Viva. Bulbous arches complete the effect. Somebody has clearly spent some money on it. Although it's beyond me as to why they didn't use that to just buy a better car in the first place.

It is less a car than a cry for help.

I slow my jog, nod to the chap leaning out of the window, and remove my headphones in a gesture of communication. He looks at me from beneath his baseball cap.

'Scuse me,' sneers the man in the Car of Shame.

I do a bit of a double-take. This is a different sort of 'excuse me'. It is not the polite 'excuse me' of a well-dressed homeseeker, with a wife named Pat, who will be genuinely grateful for my help – it is 'excuse me' as a contemptuous throwaway, as an insult, as a challenge. Not knowing quite what to make of an 'excuse me' of this ilk, I slow to a halt, there in my tracksuit, jogging on the spot to keep the breathing going correctly, the living epitome of health and exercise.

'You got a light on you, mate?'

I gape at him. Although this is hardly the vibrant metropolis of Norwich or Fakenham, I can see at least three other people going about their business in the street or in their front gardens. No matter how I try, I just cannot comprehend the thought processes that have led him to conclude that I'd be the particular one likely to be carrying a silver Zippo and twenty Benson's. I pat my tracksuit apologetically.

'No. Sorry, mate,' I reply. I almost add: 'You got a copy of *The Brothers Karamazov*?' But I am keen not to be hit.

He does not reply, but sticks his foot down on the throttle and the car accelerates away. I am incensed by this rudeness. I want to shout after him: 'Don't you know who I am? Don't you fucking know who I am?' But this would involve finding something to do, and practising it really hard, then working at it for years and years until I receive some form of recognition from the public at large. So instead I stare at his rear lights angrily. I can see him swearing as he goes.

People like that don't respect real achievements. He probably knows as much about music as he does about bowls. I guess he would have been more polite had he seen me on the *X Factor* or *Pop Idol* or whatever it is people with hair gel settle down to watch in lieu of serious programming such as *Later with Jools Holland*. He's probably never even heard of the Sultans of Ping. This small incident makes me just a little bit more determined. It is criminal to leave a talent lying dormant.

I love music, and music has always loved me. Whatever I plan to do in the future – and if I am completely honest it is probably time that I started thinking about this in-the-future thing – perhaps it will involve music. I have a few irons in the fire. Some solo ideas that are running around my brain which might come to fruition. But it is early days.

There was no big break back then. Despite our coolness and two prospective dynamite gold top-ten singles, Wildebeeste petered out after a year or so. There was no single reason. We had no gigs, we had no transport, we had no focus. I wrote a couple of songs of which I was really proud but that the others rejected as 'too Jethro Tull'. It is not quite being dumped by your girlfriend or having your home address mixed up with a paedophile's in the local paper, but being told that you are 'too Jethro Tull' when you are a teenager can be firmly placed in the mental lever-arch file marked 'Disappointing'. The BBC lost the rights to cover motor racing to ITV; the title sequence changed accordingly – including the music. And whilst this was after the band split, and I am not claiming it as a major reason why we didn't make it big, it seemed to drive the final nail into our prospects.

I don't want to live in the past, but it is quite nice to pop in there for a short visit, and perhaps a spot of breakfast. It's so easy to be embarrassed by stuff that you've done when you're a kid. But I can think back and smile, given where I am today. We were a good little outfit, a good start. Yes, it's time to do something like that again. I have to. I really have to.

FIVE

These deeply, deeply unfashionable shoes are made for walking

Lord's.

Nigel is at Lord's.

So much for well-drilled trios and mutual respect and support. Pissing off to watch the West Indies and upsetting the delicate balance of the block like this. I haven't even donned my deeply, deeply unfashionable shoes yet, and already I am thinking negative thoughts about the game. I shake my head and curse my stupidity, dragging myself back into the Zone.

The first home match is always an interesting one. Let's get some points on the board.

Immaculate, fine grass, mown lovingly once lengthways and then once on the traverse, to create a geometric criss-cross of stripes that makes you want to hug the ground or at the very least stroke it with your cheek. Manicured borders and a white picket fence, with a wooden pavilion constructed simply but in the Edwardian style, with a small verandah. Three elderly men, rooted to the same seats since time immemorial, sit watching the play knowledgeably, smoking clay pipes, whilst a couple of wives diligently cut the crusts off ham and cucumber sandwiches.

I would imagine that some bowls clubs are like this. As for us, we sit outside the draughty builders' demountable hut that serves as our rain shelter and toilet, waiting for Howard to allocate the score cards for this agricultural square of land. You need a score card before you can move on to the 'have a good game's, as this tells you which rink that you'll be playing on and against whom – and there's not much you can do until you know that.

This is the key to home advantage. It's nothing to do with being comfortable in your surroundings, or having a large crowd to roar you on. It's certainly been a bit less since we were asked to vacate the nice green beside the pub. It's the fact that by rights it should take the opposition three or four ends to work out that there's a slight slope up and down, and that when bowling forehand on the uphill you need no angle at all.

Big Andy checks the card. Three – we have been given rink three. The one with the most pronounced hump three-quarters of the way on the downhill, where the skill is to attempt to bring the wood to a halt just on the prow where the grass is barest, so that it might roll gently down the other side vaguely towards the cott. We stroll across the green, up and down, up and down its undulations until we reach the mat. Light brown patches, dark green patches.

But it doesn't matter.

The Stones, the Beatles, The Who – all the great records from the golden age were recorded on primitive equipment. The Kinks had a cheap guitar and a broken amplifier, and produced 'You Really Got Me', whilst even well into the seventies, Pink Floyd were using Sellotape to stick together fragments of master tape to create 'The Dark Side of the Moon'. But then what happened? Pristine, flat, mown criss-cross stripe technology brought us Jean-Michel Jarre and Cher doing 'Believe'. The idea that rough-and-ready is by definition not acceptable is not something that needs necessarily to be brought to bowls.

EBA-affiliated greens generally benefit from the slickest

production techniques. The English Bowling Association is the national governing body for bowls, although affiliation is voluntary and the association has nothing to do with our own club. We play very occasionally on an EBA green, and the difference is palpable – formal notices, honours boards, professional green-keepers and flat, flat, flat. It is nice, but alarmingly favours the better bowlers, and most of us are just as happy with a flattish piece of grass and the services of a bloke with a mower.

I remove my Stella Artois beer towel from my bag and wipe my wood with pride.

*   *   *

If non-believers know one historical fact about bowls, it's that Sir Francis Drake refused to prematurely curtail his game, preferring to complete the final end before engaging and defeating the Spanish Armada. There's no firm evidence that this is anything other than a patriotic tale, although to anybody who's been forced by a sadistic enthusiast to play on through howling gales, squalls and electrical storms the story does have the ring of truth about it.

'We still have time to finish the game and to thrash the Spaniards too!' is the quote that's cited. One suspects that, in the remote event that this episode did actually take place, Drake was fortunate that we didn't go on to lose. Still, it is a good legend, and 'Drake's Pride' is now a well-known brand of wood and bowls equipment, endorsed by – among others – Short Tony.

Drake was a well-to-do sort but when it came to the lower classes, bowls was illegal in England – right up until the mid-nineteenth century. Henry VIII had worried that the sport would distract workers from their jobs; that they would piss about playing bowls instead of doing an honest hard day's work. How things change. Subsequent rulers agreed with him, and bowls went underground – becoming known as a sport for drunkards, layabouts and vagabonds, a sport during which violence might occur at any minute. We've had none of that, although we did see a little undercurrent of tension at an away match a couple of years back, when the bowls people clashed with a folk club.

It's an odd concept now, but pick any era, and you'll find an interest of the common people that the establishment has identified as a threat. Marilyn Manson, rave music, the Sex Pistols – even the Beatles and the Stones. For a few hundred years, this perceived threat was bowls. The game might be the new rock and roll – but once it was more than that. It was *too* rock and roll.

*   *   *

Jason has been given Nigel's place for the evening.

He's only just left college, which makes him my generation if you look at the big picture, although clearly I am senior to him in life experience. It's great to see fellow young people playing, let alone taking the important skipper's role. We shared a block together a couple of years ago when I played in the Monday league, and hopefully have a bit of a rapport. It's a big responsibility for a youngster, and I'm looking forward to giving him the benefit of my knowledge – be it in hints and tips, or just by getting those good shots in first to take the pressure off him and to allow his game to settle down naturally.

'Have a good game.'

The away team always bowls first, so I have a chance to lurk behind their lead as he launches his first wood from the mat. Frankly, it is not a good wood – fifteen degrees wider than the optimum angle, and far too hard, coming to rest – I estimate – six feet behind the cott. He grins ruefully, and I give him a sympathetic smile.

Having carefully studied the path of his wood, I step up to take my own. This sets off at about fifteen degrees wider than the optimum angle and I have put too much pace on it – it comes to rest – I estimate – eight feet behind the cott.

'That's a good start!' calls Jason. 'Just take a little bit off it, and a bit narrower!'

I give him a nod. I am frustrated with myself, but it is good that the boy's nerves aren't getting to him too much – keeping the volume up is a key skill for any skipper, and I wouldn't want him to feel that he couldn't pipe up to offer me advice.

I take some pace off my second wood, but unfortunately miscalculate the angle adjustment, bowling it pretty well straight at the cott. The natural curve of the wood consequently takes it far to the left, drifting well out of contention for anything. I am cross.

'Absolutely perfect length!' calls Jason. 'Couldn't be a better length!'

Big Andy's woods cluster round the cott closer than mine – but he has had the benefit of being able to lurk behind me and watch for the right trajectory. As we cross, I make sure to buttonhole Jason to pass on some important words. 'Don't forget it's slightly downhill,' I say. 'Just drop it in there, and you'll be fine.'

Jason's two woods drop in utterly adjacent to the cott. Two up. It's good that he's got a bit of luck so early. Settle the nerves.

*   *   *

It's such a simple and ancient sport that it seems that systematic codification has never really taken hold. Not round our way, anyway. I mean, I'm sure there's a rule book somewhere that the EBA or World Bowls or Barry Hearn or somebody has come up with – but I don't know anybody who's read it. 'Get as close to the white one as possible, and take it in turns.' Nobody has needed to demand clarification of the dozens of ways that you might get out, or be caught offside, or be adjudged to be interfering with the scrum.

Every rule I have seen has really been a regulation. Where exactly the mat should be placed; the distance away from the cott that a wood must rest within before it can be counted as a score; what happens if you roll the cott too short. I believe that there was a letter once circulated to the league, reminding clubs to ensure that people wore the requisite deeply, deeply unfashionable shoes. But it's not a game for pedants, for jobsworths or the terminally anal.

*   *   *

'He's a fine young player, that one is,' comments an opponent, as Jason's final wood takes a wick sideways and drops in to save two points.

He's right. Annoyingly, Jason is better than me. I am not quite sure how this has happened. When we first started playing, we were much of a muchness. Suddenly, he is streets ahead. Perhaps he has had coaching, or secret practice, or hypnotism.

It hadn't occurred to me, when I had played those first couple of games, that I might not be much good. I had assumed that it would be the sort of sport that you really only needed to turn up to every week. I was never a natural footballer or runner or cricketer or tennis player – but millions of people aren't. Now it's a bit disappointing to start bracketing bowls into that mix. But I can try. I have always been a trier.

We lose by one single point.

I can't help reflecting that this is my fault as I stuff my deeply, deeply unfashionable shoes into the burgundy bowls bag. Despite my energy and enthusiasm and trying, I have not had a good start to the season. Jason, who has consistently played a blinder, tells me not to worry.

'Bah,' is my considered reply.

Perhaps I am being a bit hard on myself. Form, they say, is temporary – whereas class is permanent. It is probably something to do with the Zone. Nigel! That's it! It is all Nigel's fault for missing a game, and thus disturbing the fragile ecosystem that is a bowls block. I know he's the skipper and everything, but next time I shall have a strong word with him about his commitment.

SIX

I am a lineman for the county, on sabbatical

I miss the next match, as I am away with the LTLP. Meeting up with Eddie in the village pub a few days later, I find out that we had lost badly. But the classic line-up is back together again for the following game, and it clicks immediately. We storm to victory on our home green, winning all but five ends and ensuring that the points tally across all the blocks is well in our favour. This gives us the bonus two points, and Howard is smiling broadly as he tells me 'well played'.

Consistency. You've got to be consistent.

* * *

There is a commotion.

Glancing out through the shed window, I can see some activity at the front door. I hasten to investigate. Mrs Short Tony from next door is there with the LTLP; some raised voices are occurring.

The LTLP turns and gives me her Rosemary West look.

'She's brought you round some books from the library.'

As soon as I see the titles piled up on the kitchen table, I step back guiltily. I had been meaning to mention something about their subject, but recently all my energies have been diverted elsewhere into concentrating on not mentioning it.

'So this is why you've been pissing about clearing up at the end of the garden.' She strides indoors and brandishes the books one by one: *Practical Chicken-Keeping, Choosing and Keeping Chickens, Hen and the Art of Chicken Maintenance.*

'I had been meaning to mention . . .'

'This is another one of your plans, isn't it?' she demands. She doesn't actually use the phrase 'hare-brained scheme', but I can see her contemplating having it tattooed on my face so that she can save herself some trouble in the future by just pointing.

'I thought it would be really nice to get some chickens . . . have them pecking around . . . in the country . . .'

She explodes, like a tin of out-of-date exasperation that has been left in the sun. 'Can we just get this straight? This week I'm in London on Monday, Bristol on Wednesday, Liverpool on Friday. I'll be late home on Thursday. I am *not* spending my weekends cleaning out chickens. I am *not* spending my weekends feeding them, or watering them, or doing whatever it is you need to do with chickens. *Have you got that?*'

I stare at her in astonishment. 'But I'll do the cleaning out an' stuff . . .'

'You?' she goggles.

I gaze weakly at Mrs Short Tony for some support. But I gaze in vain. By rights she should be looking sheepish or guilty for her role in creating this unpleasant scene. But, as with all women, all compassion is set aside under the instinct to show solidarity with another female. If men had that sort of blind pack mentality then we would have ruled the world for thousands of years.

The LTLP slams the books back down on the table. I retreat to the shed. 'You're bored, aren't you?' she shouts after me. She is such a townie. Chickens! I have lived in the countryside for ages now – it is about time I had some chickens. I will be known locally as 'the man who has the chickens', and I will take people free eggs, and they will be my friends. If rock superstars like Ian Anderson and Roger Daltrey can have their salmon farms then there is no reason whatsoever why I can't have some chickens.

*   *   *

Walking out of a highly charged executive role without another job to go to is a powerful statement. Unfortunately, it is a powerful statement that you are unemployed. It is funny how things turn out. One minute you are the undisputed head of a household, the next you have made a principled Nelson Mandela-like stand against Strategic HR Initiatives and found yourself a dependant.

So we had moved to Norfolk and I became an appendage.

No. I had become a househusband.

No. I had gone on 'sabbatical'.

That is the word: 'sabbatical'. A 'sabbatical' as far as I can work out, is where people stop doing proper work for a bit but get away without being labelled a parasite on society by dint of using a well-to-do phrase (of Latin origin, I would expect) that makes them sound important and in control and not just fucking about wasting their lives because they've thrown a bit of a wobbler about Strategic HR Initiatives.

You take a holiday. He/she malingers. I have gone on sabbatical.

And when I had embraced and kissed her on her first day at work and my first day at home, when I had handed over the delicious freshly prepared packed lunch, when I had waved through the window at her getting into the car, and then at the back of the car, and then at the side of the car as it turned right out of the gate towards the village, and then just the empty street in general, I took one step back, shrugged my shoulders and wondered what the fuck to do with the rest of my life.

'Sabbatical'. I was young, I was brainy, I was enthusiastic and I had my whole life ahead of me. This would not just be a new personal dawn; it would be a new personal big bang. A million opportunities, a billion things to do, a trillion chances to do something really special with my life that morning. My time to plan and achieve some things that other men my age could only dream of, stuck in their city-centric nine-to-five drudge routines, prodding away at a keyboard whilst in glass offices, floors and floors above them, faceless managers formulated Strategic HR Initiatives.

I sat down and watched *Bargain Hunt*.

I really don't watch a lot of television – I've got so much else to do. A bit of the daytime stuff, the news, *Prime Minister's Question Time*, very occasionally *Countdown*. Now it's the season, I'm looking forward to Barry Hearn's bowls coverage; the cricket will be on Sky and there are often bands playing on Sky Arts – even if I'm not into the music in question, I like to watch these for professional reasons, to pick up some tips. Repeats of *Crown Court* are always interesting. But I ration myself carefully – you can waste your life on such stuff. *Eggheads* is fun as well.

Bargain Hunt is my favourite. I think the thing that I like most about it is the sheer good-naturedness of it. Amiable people accompany amiable presenters around amiable antiques fairs. The amiable winning team is thrilled to walk away with a twelve pound profit; they give big, amiable, enthusiastic hugs to the losers, who are in the red for the sum of two pounds. The presenter wraps it up with an amiable bad joke and the whole thing will be on again tomorrow, just with different people, unless they cannot find any different people in which case they will use the same ones and nobody will notice.

There is a lot to say for good-natured, undemanding television. It is as heart-warming as good-natured, undemanding music is bland. I don't know why this should be the case. Why should the amiable people on *Bargain Hunt* make you feel all warm and comfortable and pleased that they've done well, when listening to the equivalent sort of music – say, Dido – make you want to kill people with an axe?

I have a theory about this; a theory upon which I have been

working for some time and which I think contains a germ of profundity.

That is, when the television is on, people have to focus on it. Accordingly, they get drawn in to the exclusion of all else; watching happy people on undemanding programmes causes viewers to project the scenes on which they are concentrating into a vision of humanity as a whole. We do not resent the mindless friendliness or the clunking set-ups because we know deep down that, whilst an artificial reality, it is a version of reality that might well be better than our own. Put simply, in the case of television, we see two or three amiable people on our screen and momentarily believe that all the world is like that. That is why it becomes reassuring rather than irritating.

Whereas Dido inserts secret messages into her audio recordings, telling you to kill people with an axe.

Lumped in with the antiques programmes are the cookery programmes and the property programmes, and the programmes about going on holiday, and the programmes about going on holiday to find a new property and sitting down for something to eat at the end. The shows are all interchangeable and formulaic, but very watchable. Kirstie Allsopp – the homely, comfortable long-term cottage prospect in the countryside against Sarah Beeny's wham-bam crash pad in the city – is a particular favourite of mine. Her presenting skills give even the pokiest hovel the warm, welcoming feeling of a breast.

However, as you venture outside the antiques show community, the amiability becomes slightly forced; imperceptibly less genuine. And if you watch enough, sooner or later you will come across Max.

Max and his wife Becca are the subjects of much of the property-, holiday- or dinner-related content in the daytime hours. Stressed by their successful businesses in the City, they have a hankering to move to the countryside with their children, Harry

(12) and Amelie (8), and a Labrador. The property must be a cosy olde-worlde period cottage in a very rural middle-of-nowhere setting, with all mod cons and good transport links.

Max is very tall, due to his successful business in the City, which is probably something to do with portfolios. None of the cosy olde-worlde period cottages with good transport links are quite right, as the ceilings are too low and the rooms are too small, or they are too close to a road. Becca is dead set on having large grounds around the property. These are partly for the use of Harry (12), Amelie (8) and the Labrador, but mainly because she has spotted a gap in the market and wants to set up a small studio in the old converted garage 'for her art'. Then she will not have to be stressed by her own successful business in the City any more – which is probably something to do with recruitment consultancy – but will make an honest yeoperson's living selling hand-crafted and beautifully-framed leaf images to a market hungry for such *objets*.

Max makes some compromises to get the place he wants. The presenter suggests that he can knock through from the dining room to the living room to increase the space available, making the house suitable for modern living and getting rid of all the nice-but-impractical olde bits. A Reliable Local Builder has provided a quote for this. Harry (12) and Amelie (8) are happy enough. They are hopeful of being given a quadbike, and it is fully four and eight years respectively before they discover that there are no jobs, no off-licences, and no places to meet people with whom they might have sexual intercourse but yet not be forced to enjoy a subsequent acquaintance. This causes them to move to the city and set up successful businesses, in portfolios or recruitment consultancy. The Labrador just goes with the flow.

There is a particular scene at the end of every Max-and-Becca programme. This is the 'dinner party scene'. Max and Becca have thrown themselves into village life, and have been delighted to meet and befriend a group of solid village local types, all extremely happy as they are no longer stressed by their successful businesses in the City. We watch their perfect dinner party, with perfect jollity around a perfect country dining table. There is lots of complimenting Becca on her starter, and probably a toast. It is horrible.

I do not want to turn into Max. If there is one thing in my life that I do not want to be, it is Max. That is my aim in life – non-Maxism. It's not much, but it is always good to have a goal.

* * *

The thing about chickens is that they are a connection to the land. My Auntie Miriam keeps chickens; she is a well-respected organic permaculture farmer and land expert living in the wild part of New Zealand. The chickens peck around her land, devouring grubs and other unwelcome pests. They give her eggs, and every now and again she wrings a neck and enjoys a delicious chicken dinner.

The LTLP has insisted that the chickens keep within a specific fenced-off point, and that should they be found pecking around her land (whether devouring grubs and other unwelcome pests or no) then it will not be their necks that will be wrung.

It is a collaborative project with Short Tony from next door. The chicken enclosure will start at the back of my garden, and then extend in a large 'L' shape behind my shed and onto his land. We shall share the eggs and the responsibility of husbandry. It is our first step towards setting up a self-sufficient commune for when society finally collapses in an implosion of racial violence, terrorist outrage and the totalitarian imposition of Strategic HR Initiatives.

Cleaning them out will not be the hardest thing I've done. I've been cleaning things out ever since day zero, ever since I came to Norfolk, ever since LTLP sent me to Tesco on the very first day of my sabbatical with an instruction to buy cleaning products.

* * *

Tesco in Norfolk is nothing like Tesco in North London. There are far fewer people; there is more space and a friendlier atmosphere; you are not worried that if you turn your back as you reach for a new carrier bag then somebody will artfully reach round and steal your Cathedral City. The checkout assistants wait patiently, looking eagerly for customers; they wave at you cheerfully if there is any danger of you having to queue. It is always good to support local retailers like this. And if I leave the house at the same time as the LTLP leaves for work, I can be in Tesco for eight o'clock and have the household shopping done by nine. That is the sort of time management skill that I have brought to my role from my previous successful career in the City, and why my sabbatical is a continuing success.

I am well known in Tesco these days, and always chat to the staff. There are the Eastern European guys who you sometimes find stacking the shelves, a nice chatty middle-aged lady on the tills who is new and just getting to grips with things, and the man with glasses who supports Spurs. A man on the tills! That is not even worthy of comment these days, thanks to Dawn French and her associates. People might criticise Tesco, but it has led the way. It is commendable. He packs at least as fast as the ladies, proving the dinosaurs hopelessly wrong.

Despite their enlightened social policies, I am, of course, aware of this well of criticism, and that Tesco verges on Evil Corporation status. Colin, whose family have farmed in the village since about 489 BC, stringently boycotts them due to their perceived shabby treatment of the farming community – and there is the very real problem of local shops and businesses being forced to close whenever a Tesco moves in nearby, despite the store's protestations that its presence increases consumer choice. On a wider level, the 'food miles' issue is a serious one, the extra packaging used by supermarkets contributes to our landfill surplus, and the 'big brand' mentality is a key factor in the homogenisation of Britain. But you have to balance all these factors with the fact that you get points whenever you shop there.

Personally, I have a rule that governs my Tesco use – I try not to buy vegetables, as I can get nicer and better and more local and cheaper ones elsewhere, and for ethical reasons I don't buy meat there, unless it is heavily reduced in price. Tins, frozen stuff, drinks, cereals – they are OK. And cleaning products. Cleaning products.

It is not as if I had never been in a supermarket before – it's just that I could not remember ever having been in one on my own. On sabbatical day one I had no idea that I would eventually become close friends with the Eastern European Shelf Stackers, New Middle-Aged Lady, or Man With Glasses Who Supports Spurs, the Rosa Parks of the Tills. It was not my comfort zone at the time. The second sexual revolution was all very welcome and overdue, but you cannot overturn millennia of evolution in eighteen episodes of a thirty-minute situation comedy featuring a girl vicar.

I stared at my list.

'Cleaning products,' read the item.

'Cleaning products.' Cleaning products. This was typical. How was I supposed to know exactly what to buy? The rest of the list didn't simply read 'food' and 'drink' – it was broken down properly, by item. Lettuce. Tomatoes. Low-sugar lemon squash.

'Cleaning products.' I noted with irritation that the list wasn't even properly arranged. When you walk into a Tesco, the first thing you get to is the fruit and veg, and then, after you turn left and progress from aisle to aisle, there are the household items (including 'cleaning products'), then general groceries, followed by the frozen stuff and, finally, soft drinks and alcohol. Therefore, that is the logical way to structure the shopping list. Yet 'Branston Pickle' was right at the bottom, 'beer' was in the middle, and salad items were sort of dotted all the way through. I made a note to talk to her about this. No wonder the CD collection was in such a state.

The cleaning products aisle was colourful and shiny and

absolutely full of choices. I wandered up and down the planet Og, amazed and enthralled by the options available.

There were things that would clean wooden surfaces, and things that were good for stainless steel. Kitchen dirt was obviously different to bathroom dirt or living-room dirt, so there were different products for each of those rooms. There was special stuff for the windows, for the shower, for the inside of the dishwasher, for the oven, for wooden floors, for vinyl floors, for floors (unspecified), for those difficult-to-reach surfaces, for putting down the plughole to remove blockages, for putting down the plughole to remove stale odours, for putting down the toilet to remove both blockages and stale odours, and for 'all general cleaning tasks'.

It was difficult to quell my panic. If I inadvertently effected a spillage of, say, coffee on the dining table, some would be likely to drip over onto the floor. I would then get it onto my hands, and need to wring a cloth out down the sink. Several products displayed a 'helpline' number, but I was not entirely convinced that their help would be truly impartial.

There were Cif cleaning products. There was Mr Muscle. There was Fairy and Domestos and Tesco's Own and Weirdy Beardy Ecological Brand that doesn't cause the creation of grotesquely mutated hybrid monsters in your toilet pipe. I realised that I had never bought a cleaning product before in my life. They all looked super, like they would get things really, really, really clean.

I swung my head from side to side, casting my eyes up and down the aisle. From what I have read in the magazines, if you look a bit lost and helpless when you are on your own in the cleaning products aisle of your local supermarket then an attractive divorcee/single mother will probably sidle up to you and start giving you advice, and before you can say 'Bang! And the Dirt is Gone!' you are having sex on her kitchen floor in the half-hour between dropping off for playgroup and morning yoga class. I swung my head and cast my eyes for ages and ages, but nothing whatsoever like this happened. Perhaps I looked too on top of things. That can intimidate women occasionally.

Being a countryman, what I really wanted was something that was very good for the environment. But this would need to be combined with a formula that I could just spray on and it would dissolve every single bit of dirt there, without me having to touch it with my fingers or do any scrubbing or wiping. I got a portfolio of Mr Muscle in the end, as it seemed to fit my lifestyle profile more than the Cif or the Fairy.

I was cleaning-products-upped; primed with detergent and ready to go.

* * *

My mobile phone bursts into life! I fumble in the pockets of my jeans as I survey the land intended for chickens. The name flashes at me from the dainty LCD display. It is Unlucky John.

'Mate!'

'Mate!'

'Mate.'

'How are you, mate?'

I grew up with Unlucky John. We went to the same school and then, when the time came, got jobs in the same sort of professional areas, in the same city, sharing the same sort of experiences that any young men do when they taste freedom for the first time. Of all the people in the world aside from the LTLP, I am probably closest to Unlucky John, which is why we try without fail to speak to each other on the telephone at least twice a year. That is the male way.

He's never played bowls, but I was in a band with him once. To expand my musical horizons, I put together a group of local musicians, to play at birthday parties and other functions. Every serious musician should spend part of his life in this sort of outfit.

You learn so much about songwriting and arranging by working out exactly how to play other people's material to an audience, and it's a good way of making you think about what an audience wants to hear and learning how to construct a coherent set list. We learnt 'Hammer to Fall' and 'Smells Like Teen Spirit' and 'Deeply Dippy'. Covers bands also teach you discipline, and force you to adopt a professional attitude.

So Unlucky John became the singer and frontman of Brian Cant and the Flaps. He wasn't actually a singer, and had never been a frontman, but none of the rest of us was either, and he was a friendly, popular chap, who we thought could work an audience. It was my birthday party coming up, and we were awarded that gig, after which bookings dried up. I wanted to persevere, but the others sort of drifted away to do other things – perhaps discipline and professionalism was not for them. Unlucky John had unfortunately got a bit pissed off that the dried peas had fallen out of the adapted plastic cup we'd given him for the shaky bits in 'Sympathy for the Devil', so his enthusiasm had waned also.

It was their loss. Their musical projects elsewhere came to nothing in the big scheme of things, whereas I went on to support the Sultans of Ping. I wouldn't gloat about my success if I saw the guys again – I'm a bigger man than that. And I don't want to live in the past.

* * *

'I'm good! And you?'

'I'm good as well! What've you been up to?' I ask. It's great to hear from Unlucky John again – I really should make time to keep up with friends a bit more. Daylight, reflected off the phone's smooth plastic, bathes pink on my chin.

'Well,' he takes a deep breath. 'I've been working really hard, I guess – the stuff with the new agency is going really well although it's pretty demanding and there's a bit of a situation as I ended up with one of the incredibly fit receptionists after we all got totally shedded at a leaving do last week, although I'm not altogether sure how that happened. So I've been out most nights with them, and I stopped smoking and started again, and I only made it in at eleven this morning as I was so hungover I fell asleep on the bus and ended up going south again until I realised. Then it's been Arsenal most Saturdays with the lads, and I guess we normally go on for a few more beers and a curry after that, although we don't do the strippers so much these days, although the other night – oh! Disgrace! Disgrace! – there was, well I'll tell you about that in a bit. And in my time off I guess I've just been hanging around the bars and pubs round here, just chilling out and stuff, although Aaron – you remember Aaron? – has ended up moving in for a bit and sleeping on the floor as it all went horribly wrong with his other half for a bit, so I guess we've been out quite a bit and shared the odd kebab and cheap late-night bottle of port and all that, but if I'm honest it'll be good to have him out in a bit as it's getting to be a bit of a bind sharing the Playstation and Sky, if you see what I mean.

'How about yourself?' he continues.

I think for a bit.

'Oh you know – this and th . . . we drew against Albert Victor!' I recall. 'Who are pretty good. So that was exciting.

'I went to the village pub afterwards,' I add.

There is a short pause.

'How's the LTLP?' he asks.

'Oh she's very well,' I reply. 'Working hard, you know. We both are.'

'Anyway, it's been great to catch up like this!'

'Definitely, mate,' I agree. 'Definitely.'

We ring off. Later on, I remember that I have not told him about my tooth abscess surgery. I might email him to follow up. I'd hate him to think that I didn't have any news.

* * *

Sabbatical. And then the clock had tick-tocked onwards: four, five, six. The end of my very first sabbaticalised twenty-four hours! I'd had a productive day; cleaning products nestled safely in the cupboard under the sink.

'Are you hungry?' I asked the LTLP. We had kissed, she had put her bag down, I had asked her dutifully about her day.

'Starving!' she replied. 'I didn't really have time for lunch. What's for dinner?'

I had been anticipating the question and was excited, having spent the afternoon making a huge effort in that direction. Donning the oven gloves, I dramatically removed some chicken thighs.

'It's chicken!' I exclaimed, making an orchestral 'daa-naaaa' noise before reaching in once more. 'And . . . potato!'

'A potato!' she repeated, gazing in wonder at it. I have fairly simple tastes in food, and chicken and a baked potato is one of the best meals that there is.

'Is there any salad, or green veg, or anything?' she enquired.

'Oh yes – I've done a salad,' I assured her, fetching a bag of Tesco salad from the fridge. I pulled the plastic seal open and plonked the bag in the middle of the table. We munched our chicken and a potato with Italian Bistro-style salad contentedly. Despite the pressures of my sabbatical – to regroup mentally, to refocus and retrain, to get a band back together again and resume the upwards trajectory of my musical ambitions – I knew I could accomplish one other thing. Buying the cleaning products had filled me with confidence, had convinced me that I could do it. If she was going to treat my sabbatical as mere househusbandom, then I would play along with it and become a sizzlingly hot one. The best househusband that there ever was. I would show her, oh yes I would.

'Is there any pudding?' she asked.

'No,' I replied.

SEVEN

Working on a coop gang

'Here you go,' I offer generously, as she picks up her sandwich box. 'This could do with using up.'

The god of regretting what you've just said appears in a flash of smoke and lightning and starts hitting me in the face with a hammer.

'What do you mean: "using up"? What's the date on it?'

I hesitate. 'The fourteenth.'

'That's four bloody days ago! Throw it away.'

'It'll be OK!' I plead.

'It's yoghurt! It will not be OK.'

Her eyes narrow to threatening slits, like the Tony Blair poster with the scary devil bits. 'What flavour is that?'

I pretend to examine the carton closely, raising my eyebrows in surprise at the information gleaned from the fruit graphic.

'It's . . . apricot.'

'I knew it! I am not taking out of date apricot yoghurt for my lunch!'

'You like apricot yoghurt!'

'I know I like apricot yoghurt! But I like the other flavours as well and I'm sick of being given the apricot just because you only eat the fucking berry ones!'

'But otherwise it's a waste!'

She snatches it from me and stuffs it into the bin.

'You are the fucking tightest man I have ever met in my life,' she spells out, pretty unreasonably in my opinion. 'I am fed up with being given manky stuff from the fridge. Just throw the things away if you don't want them.'

I nod, knowing better than to argue for fear of another face-hammering. Managing a household isn't really that different from working in an office – there is always somebody higher up than you who ostensibly puts you in charge but then sticks their oar in at every opportunity.

'Is there another one in there that I could take?'

I reopen the fridge, then step in front of it, guiltily. To claim that it is stuffed top to bottom with apricot yoghurts of various vintages would be an exaggeration. But it's fair to say that if someone suddenly starts hammering on the door, desperate for my help as they are suffering from some form of emergency apricot-dependent diabetic attack then I will be in a reasonable position to give them a bit of assistance.

She sighs.

'Just give me one of those, then.'

There is no more conversation before she departs for work.

* * *

Making a good first impression on the neighbours is always desirable when one moves house, or acquires new people next door, especially in a small community such as this. People want to be on friendly terms. As it was, I had sent the LTLP ahead to pick up the keys from the estate agents and to take possession of the empty cottage, whilst I had dropped into my parents' in Essex to say a loving and dutiful 'hello' and to leave boxes and boxes of shit in their loft. That was at about 4.30 p.m. At about 5.15 I had received a message that she had been kidnapped, followed by a barely coherent rambling telephone call at 10, telling me that she had encountered the neighbours and a box of wine. At 11, I had opened another text message that seemed to have been automatically generated by gibbons, at 11.05 a duplicate of this, presumably by somebody slumped asleep on their phone.

The LTLP had met Short Tony.

Short Tony does not play a musical instrument. He claims to have once learnt to play the saxophone as a hobby but I have never seen any evidence of this, and even though we have cajoled and encouraged him to show us, he has always proved unwilling. He's never been driven towards rock-stardom, which is probably just as well as nobody wants saxophone players these days as it is not the eighties. Instead, his speciality is vocals, via his home karaoke machine. I would not ever admit it to him, but he does, in fact, have the voice of a hundred thousand angels descending from heaven on golden wings singing into heavenly karaoke mics, his speciality being Meat Loaf.

He does, however, play bowls – or did. Having joined the club at the same time as me, bought all the gear including an identically pristine bag and equally deeply, deeply unfashionable shoes, Short Tony developed a consistent and mechanical drawing style before moving on to snooker as a hobby and deciding that he would rather spend Friday nights drinking in the village pub. He plays intermittently now; it is a shame when talent goes to waste, although it is arguable that his talent for bowls doesn't approach his talent for drinking in the village pub.

So Short Tony is my next-door neighbour, and we are getting chickens together.

The flat-packed coop looks promising. Short Tony and I rub our hands in anticipation of its contents.

'What do you mean?' I ask him, when he has dropped his bombshell.

'Andy. Big Andy. He's getting chickens as well,' reports Short Tony.

I snort crossly. Copying my ideas. Ask any musician – plagiarism is not big and nor is it clever. It is easy to get a bit competitive about these things, even if Short Tony and I are bigger men than that. However, we have spent a decent amount of money on accommodation, and I am immediately confident that our chicken coop will be better than whatever Big Andy comes up with. Apparently, he is looking to get some rescued battery hens, so basically in terms of housing, they'll be happy with anything. Whereas ours will be used to frolicking and free-ranging in the meadows so will be expecting their personal space.

Nevertheless, I am a tad peeved at Big Andy trying to steal our thunder with his own chicken project. I gaze at the box, freshly delivered from eBay, and clench my fist in determination. Our chicken house will be better than his. It will be more professional-looking than Len the Fish's, more spacious than Narcoleptic Dave's. The Chipper Barman used his DIY skills to build Viney's, which is cheating and, after all, has turned out more of an aviary than a coop. Kingy doesn't really have a coop as such – just a bunch of wild chickens who have set up nest in his hedge.

I am enthusiastic. Getting chickens for the garden will provide a unique feature.

'Do you want to get a coffee?' I ask Short Tony some hours later, when the flat-packed chicken coop has been unpacked but is still flat. We get a coffee. For some reason we have chosen the most bitterly cold day since chicken-coop-building records began to construct ours – the wind is howling and swirling around the Scots pines; gripping a screwdriver is physically painful to the fingers.

The instruction leaflet is gibberish. I know there is some sort of academy of gibberish that awards diplomas to the writers of flat-pack assembly instructions, but this tests our gibberish tolerance like nothing has before. I give Side Panel B a hefty kick in frustration. At one point we have the egg-laying nesting-box bit constructed but discover that it is larger than the coop itself with no way to get at the eggs that have been laid; later I make a triumphant breakthrough in panel/bolt identification only to find that there is not a hole where I am expecting one. I feel like Ray Davies in the song 'Lola'.

Short Tony is staring thoughtfully at the bits and pieces. He strokes his chin and starts nodding his head very, very slowly. An idea is clearly forming in his mind. I wait patiently for it to emerge, enthusiastic that he is hitting on a simple solution to our problems.

Eventually, he speaks. 'I was thinking,' he says ponderously. 'Can't we just stick the chickens down, give them the tools and wait for them to evolve opposable thumbs?'

He is an idiot. I take up the Allen key once more and grit my teeth for one last push.

Chicken coops should be placed in a sunny, well-drained area, where there is also shade and wind-protection. So writes Katie Thear, author of my new book: *Starting with Chickens: A Beginner's Guide*. Katie Thear, from her photograph, looks a bit like a cuddly hen, so I would trust her every word. The chicken world grows more fascinating to me with every passing day. All the different breeds of chicken – the Buff Sussex looks cute; the traditional country-dweller in me fancies going for the Old English Pheasant Fowl, but then it is tempting to acquire a flock of Transylvanian Naked Necks. The rare and ancient traditional breeds, some of which date back to as far as the 1920s, all appeal.

There is some conflict as to where precisely to situate the coop. As the boundary between my garden and Short Tony's is imaginary at this part of the garden, we have to plan for the future – we are friends now, but who knows what could escalate from a petty disagreement over gapeworm? In the end we compromise and carry the structure across the lawn, placing it to rest directly and exactly across the line where the fence would be. But due to its construction, the egg-laying box bit is on my side! I win! It is like Steptoe and Son and their television set. Happy with a job well done, we retreat indoors for another hot coffee, pausing only to replace two of the feet bits that have already dropped off in the wind.

* * *

We do not use the term 'semi-detached' about our cottages, as that is for housing developments rather than desirable brick-and-flint conjoined residences near the Queen's estate.

Ours are, we understand, the second-oldest dwellings in the village. According to the surveyor's report, they were built in the 1700s and then extended in the 1800s, but then again, according to the surveyor's report everything about ours should have fallen down by now – but to be honest he might be wrong as he couldn't peel the wallpaper back and whether it falls down or not we can't sue him or ask for any sort of money back, as that's how surveyors work.

Originally they would have comprised a single agricultural building – perhaps a piggery of some sort. They certainly weren't always cottages, but at some point they were developed from this single building and upgraded into hovels, with all sorts of roof-raising and wall-extending and stuff. You can see the old line of the roof if you climb into my loft, although I recommend that you do not try this as I will call the police.

At one stage, the building consisted of three conjoined dwellings (N.B. not a 'terrace'), and then just the two as more partitioning and knocking-through was done by the property developers of yore. And then came Short Tony and I. The party wall between us is a single layer of ancient wood and brick, a flimsy reminder of the once unitary state of the building. It is good that we get on well, as it is very possible without even trying to share in the muffled sound of the television or of raised conversations or of 'Dead Ringer for Love'.

At most times of day there is just a mysterious 'thud thud thud'.

The most interesting thing in the world would be to get a time machine together. Not only to travel back to Merrie England to see the place in its early days, but to bring back to the present day the peasant who first lived here. He would be so amazed and incredulous that his piss-sodden shanty-hovel was now a desirable residence for successful professional people. He would probably laugh and laugh and laugh, after he got over his terror at a man arriving in a big metal machine with flashing lights and a small pointed fin on the back, whisking him off into a world of motor cars and Noel Edmonds. How things change over the years. The cottage was once a simple shelter for working agricultural people. Now it is a pretty dwelling with roses in the garden and an annexe for chickens. In its own way, it is on 'sabbatical'.

I've never felt any snob-appeal about living amidst the Queen's estate. A lot of this part of Norfolk is hers: the cottages, the farms, the woodlands – even the bowling greens. This cottage was once hers, although there is no evidence that she ever actually *lived* here, and it has been in private hands for some decades. So there is no snob-appeal, just a quiet satisfaction that I have found somewhere that suits me perfectly in my escape from the big city – a cosy olde-worlde cottage, nicely in the middle of nowhere but with good transport links.

In fact, I've always found the connection a bit spooky. One

minute I am being boyishly inspired to pick up the electric guitar by listening to 'We Are the Champions' by Queen – the next minute, I am contemplating a new musical direction whilst living in a cottage that was once owned by the actual Queen! If that's not proof that some higher power is looking over me then I don't know what is.

* * *

I pause before entering the builders' yard. The list in my pocket is comprehensive. Posts, chicken wire, supporting wire. The plan for today is just to suss out how much we will have to pay. I am a good negotiator, and we have worked out the exact lengths of wire that we will need, using the medium of Short Tony's stride, which is probably about a yard. It is important to be totally accurate when you order building materials, as otherwise there is wastage.

But I hate going to builders' yards. It is intimidating.

How do they know? How? What sort of sinister telepathic powers do they have that lets them know that you are, for instance, a musician and not a genuine builder? Why am I on the back foot immediately? Why?

I cross the threshold with a bullish air, determined this time round to radiate confidence in my abilities to choose building materials and not be ripped off. Unfortunately, loud sirens immediately wail out and a big neon sign with pointy arrow things starts flashing 'not a builder! not a builder!' in bright yellow and electric blue above my head.

I swat at it, irritably.

'Er – how much is that?' I ask the man, waving at some fencing and attempting to look as if I spend my entire life buying and putting up fencing. I give the fence a sneer.

'That's . . . about twenty,' he replies, having sized me up. Damn him. I do not have the courage to ask what factors affect the 'about'

76

aspect of the cost. I nod sagely, before remembering to shake my head at the ridiculous price he is asking for his fencing when I could get it for half that from any number of my usual fence suppliers.

'Is that including or excluding VAT?' I ask, cleverly.

'Including,' he replies. This is annoying. He should have quoted me excluding, as I am clearly in the trade. I do think of pulling my phone out and having a loud 'look, boss, I am not sure this builders' yard is up to our usual suppliers' conversation, but I have a nagging doubt that my personal stature will be enhanced in his eyes by my telephonic prop from the 'My Little Pony' cartoons. So I give a 'that is inconvenient as now I am going to have to work it out excluding the VAT as actually all this stuff is to do with my successful fencing business'-type shrug instead. 'Fine,' I tell him, before asking my next question. 'Have you got any – ummm – I need some wire like chicken wire.'

'What sort?'

'Well – chicken wire,' I clarify, trying not to give him the erroneous impression that I am one more Max-type idiot who has decided that by keeping half a dozen hens in his back garden he is suddenly an important part of the stewardship of the countryside.

'What size holes are you after?'

I am stumped by this. I haven't a clue how big the chickens will be. There is probably an average size, but I guess some are smaller and some are bigger, especially if I get the Transylvanian Naked Necks. I pretend to knowledgeably ponder.

'One inch, or two inches?'

Relief. I'm fairly sure that even Short Tony and I will be able to breed the chickens to the sort of size where they won't be able to get through either of those gauges. He gives me his price, which I scribble on a scrap of newspaper that I find in my pocket. Shit! It is the *Observer* and not the *Sun*!

'Thanks,' I say, all my price research complete.

'You're welcome.'

'Yes – I'll measure up and pop back to order it,' I promise. 'With my van.'

* * *

Len the Fish lives in a cottage almost opposite the village pub, which saves him miles and miles of walking. He has many hats: gamekeeper, grounds-keeper, butcher, bacon-smoker, shooter and, of course, fish and fishing expert. He is also an all-round nice bloke; one of life's genuine people. He's given me mackerel, and pigeons, and duck; he's come round with home-smoked salmon and pork pies, mussels and razorfish. What he doesn't know about genuine things in the country isn't worth knowing.

Classing 'building a chicken run' as a genuine thing in the country, Short Tony and I have been hinting to him for ages that he might come round and 'give us some advice' – this being code for 'do all the work for us'. As it is, he has agreed to turn up to help for the couple of hours that we anticipate the job taking.

'And grip it like this,' demonstrates Len the Fish, 'and . . . twist.'

I watch him gripping it like that and twisting. He works along the length of fence, doing his expert gripping and twisting, whilst I hold something for him that does not seem to really need holding but that he has given me to hold out of exasperation and pity. There is a nagging worry that I am not being much real use. Boooooo – it is my own chicken run, and I was going to make it, and it was going to be brilliant, and it would have been made with the sweat of my own labourer's brow (plus Short Tony's). But I am just not much good at these things. I am also suspecting that two hours was a slightly low estimate on our behalf.

The sun creeps towards the horizon.

By day two of construction, I am feeling even more down. Short Tony has disappeared to buy the extra lengths of wire that we need to finish the job, and I have been struggling for ages to hammer the same small staple into a piece of wood. Meanwhile, Len the Fish is erecting, wiring, twisting, hammering, digging, measuring and fixing.

'Thanks ever so much for your help again, Len,' I mumble. Abusing his kindness like this has embarrassed me. 'If you ever need some . . . ummmmm . . . something done, then just . . .'

I tail off lamely. It is shameful. Len the Fish has given up his entire weekend to do our fencing for us, and I have cock all that I will ever be able to help him with in return, apart from the purchase of a pint of London Pride, which doesn't count as he will buy me one back immediately and we do this every Friday anyway. I continue grafting on my staple, feeling a bit useless, humbled and humiliated.

* * *

All my professional skills were acquired whilst working in the music business.

This was before the Strategic HR Initiative people, back when I was young and full of the idealism of rock and roll. Before I took the corporate shilling; when the idea of a desk job working for suits and squares and drones was anathema to a kid with effects pedals running through his veins. The music business! I was the envy of all my friends, as the office boy for the company that booked advertising space in the *Daily Telegraph* for the Royal Philharmonic Orchestra.

The Royal Philharmonic – alongside all other orchestras – was worried that people did not go to classical music concerts any more – particularly young people. In fact, live classical music was struggling, full stop. I felt a bit bad about this, as it was bands such as Wildebeeste that had been set up specifically to rail against these once great institutions, although the challenges faced by this centuries-old art-form were by no means all Wildebeeste's fault.

The company was busy at that point, as a promoter had paired the Royal Philharmonic Orchestra with a lighting rig that Genesis had just discarded as not up to their needs. Obviously the young generation would be blown away by the visual show that had so recently been adjudged adequate for their pop heroes, and lots of publicity was needed to promote the fact. But it wasn't just the Royal Philharmonic Orchestra on our books – that would have been deadly dull. There was the London Philharmonic, the Philharmonia, even – in short bursts of gigging activity that would visibly lift the air of excitement in the office towards an electric frenzy – the London Mozart Players. I was hungry for knowledge and I watched and learnt.

I learnt to be an expert on a pre-Apple-Macintosh patent computerised typesetting mark-up system that sent instructions via an electronic modem to a plant in Watford that then couriered back finished typesetting at twice a day intervals.

I learnt how to use the enormous hardback pre-internet printed directory that could tell you the names and circulations of all the pre-internet local newspapers that covered all the towns in the UK.

I learnt to check telephone numbers at least twice, or at least I did a bit later on.

The owner and Director called me to his office. He was a Welshman on the small side, of well-spoken demeanour and an air of satisfaction with the status of Directordom. Keen to hand down some of the wisdom of his many years, he had offered me a session of Media Training.

Media Training was something for which I was particularly hungry – if whatever was to come after Wildebeeste was going to crack the publicity nut then I would need to employ every trick in the book. When you are starting out in a band, you can't just play your guitar and wait for everything else to fall into place – you need to be a jack of every possibly relevant trade that there is. So Media Training from a genuine advertising agency was not something to be passed up.

'Now,' he said, having taken a small sip of tea, paced the office to collect his thoughts and plonked himself back behind his vast leather-topped desk. 'What you need to know is this.'

I sat up straight and alert, ready to absorb the Media Training.

'People who buy the *Times* during the week,' he began, 'buy the *Sunday Times* on Sunday.' He took another sip of tea and nodded slowly.

'But people who buy the *Telegraph* during the week,' and at this point he leant forward across the desk and lowered his voice in order to deliver the killer fact, 'don't necessarily buy the *Sunday Telegraph*. They often buy the *Sunday Times*. And their wives get the *Mail*!' He leant back triumphantly, to conclude the Media Training.

There was a short pause. I eventually rose from my chair. 'Right,' I said.

*   *   *

Directories of local newspapers. Typesetting mark-up systems. Multifaceted print media buying strategies. I cannot help but reflect that these skills have not held me in the greatest of stead throughout my later adult life. Even the thing later on about Strategic HR Initiatives might have been a bit useful here, managing Short Tony and Len the Fish – perhaps I should have given these concepts more of a chance and thus been equipped to step in should there be some form of diversity conflict between them. I can't do fencing, I am a lousy hammerer, my accuracy with an electric drill is risible. I am not even to be trusted with the gripping and twisting.

Once, I was excited about learning new professional skills. But these skills turned out to be useless ones in the big scheme of chicken coop construction. All obsolete skills. Boooooooo, booooooooo and triple booooooooo. I have lived my professional life in Betamax. I will be no good when society finally collapses and we have to live as savages in one commune, like in William Golding and his thing about the flies.

Perhaps Len the Fish might need to promote a rock festival at some point. I could play for free, or do the musical direction. This is more like it. I turn to him, but something about the way he is expertly fitting a cabin hook to the wooden upright tells me that he is unlikely to be promoting a rock festival any time in the near future.

'A pint. Just buy me a pint,' he insists, not even asking me about local media in Exeter, or Mansfield, or Leigh-on-Sea, or even giving any indication that he requires something put together in fourteen-point Bodoni – something for which he is happy to wait for a courier from Watford. I return morosely to the single supporting wooden post that I have insisted on putting in myself – it is at an odd angle and doesn't appear to be set into the ground with any stability whatsoever.

'Huge gales forecast for tomorrow,' he advises, not entirely reassuringly.

* * *

There is a path running the length of the cottages and underneath their front windows, with a gate that is riddled with wood disease at the boundary between the properties. The dwellings were once owned by two brothers, who clearly spent much time pottering about together. Now Short Tony and I use the path, to flit in between each other's places – the gate is never closed.

I think it is unusual for men to make friends later in life. Women are different. Women can join a bus queue and have formed intense and lasting bonds with their fellow potential passengers before the number 72 has even left the depot. Men are naturally more private. The pub or a sports team are the only venues where it is acceptable to share conversation with total strangers, and the deal is that any conversation made there remains there, and must be about the pub or sports. Inviting somebody from the bus queue for coffee is strictly off-limits, and would be regarded with suspicion and alarm.

But we have got a path. A path, and now a mutual chicken coop. I used to think that I was good friends and neighbours with Adam, as we saw each other occasionally and shared the noise of his weeing. But that was nothing compared to this. Short Tony and I have a chicken coop! We share a chicken coop together, as men. A chicken coop that, admittedly, hasn't got any chickens in it.

A coop.

EIGHT

Got measure, in pocket

'That's the green. Come on. Come on. Come on.'

My wood skips through the wet grass, curving towards the glistening cott, homing in like a well-trained chicken.

Nigel watches it in glee. 'I like this one! Roll it out! Roll it out! Well you bowl!'

'Well you bowl!' I got a 'well you bowl!' 'Well you bowl' is what you say when somebody has bowled well. It is a convention, like saying 'have a good game'. I wave modestly at Nigel and turn nonchalantly away from the mat to locate my second wood, which is covered in wetness and grass clippings. My beer towel is deployed ineffectually.

'Well you bowl,' offers the opposing lead, genuinely. It is a sporting game like that.

'Well you bowl,' adds Big Andy, slapping me on the back.

It is always good to get a 'well you bowl'.

Having done reasonably well in our first few games, there is a mood of distinct optimism among the team. After a small wobble with line-ups, we seem to have found a solid bunch of regulars for Friday nights – everybody is settling into their roles and the evenings are relaxed and enjoyable. I place my right foot on the mat to take my second wood, and my pride in the chorus of 'well you bowl's is not dented by this one being too short, too straight, too not in contention and too in the way of everybody else's. It fleetingly crosses my mind that if we continue playing like this I might be adding to my bowls trophy collection at the end of the year.

Across the green, seventeen other people bustle around, bowling, crossing, milling to and fro, advising, scoring, setting down the mat – smiling as they go about their bowls business, wrapped up gamely against the cold and damp, slapping their foreheads as they realise that they've let loose a hopeless one. From the large house that adjoins the green comes the unmistakable waft of a newly lit barbecue. I shake wet grass from my towel.

The bowls trophy collection amounts to one. A couple of years ago I was awarded a small plasticky plastic cup that now nestles in an alcove in the bedroom. It was my first season at the club, and my contribution towards making the team championship runners-up had been minimal: the odd wood vaguely near the cott and once being responsible for giving a couple of the good players a lift to an away match. Nevertheless, I am proud of my plasticky plastic runners-up cup, even if I did come into it by default. It is the only thing that I have been awarded since I was a cubs chess champion in 1980, and the latter trophy is starting to get a little worn at the edges, lessening its impressiveness to visitors being shown round my home.

If we can challenge for bowls league honours this year then it will feel different. It will feel like the trophy is deservedly mine.

Big Andy draws one in directly behind the cott. He gives a little air-punch as it comes to rest, falling to the weighted side exactly where he'd wanted it.

'Well you bowl, Andy,' I assure him, determined not to be out-'well you bowl'ed.

It's not always like this – some people take it very seriously, of course. You get skippers who shout petulantly at their teams, who shake their heads theatrically at the human shortcomings of their lesser players. You get husbands and wives bickering with each other, forty years of marriage being metaphored in microcosm on the bowling green. You get younger players frustrated at their own inability and with youth's horror of looking foolish, winding themselves up into a frenzy of counterproductive defensiveness. You get older people who were clearly once magnificent sportsmen or women, railing against the onset of physical infirmity, driven to fury by their new limitations. You get the odd person who just isn't much fun.

But these are the exceptions, the very rare exceptions. On the whole, everybody is so incredibly, incredibly amiable. *Bargain Hunt* amiable.

* * *

Ritchie Blackmore famously kept sacking musicians in a strop, changing line-ups for each Rainbow album in a fruitless effort to achieve the perfection that would never ever be attainable. He had the reputation of being autocratic, of being difficult to get along with. He returned for a while to Deep Purple, the band that he'd co-formed in the sixties and with whom he'd enjoyed his finest moments. But after one falling-out too many, the tensions grew too great and the band parted company with the legendary guitar god himself; like a brilliant yet frustrated skipper, his outstanding playing abilities were subverted by his own lack of interpersonal skills. Now Deep Purple continues playing all over the world, whereas he is a weird man who plays medieval music in a funny hat, locked in a downwardly spiralling solo career. It is a tragedy that Ritchie Blackmore never played bowls. He would have seen the writing on the wall.

He was a big influence on my guitar playing, Ritchie Blackmore. I admit I don't actually sound much like him, but I wanted to, and that is almost as good. His natural style is a fat, round tone that is unfashionable these days. His influences clearly stem from the blues, a medium that was beyond my comprehension whilst growing up in a comfortable semi-detached house but that I've come to truly understand since I've moved to Norfolk and got a chicken coop (without chickens).

I saw Deep Purple play once, at the Hammersmith Odeon. Despite the classic songs, despite the aggression of the Hammond organ, despite the sheer volume, they were terrible. Turgid and uninteresting, like five Strategic HR Directors presenting the preliminary findings of a consultation process on heavy rock music. Ritchie Blackmore seemed to be sulking all the way through – he stood apart from the others and stared at his fretboard, pulling glowering expressions.

At the curtain, not having played 'Smoke on the Water', the five surprisingly reappeared to play it.

Except that it was just four. Ritchie Blackmore didn't reappear. Presumably he was continuing his glowering expressions back-stage. So they played 'Smoke on the Water' without him.

They played 'Smoke on the Water' without the guitar player. And it was brilliant. It clicked and took off, it soared and it swung. I sometimes think of this moment and wonder if it really happened, whether I was really there. It was almost too perfect.

Nobody is indispensable, Nigel. You might be leading the team to new heights on the bowling green, but we did all right with Jason, and I'm now getting my share of 'well you bowled's. There is no indication, as he peers through his spectacles towards the pack, gently wiping his own wood with a cloth, that he is about to turn into a Blackmoresque figure. But we will be ready if he does.

* * *

'That's two? Two to us?'

'Isn't that one closer?'

'It looks closer from here.'

'But if you stand over here, I favour that one.'

'Yes, it looks closer from here, but if you stand over there, then I definitely favour ours.'

'Do you want to have a measure?'

I back away immediately. I hate having a measure. That is why I let Big Andy look after the measure, in his back pocket with the team pencil. I scurry off to clear up some of the more distant woods. The two skippers glare impatiently from the other end.

'What is it?' calls Nigel. 'One or two?'

'We're just having a measure,' I reply.

* * *

Pink Floyd sacked Rick Wright. Rick Wright – the man who played the keyboard bits that made their songs sound like Pink Floyd – sacked from the band that he'd co-formed in the sixties and with whom they'd enjoyed their finest moments. He used his piano, or Hammond or Farfisa organ, to add beautifully expressive washes of blues- and jazz-influenced sound over their languid early music. Then, as the group progressed, they discovered that he was not much good at writing angry songs about Mrs Thatcher. So they all fell out, and he went. What is it that leads people to fall out with their band mates – the people with whom they have shared everything?

Rick Wright. Sign on you crazy diamond.

Perhaps if we started playing indoor bowls or – God help us – crown green, I would be the one to go. It was a shame when Wildebeeste died a death, but there was no animosity between us, no falling-out among friends. It was just time to move on.

* * *

You have a measure when you can't agree which of the woods are closer. It can be deceptive occasionally. The fact that they are not perfectly round complicates things, and depending on where you stand, the angles can play tricks with your eyes. Anybody can ask for a measure at any time – this ranges from a perfectly reasonable request (if there is clear doubt) to a fucking rude sign of desperation (if it is totally obvious to everybody). Big Andy sighs and kneels gingerly on the wet grass.

The measuring device is clever: a plastic square containing a piece of retractable string with a pointy bit on one end. You place the plastic square against the cott, stretch the string, and then touch the pointy bit on what appears to be the nearest wood. By waving the pointy bit around and attempting to touch the other nearby bowls then you can ascertain which one is, for sure, closer.

If the woods fall so close to the cott that the plastic square is too big to squeeze in, then there is a backup option of some small metal extendable callipers. These require a delicate touch and a careful eye. Fortunately, we do not require the small metal extendable callipers very often.

I have horrible nightmares about measuring. It is something that I simply do not wish to get involved with. It is not the technology that intimidates me, it is the fact that I have done it before, and always think that I am going to press the square too hard against the cott, causing it to move, or just overbalance and fall face forwards into the entire head of bowls, scattering the disputed woods in every direction. Or that somebody will challenge my measuring, or accuse me of illegal string-retraction, and social embarrassment will ensue, probably with a man shouting at me.

'There you go. That's closer.'

'By some way, in the end.'

'Well I'll be damned.'

'Two, Nigel,' I call. 'Two up.'

The measuring is complete. Big Andy swats at the wet patches on his knees. There is no social embarrassment. The game resumes, two up.

We win the match quite easily. The final end oozes with good-will, and there are handshakes. Nigel is chuffed – his name will be in the *Lynn News* in a positive sense next week. Big Andy is chuffed; I am chuffed. It does seem possible that my alcove might sport a new occupant in September. Howard is chuffed – smiling through his beard as he fills in the scorecards. There is nothing that puts you in quite such great humour as having a good gig. We pack the mats away, change out of our deeply, deeply unfashionable shoes, and head off to the village pub.

*   *   *

After Dave, Iain and I moved on, I drifted musically for a few months. And then, completely out of the blue, I was – I guess the phrase is 'talent spotted'.

When I was a teenager, my local pub wasn't local at all. It was three or four miles away, past several other pubs; a real small olde-worlde village tavern with a crooked roof and horse brasses. Tankards hung above the bar; the local morris dancers congregated outside periodically to do their morrising. Not the sort of place where you'd expect to recruit electric guitarists. But where is?

I remembered him from school – he was in the year above me, a fashionable and bohemian type who everybody with a creative bent looked up to – he'd been in one of the big local bands that, whilst not exactly getting a major label record deal, had distributed their songs to some pupils on a C15 cassette. I was drinking with Unlucky John and our friends, and was waiting to buy my round when I felt a tap on my shoulder.

'I heard that you're a really good guitar player,' he said simply.

Back then I was unused to being approached by members of

the public. 'Who told you that?' I replied, blinking, embarrassed by the compliment.

'Him,' he replied, indicating the bloke standing next to me at the bar whom I'd been telling about my really good guitar playing.

Wildebeeste had been a bit of a joke – a chance for three friends to plug in and to mess around playing some songs. But I felt in my bones that it was time to get something more serious and solid together. Indie, shoegazing, Madchester – a great renaissance in British pop music was bubbling under and about to explode. To be part of this . . . well, the teenage pretensions of Wildebeeste seemed risible set against the seismic happenings that were shaking the nation.

It was well known that he was a gifted songwriter, singer and guitar player, an ambitious guy who was going places. He'd got a new band together with a renowned local drummer and two girl singers. We talked about our ideas for a few minutes and I was in.

This is how it happens in the music business, unfair as it may sound. It's ten per cent talent, ninety per cent luck, although obviously my talent had a huge part to play, and the luck was just lucky. But one minute you are just mooching around, writing songs and honing your craft, and the next minute you're standing in a pub and your big break arrives out of the blue. I'm kind of hoping that this is what is going to happen again soon, although I might have to make my own luck if the current quiet spell continues. But Bono could walk into the village pub tomorrow, or the four non-guitar-playing members of Deep Purple. It is as well to be prepared for such an event. Stranger things have happened.

The rehearsal facilities were excellent – a school hall just a few miles from where we lived with our mums and dads. This is something that non-musicians do not appreciate – the difficulty of securing a good rehearsal space. A school hall is ideal – echoing acoustics aside, being on a raised stage in a large room is more realistic gig-practice than standing round in a circle in a recording studio. I admit to being nervous as I got my stuff together for our first session – this would be a big step up for me. I was confident in my abilities on the fretboard – but how would I fit in with the others who knew so much more than me?

Simon helped me carry my gear from the car. 'There's been a bit of a change of plan,' he said as we walked through the entrance corridor, past fading photographs – group gatherings of form 3C and of the senior hockey team. Apparently the renowned local drummer had got a job cheffing in London, and then there had been some form of bizarre love triangle between Simon and the girl singers, leading to them walking out in high dudgeon, taking their voices and microphones with them. 'So we've got a completely new line-up,' he explained.

I pushed my way in through the regulation double fire doors at the back of the hall. 'Hullo!' said Dave, from beside his bass amp. 'Hullo!' said Iain, from behind the drums.

* * *

'And then Daltrey walks in,' he continues. 'And Townshend says to him . . .'

The Well-Spoken Barman has a story for every occasion. He appeared out of the blue one day. First, he was sleeping on someone's sofa. Then he got a barman's job in the village pub. Then he started looking after the village shop. Then he started managing the village pub, before going off to manage another village pub and then returning to our village pub. It has been like the American Dream, but with Norfolk retail outlets.

He still drinks in here and, indeed, everywhere else. Placing his pint of Wherry down with a thin arm, he blinks a couple of times whilst he remembers his thread. Apparently he had some connection with The Who back in the eighties or nineties. Short Tony and Big Andy lean in appreciatively. The Well-Spoken Barman's tales are always good value, and I'm sure are occasionally true.

'And then Daltrey says . . .'

I listen, but do not chip in. I could mention the songwriting, the gigs, the prestigious support slot with the Sultans of Ping. But I hate trumping other people's stories. And, like I say, I do not want to live in the past.

If I could meet some other musicians then that would be a good start. Short Tony's karaoke prowess is impressive, but Meat Loaf and I are a million miles apart in terms of musical direction. The bowls club is a dead loss – Big Andy once played the cello for a youth orchestra, but hasn't picked the instrument up for years, and Nigel doesn't really like music, his car radio always being tuned to Classic FM. I suddenly feel isolated and melancholy.

Big Andy leaves early, for reasons of self-preservation. And some time later, a lot later, I push through the double doors with Short Tony, weaving on a very slight zigzag down the short hill towards the cottages. There are no stars tonight, just a general North Sea-type dampness in the air, and I pull my coat tightly round myself, wishing that I'd brought something more suited to the conditions, like a car.

We bid each other farewell at the street's single lamp that spews out its doleful orange glow from its position at the end of my path. That's me in the spotlight, and I could be again. I will have to start asking around. I'd love to do it again – I'd love to.

NINE

Dust reign o'er me

If you had an American tourist to hand and wanted to impress him or her with ye olde England quaint and picturesque bowling green, then you'd take them to Sandringham.

Other quaint and picturesque bowling greens are available, but Sandringham's has everything. It nestles, hidden from the narrow road, beside the shop and social club in the tiny village of West Newton. The land drops down to the south here, providing you with a vast panorama across the fence of the fields and woodlands of the Royal estate. The church tower sits lazily opposite, occasionally punctuating the peace with a leisurely 'dong'.

An immaculate wooden pavilion has been built in one corner, to provide shelter from the sun and rain, although the hypothetical American tourist would be better advised to plonk themselves down on the raised patio area that provides a vantage point for the game and, incidentally, a beer garden for the social club. As I study the head of woods that's clustered on the eighth end, a man with a beard bustles busily with a watering can, visiting each of the various spring blooms that have been lovingly potted against the fence and up on the path, before returning to his jar of Greene King IPA.

I played one of my very first games of bowls here at Sandringham. As a beginner, I hadn't been particularly good – but I was enthusiastic, and the environment had inspired me.

It was early in the season, a pleasant yet cool evening. Kevin had been detailed to show me the ropes.

'*Be there!*' he had screamed. '*You gotta beeee there!*'

One of the classic mistakes made by beginners is to be timid and to bowl far too short. Granted, distance is very difficult to judge, even for experienced players – but a wood that's far too short is no good to anybody. One that's only a little bit short can be knocked forwards by a subsequent wood; one bowled too long brings the possibility that the cott itself might be hit and cannon backwards, bringing your wood once more into play. But far too short is useless. You have to be there.

'*Beeeee there!*' he had yelled, jumping up and down in frustration as my second wood had pulled up all of eight feet away from the head. I recall my embarrassed and apologetic wave. I was new and I was rubbish, but I knew a season with Kevin, playing under his guidance week in and week out, would do wonders for my game. And it would be a mutual thing. As the TV adverts pleading for new teachers always stress, there is nothing quite so rewarding as getting your knowledge across to a raw recruit, watching them develop and blossom under your guidance until they fulfil their full potential as a bowls player.

Despite having played every week for years and years, Kevin inexplicably gave up bowls completely at the end of that season. It was a shame – I never found out why. He'd be very proud of me now, I think, as I set down the mat for the ninth end.

'Wherever I lay my mat . . .' I croon.

The spring shower is not heavy, and the sun beaming down over the church contrasts dramatically with the black, black skies that loom above the fields. A rainbow forms, first in a shapeless blur, and then resolving into sharp, sharp clarity – a perfect one-hundred-and-eighty-degree arc such as you rarely see, its two ends meeting the Norfolk landscape miles and miles and miles apart. Birds tweet in the trees. The scene is utterly beautiful and serene.

My wood pulls up a good eight feet short.

'Fuck!' I shout. '*Fuck!*'

* * *

'You haven't kept chickens before, then?' the lady asks us over her shoulder, heading towards a bunch of sleek, befeathered show-hens.

'No,' we affirm, absent-mindedly.

The lady bypasses the show-hens with a cackle, and veers towards the deepest depths of the enormous poultry shed.

Shortly afterwards, Short Tony and I are speeding back along the A47, a half-dozen chickens confined to the dog cage on the back of his truck. The sun is out, the road is open and we have the satisfied feeling of two men who have bought some chickens.

Short Tony knows about livestock – he has a dog, he goes shooting and fishing, he's lived in and about the countryside all his life. No stupid townie Max incomer he. But I can sense that he is as child-ishly excited as I am as we head for home – the chickens will give him a nice new hobby.

'We should decide a few things. Are we going to give them names?' he ponders.

'I hadn't really thought about that,' I reply. And I haven't.

'Maybe we should leave that sort of thing to the kids.'

I am quite happy to let Short Tony's children name the chickens if that's what they want to do. I've only ever named bands, and that requires a different skill-set altogether. 'Let's be clear, though,' I warn, resolutely. 'No comedy names. Like Gregory Peck, or Princess

Layer, or Hen Livingstone. And no bloody post-irony, like when people call their cats Chairman fucking Miaow.'

'Fair enough.' We drive on, before Short Tony pipes up again, this time with a note of mild concern in his voice: 'Can you still see them?'

My neighbour is peering into the rear-view mirror and frowning hard. I turn to look through the glazing at the back of the cab. No chickens are visible. I undo the seatbelt and strain my neck upwards and towards the window, like a chicken. There is no sign of them. I have a brainwave and take my phone from my pocket, switching it to the camera setting; reaching up as far as I can and guessing the angle, I take a picture through the glass into the base of the load area. Short Tony snorts as I wave the pink Motorola around – even in a prospective emergency he can still be immature and sexist.

The picture is inconclusive.

'I'd better pull over,' he mutters, flicking the indicator switch as a lay-by approaches at a rush. We hop out anxiously and hasten round the back. Six chickens peck away at us from the security of the dog cage.

'Perhaps they were crouching down when we looked,' I shrug. 'Just to fool us.'

We are relieved. I give a weak smile to a lorry driver who is staring down at us from over his sandwiches high up in his parked cab.

'Vets?' asks Short Tony when we have got going again.

We agree that running up a vet's bill for a chicken would be lousy, lousy economics.

'And no puns,' insists Short Tony. I nod vigorously in agreement – he has hit the nail upon the head – there is something about chickens that invites even the most level-headed people to pun. 'No

"Oooh, aren't they egg-citing!" or "This one is eggs-traordinary!" or that sort of stuff.'

We are reassured that there is strong consensus on that topic. No puns. We have built the coop together; we will go halves on feed, straw and upkeep; we will take eggs on alternate days with a free-for-all on Sunday, and we are agreed that there will be no puns.

A roundabout approaches, which Short Tony negotiates hearse-slow. I might get a truck like his at some point. That's the thing about living in the country – you never know when you might just want to throw some chickens in the back and go for a drive.

'How much were they again . . .?' asks Short Tony as he twists the wheel to bring us round onto the minor roads.

'Seven pounds fifty each,' I confirm. 'No VAT.'

'Forty-five quid,' calculates Short Tony. 'That's a poultry amount.'

We continue the journey in silence.

* * *

Chickens are completely new to me.

I didn't have a pet when I was a child. We weren't really a 'pet' family. My mum had her badminton, my dad had his Sinclair ZX81 and I had my music. In fact, music was all around me from an early age, carried in the genes of the Marsh family – it seemed predetermined that I'd end up in the industry.

My Uncle Ted was an excellent violin player in his youth, perhaps never fulfilling his potential – he became an in-demand music photographer in swinging sixties London. My cousins formed a band with the young Phil Collins, whose ex-lighting display would impact on my own life so much at a later date. I have a signed copy of the early *Genesis Live* album accordingly, and have always felt close to the band.

My cousins moved on. One is now a respected professor in a

leading European music conservatoire; his daughter is a celebrated violin soloist, who has played and recorded with leading symphony orchestras. My other cousin became a much sought-after guitar and violin teacher. And then there was my grandmother – in her youth, she was the piano player for a dance band in London. You can't get more rock and roll than that. She died very recently, at an extremely old age.

It feels wonderful, deep inside, to be part of a family lineage like that. I hope my descendants will look back on us – the music professor, the internationally renowned classical soloist, the man who supported the Sultans of Ping – and be a tiny little bit inspired by our achievements.

I fretted that I had caused my family concern by leaving a safe, comfortable job based around Strategic HR Initiatives in order to follow my dreams, going on sabbatical, being a househusband and playing bowls and having some chickens. But they needn't have worried. Everything was going idyllically in the cottage – I was managing the stresses and strains of my new life well and, whilst she might have got a little bit tired from her working day, the LTLP knew that she would be returning home to an immaculately househusbanded dwelling and a beautifully prepared and arranged meal of chicken and a potato, or chilli and a potato, or lamb steaks with salad and a potato.

So life was superlative for both of us. Until it all went a bit tits up.

* * *

Solitaire is no bowls, but it does qualify as one of those games that shouldn't be interesting but is. You see the cards. You check the cards. You move the cards. You see more cards. You check the cards. You move the cards. You see the cards. You check the cards. You move the cards. All whilst the clock is ticking away against you, challenging you to go faster and faster. It is a welcome escape from the routine drudgery of work.

I did enjoy the odd game, when I was a bit stuck on whatever job I was doing at the time. I would sit at the makeshift desk in the back room, whilst rabbits gambolled on the patio outside the French windows. They probably wondered what I was up to.

I noted with concern that Solitaire had worked its way above Microsoft Word on the list of frequently used programs on the computer. I thought about this for a bit, and decided to leave the game open all day, rather than keep launching it from the Start menu.

The telephone trilled into life.

The sound was an unexpected one – people very rarely call me during the day, and it made me jump. The sound shrilled through the house and round and round my ears. I picked up the handset, tentatively. It was the LTLP on the other end, using her Voice.

'Have you spoken to the cleaner?' she demanded.

I explained that I had not, as I had been busy. Her Voice didn't like that, and shouted at me in a threatening tone. I held the receiver six inches away from my ear; I felt my hair blowing horizontally in the opposite direction, like in cartoons.

'Look.'

There was a microsecond of thunderous silence, like the imperceptible gap before the final chord.

'Ring the cleaner. Speak to her. Get a cost. Find out about things. If you haven't telephoned her before I get back then I'm not speaking to you. Get it?'

I nodded at 350 nods per minute. The conversation was closed. We assured each other of our mutual love before I replaced the receiver, and stared at it hard for several minutes. Pondering her words, there seemed to be some ambiguity about them. I resolved to wait until she got home before doing anything stupid like ringing the cleaner, and, anyway, my plan of a delicious meal of pork chop and a potato would put her in a better mood.

But it was good to hear a human voice in the daytime. Even a shouty one like that.

I'm not sure how it became the received wisdom that I was shit at cleaning. I certainly didn't think that I was, and as I form fifty per cent of our household partnership it struck me as a bit unfair. However, there will always be different standards applied to household jobs, and these are usually gender-related:

HER: 'Oh dear. There is a speck of dust on this ornament. I shall initiate a full spring-cleaning programme immediately.'

HIM: 'Golly. This mantelpiece is dusty. I'd better – hang on! I can make tracks in the dust with my finger! Cool.'

The LTLP explained at some length that her problem lay with my interpretation of these standards. Essentially I was told that if she was going to go to work all day and leave me at home, then she wanted the cottage spotless on her return. Which I thought was understood. But I am afraid that there will always be conflict if a woman with obsessive-compulsive anti-cobweb move-the-ornaments-before-you-dust and more-than-once-a-month fundamentalist tendencies decides to set up home with, say, a tramp.

So some conflict arose between us, exacerbated, I can freely now admit, by the fact that I think she did not quite understand the pressures I was under on sabbatical. I do not think I am being sexist if I say that women are generally better at housework than men, but we seemed to have reached a stage of no compromise, which, to me, was worrying.

On the face of it, her suggestion to employ a cleaner was an extremely attractive proposition, viz. I would not have to do the cleaning any more. But a million objections churned round my brain as I wrenched my eyes away from the telephone and realised in dismay that the Solitaire clock had reached seventeen minutes. We had employed a cleaner before, a long time ago, and I knew the score. They're always hoovering around you, disturbing your concentration. And they move your things. And they have this uncanny knack of starting work on the bathroom just when you really really need to use the toilet. Like many creative people, I need my personal space.

My bare feet thwapped against the cold tiles as I wandered through into the bathroom. Objection number two was this: it's a small community, and I did not want to walk into the village pub to find Mrs Short Tony or Mrs Big Andy or Mrs Len the Fish discussing intimate details about my pants, or anything else that a cleaner might hypothetically have found at the back of my chest of drawers (2nd one down). The problem with the LTLP is that she sometimes just does not understand.

My wee was dark yellow, which caused me a pang of anxiety; I studied it closely for signs of cloudiness in the bowl. Whilst I was in there it seemed like an appropriate idea to clean the bathroom, so I squirted some I Can't Believe It's Not Toilet Duck around the rim and initiated a full flush by holding the handle down.

Bathroom cleaning duties complete, I sat down on the soft chair with my tea and rested for a good ten minutes in front of a property programme. It was almost halfway through, but fortunately they did a convenient 'recap' so that I could catch up.

Disturbing me; small community. There were two serious objections already. But of course it was the big one that was really bothering me. The fear of redundancy. I would become the only man in living history to be made redundant from not having a fucking job.

I fretted about the cleaner issue for the rest of that day. I fretted so much that I decided that I should perhaps do some dusting myself. A clean house, a pork chop and a potato – she would calm down and, in fact, be putty in my hands. I might as well be changing into my best love pants there and then. As I located the dusting equipment I racked my brains to work out what our earlier tiff had been all about.

Dust! Dust! Dust! Too much dusting must surely be bad for the furniture. It would wear it down to nothing, especially with the dust spray stuff which must be full of chemicals. What the fuck was she talking about? A cleaner? I was clearly pretty proficient at this now, scuttling expertly from surface to surface like Edward Dusterhands. The spray smelled strong and disgusting; I felt a rising concern about getting too much of it on my skin and ending up like the Joker from the Batman films. But fuck it! I would move the ornaments as well. Dust! Dust! Dust! Fuck it! I would get the Hoover out! Dust! Hoover! Hoover! Hoover!

A poke around a seldom-visited corner revealed the old black leather shoes that I had last worn to the office. I had forgotten that they existed. They were caked in months of dust, that particular dust that gathers only in corners, so I hoovered these as well then ran the vacuum over the rest of the flat surfaces that I'd got bored with wiping manually.

One more thing to be cleaned. But with that I sat down and took care and used a soft cloth and a small amount of chrome polish, and those cotton buds that you're absolutely totally forbidden to put in your ear but that people buy for putting in their ear. The Fender Telecaster emerged shiny and gleaming, and ready for action once more. I played a very quick acoustic gig to the banisters before replacing it.

The banisters proved not to be the most receptive audience in the world, but a gig's a gig. On a whim, I decided to chuck in some old stuff. I can still remember some of the chords to the aliens song, and included an abbreviated version for the benefit of the newel post. On impulse, I added in a new bridge section.

'We bring you Strategic HR Initiatives! We bring you Strategic HR Initiatives!'

It did not scan at all, but made me feel a bit better. I replaced the guitar with a long sigh and mooched back downstairs for a tea.

Cleaners, dusters, domestic help.

I couldn't have accepted that. Because it would have meant that I had failed.

I'd never failed at anything, ever. Not in my personal life, not in my professional one, not in the music business. Because I am the sort of person who keeps going until I get what I want. That is why I'd joined Simon, Dave and Iain in the brand-new band. That is why I'd moved the ornaments when I dusted. That is why even now I am looking round seriously for a bass player, a drummer and a singer. The fear of failure is everything to me, more so even than being shouted at by a man.

When you play bowls, it does not matter one jot whether you win or lose. What matters is that you overhear the opposition whispering: 'That was a good win, as the young bloke that leads for them is a really strong player.' The Velvet Underground never sold very many records, but influenced a hundred thousand other bands to get going. The LTLP has always looked up to me, and I was determined not to let her down. There had been a small blip, that's all.

I just needed a plan.

*   *   *

The chickens are Black Rocks, a hybrid breed that love to free-range and are both docile to live with and hardy in the cold weather; accordingly, they are considered ideal for the beginner chicken fancier. My only concern is that I will grow out of them soon. The chicken lady did not have any Transylvanian Naked

Necks on offer – in fact, she didn't seem to have heard of them. I worry about the legitimacy of her supply operation.

Black Rocks are reported to lay an egg a day for most of the year, production only easing off as the daylight hours reduce in winter. With a half-dozen birds between the two of us, we would not go short in that department; I make a note to look up some egg recipes when I get back inside. The chickens have sleek and shiny dark reddy-black feathers that become a warm brown closer to the neck; their little red faces are crowned by a small red comb. They really are the most attractive animals, although not in a sexual way.

Initially, they are reluctant to leave the dog cage, huddling at the back as we place it gently down on the bark. But we tempt them out gently by shouting things like 'Get out of the fucking dog cage!' and soon they are pecking around curiously in their new home. Chickens! I finally have some chickens. I feel like there should be some form of fanfare. Forget computerised typesetting, forget local newspapers, forget it all. I finally have a role for myself in the village. I am the man with the professional chicken setup.

Big Andy appears from the path beside the cottage, shepherded towards us by the LTLP. He takes a brief look at our handiwork, and gives one of the posts a critical poke.

'Nice chicken run,' he comments. 'Now come over the road and see mine.'

'A letter box?' I spit.

'I'll show you,' offers Big Andy.

We wander over the road in silence, one punctuated only by a single 'cluck' from behind the wall of the village doctor's.

'Here you go.'

I do a double-take as I pass down the narrow path between his house and his garage, stepping out into the expanse of his back garden. A shady corner has been fenced off ready for the arrival of chickens, the wire reaching six or seven feet high and then stretching across as a roof. At one end of the run is a salvaged old wooden front door, a familiar open rectangle in its very centre.

Big Andy's new chicken run does, indeed, feature a letter box. I stare at it in both amazement and annoyance. He is being ridiculously competitive about his new run. It is not even as big as mine.

'Have they had any mail yet?' I enquire sarcastically, as he twists the handle and gives me a tour of the facilities.

'I've concreted the posts properly, right into the ground,' he mentions, ignoring me. We take a walk round the run before exiting back through the front door, which he closes carefully behind him. I consider lying about our own post construction techniques, but do not wish to descend to his level.

'Some of that wood you've used looked quite rotten,' I point out, as we wander back through the garden.

I won't have it said that I have failed in having the best chicken coop in the village. It is ridiculous, him going to those sorts of lengths just for some scraggy old ex-battery hens. My pedigree Black Rocks will put them to shame, and it will serve him right. I will be careful not to let them mix, so mine do not get into bad habits. But I suppose they can write to each other if they like.

TEN

The great gig in the hall

There is a knock at the door.

I blink in surprise. There is never a knock on the door these days, let alone at this time in the morning. I mean, telephone calls are quite rare, but knocks are unheard of. The weather outside is poxy; I have only just scuttled back in my overcoat and pants from waking up the chickens to let them out from the coop into their run. Now, I am looking forward to a nice cup of hot coffee and perhaps a date with *Bargain Hunt* before I settle down to do some important work.

I trot through the kitchen and open the door to find Mrs Short Tony shivering in the unseasonably arctic conditions. Mrs Short Tony works at a school, so gets loads and loads of time to mooch around at home whilst the rest of us are working hard.

'The chickens are escaping,' she reports.

There is a short pause whilst I digest this news. Being a man, I really am no good whatsoever at multi-tasking, and therefore there is some comfort in the fact that I am able to combine my eventual reaction with some much-needed practice for the following week's National Face-Falling Championships. She gives me a helpless shrug and I grab some proper clothes in order to investigate.

Outside, I find Short Tony grimly banging in nails. The wind howls pitilessly through the trees. The chickens peck around innocently.

'I caught them sitting on this fence,' he explains, indicating a piece of the back fence that is surely too high for chickens to get up to. I look at the chickens. I look at the fence. To be fair, we had identified it as a Point of Potential Weakness, but had assumed that they would not be able to jump that far up.

We spend the next bitterly cold hour raising the height of the fence by two feet. Len the Fish not being available, our fence-raising is slow and ham-fisted – but I am encouraged as I realise that I have taken some of his skills on board; I grip and twist like somebody who has been gripping and twisting all his life. My neighbour on the other side, Harold, hears the banging and peers over the fence from his garden; I give him a chill-handed wave. Meanwhile the chickens continue to potter about inquisitively.

Pausing in my gripping and twisting for a moment, I cast my eye around the fenced area. It runs to several square yards of my and Short Tony's land in a desirable part of our gardens backing onto the woods. The posts are still new and clean; good-quality tree bark lines the ground. On my side, I've taken some large old flints that had previously formed a garden wall and created a banked-up area, a short path and a gallery for chicken-viewing purposes. I've also strung up a washing-line arrangement for the chickens so that I can hang up small bits of food in order to keep things interesting for them. Stopping your chickens from getting bored is key to good husbandry.

It is a lovely enclosure. I do not see why they would wish to go elsewhere, and I am a very tiny bit hurt by their attitude.

*   *   *

The rain whips horizontally across from the south-west, blattering us, threatening to sneak its wet fingers inside my anorak like a drunk girl at a bus stop. I grit my teeth and search the horizon for some blue.

My opponent's wood skids across the green, water spraying up behind it as it goes. She is a very pleasant elderly lady, with whom I have already enjoyed a laugh and a joke. Her wood comes to a halt several yards short of the cott. Again.

One of the key skills for the lead is judging how far to roll the cott. Sometimes, you will find that your opponent is very good when the cott is a long distance away – in which case you will try to roll it short. Conversely, some prefer the shorter game – at which point you try to bring it to rest right at the end of the green.

'It's no use,' she turns to me. 'I just can't get it that far. I'm not strong enough.'

I return her a weak, guilty smile.

It is one of those accepted things that is not exactly gamesmanship or unsporting or cheating, but is just a bit awkward, especially when you are playing a nice old lady who is a little bit weak in the arms. I avoid her for the rest of the end.

'Put in another long one,' hisses Nigel as we cross over for the next go.

I make mumbling noises. I do not want to be unkind. I am not Robert Mugabe. But nor am I Nelson Mandela. I am somebody in the middle, like Kenneth Kaunda. Laying the mat down, I throw the cott quite long; long enough to be a bit difficult for somebody with a bad arm, but not as long as I clearly could, thus giving the impression that my long(ish) throw was a complete accident. She gives me a reproachful look. Nigel gives me a reproachful look. I have tried to please everybody and now they all hate me. It is typical.

Ironically, my first wood pulls up about ten feet short. My opponent's rests next to it. I glare hard at the playing surface – there was surely a bobble somewhere that took the pace off the wood. The lead should know his lengths.

'Never mind,' calls Nigel.

I trip slightly as I release the second; it bounces rather than rolls and finishes even shorter.

'Never mind,' the skip reassures patiently. I give him an angry look. People are always reassuring me patiently to 'never mind'. I gesture my strong disappointment with a sharp sweep of the arm and turn away. 'Never mind?' I hiss to Big Andy. 'I want to get it fucking *right.*'

Howard's been struggling for players on Thursdays. Thursdays are difficult, as four rinks play – twelve players per side in total.

He'd brought it up at the annual meeting, the one that I'd returned from very late at night with leg injuries, but we thought we'd be all right. But we've lost Ron and Vicky, and a couple of other prospective players, and John Twonil has decided to take up golf, and Richard's shifts have all changed.

'I've rung so many people now,' complains Howard.

'My daughter used to play when she was seventeen, eighteen,' recalls Tim. 'Then she went to university, and I said to her: "Find a good bowls team there." But she didn't want to know.'

We promise that we'll try to find more players. Personally, I think a major part of it is not having a bar. We have some benches, a dry cabin, somewhere where we can go to the toilet and a nicely stained fence, but no bar. That doesn't make us unusual on the circuit, and to make up for it one of us will usually bring a couple of tins, but it means that we're missing a selling point for the young people.

There are very few sports which can offer you the solid enjoyment of balancing a pint on the grass before you have your turn; even the professional darts appears to be teetotal these days. Bowls can be a very self-conscious sport – all eyes are on you – and a relaxing drink to calm your nerves and help get everything in perspective can help a lot. There is very rarely drunkenness or hooliganism at bowls. We are above all that.

'Well they were bringing neat vodkas over from the pub opposite,' Nigel recalls. 'And in the end the opposition complained. And then, of course, the following fixture was the one where she fell over.'

'Yes. I do remember that one,' I assent.

'That was the one where there was the pushing and shoving at the end,' muses Big Andy.

I order another round on my bar tab.

The village pub is busy. A customer tries to ease through us to the bar, but is thwarted by the sleepy form of Len the Fish's dog lying in the gap between barstools. The man halts and stares down at the animal, which raises its head and gives him a lugubrious and slightly disapproving look, like Stephen Fry confronting some burglars. I make some room, and the Chipper Barman glides over to serve.

Eddie arrives.

Eddie rarely plays on a Friday, as it's the evening that traditionally he spends with his wife, Mrs Eddie. As it is, Mrs Eddie is away at their daughter's, and so Eddie has free licence to join us for a few pints.

'Bloody hell . . .' he gasps as he walks through the door, catching sight of the new upholstery.

'Have you not seen it? Quite striking, I thought,' I reply.

The Well-Spoken Barman pushes past us to rest some empties on the bar. He has the leave-me-alone air of a man who has been defending haberdashery all day. We tactfully wait for his withdrawal before resuming the discussion.

'There's reupholstery. And there's reupholstery,' says Eddie.

The glow from the fluorescent pink seat covers now seems to fill the room, transfixing and hypnotising all who behold it.

'It's like – it's like we're in a gay bar . . .'

'No,' I correct him. 'It's like we're in a heterosexual notion of what a gay bar might look like. Actually, most of the gay bars that I've ever been in have been horrible dives.'

'You've been in gay bars?' someone asks.

I used to live in London and work for a company that was developing Strategic HR Initiatives. I see no reason to defend the fact that I've been to a gay bar to anyone.

'Was it with that phone?' asks John Twonil.

'Were you in at lunchtime?' I ask the Chipper Barman later on, when the crowd has thinned out to a few regulars and he is slowly wiping down the pumps. The whole upholstery situation has been causing comment all night – it looks like the village pub is moving upmarket. Will this be a problem? There are so many incomers to the village, I strongly worry that the village pub will cease to cater to us locals.

The Chipper Barman places a full pint down in front of me. 'Naaah.'

My strong worries vanish.

'Wife and kids went shopping into town, so you know what I did?' At this, he leans forward at me, resting both hands on the bar in front of him, and nodding his head slowly as if he has a great secret to impart.

'What?' I ask.

'I got my bass and amplifier out and just started playing a few things.'

There is a short pause, while I feel my entire inner body leap.

'I didn't realise you played the bass?' I hear myself saying.

* * *

Simon, Dave, Iain and I were gelling as a unit, and were going out under the name 'Where's Johnny Christmas?'. Finding names is hard, and every band goes through this. You need something memorable but not forced, clever but not clever-clever, intelligent but not pretentious. You need something that will work typographically on a record sleeve; something that will point towards your sort of music and attract the casual browser in HMV. Above all, we were determined not to call ourselves anything that would allow the national music press to make a derogatory pun in the headlines at our expense. You have to keep looking forward in music. Anyway, we were pleased with Where's Johnny Christmas?, which would clearly get us vastly more respect than the juvenile Wildebeeste and reflect our more sophisticated and original songs. When you hit on the right name for a band, you just *know.*

Our first song was called 'Where's Johnny Christmas?'. It was a really catchy name for a song, and fitted the rhythm of the chorus well. The lyrics worked on many levels, and were about this guy called Johnny Christmas and trying to find him; the arrangement introduced our trademark sound of a mix of twelve-string and electric guitars. Other songs followed, but we deliberately stayed clear of the subjects of motor racing or alien life-forms. We had a more refined approach than the rawness of Wildebeeste; Simon was coming up with impressive song after impressive song; despite my early promise I was steering clear of writing in favour of finding my sound.

On reflection, when I say we were 'going out' as Where's Johnny Christmas?, what I mean to say is that we were going out to rehearsals and then to the pub under that name. Rehearsing hard in that school hall. Getting our act together, becoming potentially one of the top bands – if not *the* top band – in Billericay.

But we didn't have any gigs. We were tightly, tightly rehearsed, and raring to put on an industry showcase, but we didn't have any gigs.

So we hired the local church hall.

* * *

The church hall was a natural progression for us. The thing about being a local band is that until you make a name for yourself, you don't have much control. You turn up and fit in with the promoter. It's like being a bowls club that doesn't have its own green, clubhouse and bar – you can't make any money and you're at the mercy of the groundsman's every whim. By taking the reins and promoting ourselves at the prestigious church hall venue, we knew that we could play what we liked, when we liked, the room would be set up exactly as we wanted it, and after expenses all door receipts would go to us.

It was a lot of work, but it would be worth it. We hired a PA, employed some big blokes to work the door, engaged a promising young girl photographer to get some proper shots of the band playing, ones which we could use in subsequent publicity. We made flyers, created a backdrop, sold tickets, packed the place out. We sat in the backstage area, listening to the hubbub of people filing in, nervous energy flying round the room. The first gig with a new band is always a special, unique shared experience for its members.

'Have a good gig,' I wished Simon.

'Have a good gig,' he replied.

'Have a good gig,' I wished Dave and Iain.

'Have a good gig.'

People talk about The Who at Leeds and the Stones at Hyde Park, but – in its way – Where's Johnny Christmas? at the church hall made the same sort of impact. Granted, the national music press didn't cover the event, wrapped up – as they were – in the establishment cliques of Manchester and London. But I would be surprised if most people who were there that night, who packed themselves into the sweaty venue up against the stage and beside the hatch for the tea urn, who were battered and whipped by the Where's Johnny Christmas? sound, didn't find afterwards that their lives had changed in even some minor way. At the end of the gig, as the last chord was dying away, as the cheers and applause of at least fifty star-struck music fans – some of whom we didn't even know from school – came to an end, I generously stepped up to the microphone and invited the entire audience back to my house, my mum and dad being on their holidays in Cornwall. This wasn't just the first step to becoming one of the top bands – if not *the* top band – in Billericay. This was the first step to conquering the whole wide global rock and roll world (starting with south-east Essex).

Some time later, as I climbed square-jawed into bed with the promising young girl photographer, listening to breaking and smashing noises from downstairs, I replayed every note, every chord in my mind. Rock and roll. Rock and fucking roll! We had made a sonic assault on the church hall, we had battered and seismically drilled the youth of the town with a tidal wave of rock and roll. I was a member of a smash-hit band, I was at a wild post-gig party and I was just about to give a promising young girl photographer a personal rock and roll seismic drilling that she'd never forget.

'Never mind,' she reassured me patiently, about three minutes later.

*   *   *

'The thing is, I can play anything on the bass, me,' explains the Chipper Barman later on, when but three people are left in the bar. 'That's what I used to do in my old band. Just tell me what to play, and I'm quite happy standing there at the back playing it.'

'Yes, that's exactly what a band needs in a bass player,' I agree. 'As a matter of fact, I supported The Sult—'

'Anything at all, really,' he continues. 'Quite happy, just playing it. Dum, dum, dum, dum.' He mimes some bass playing with his fingertips.

'Good stuff,' I agree.

'So if you want to get together for a jam sometime, I'm quite happy to,' he says.

I have something a bit more solid than 'a jam' in mind, but 'a jam' is probably how Debbie Harry started. I agree vigorously.

'Well, we'll sort a date out the next time you're in here,' says the Chipper Barman.

There is a full moon, and no need of torches as Short Tony and I trot down the hill towards the cottages.

'So anyway,' I insist. 'It was after a Christmas party, and nowhere else was open, and one of the guys – Big Mike – knew some people who were gay, and that their pub was open late and that we could get in, and that was really the only time.'

'I need a slash,' Short Tony mutters.

The orange-hued lamp glows away at the gate, washing mournful colour across the tarmac. I have never worked out why my street lamp is this horrible orange sodium thing. There are a couple of lamps at the far end of the village, up towards Colin's farm, and they are both a nice rural old-fashioned white – the epitome of old-English street lighting. Whereas this one is grim and dull and out of place; it seems to scream 'municipal!' louder than the Reverend Ian Paisley being chased down the Falls Road by a giant Municipal.

But my optimism alone would light up the street.

Somehow, completely out of the blue, it has happened. As I said – hang around the village pub long enough and a lucky break will come along. Granted, it was not Bono, or the four non-guitar-playing members of Deep Purple – it was the Chipper Barman and the revelation of his bass-playing prowess. From nowhere, from out of the blue, I've got the beginnings of a band again.

ELEVEN

I'm in love with my bookcase

'Do we really need to pay for one? There are loads in the field just past Glen's place that we could . . . acquire.'

I frown at Short Tony, wondering whether he's serious. He takes another swig of red wine. I take another swig of red wine. He takes another swig of red wine. I have always been quite competitive so I take another swig of red wine and pour some more. The LTLP and Mrs Short Tony sip their girls' drinks, daintily. I lean forward from the depths of the worn orange sofa, stroking my chin to help me think.

Within the immense brick fireplace, an ex-apple tree spits and bursts. The renovation work that we had carried out – ripping out the chipboard, scraping off the artexing, revealing the old lintels and beams – had provided us both with previously hidden inglenooks. Among other intriguing artefacts.

Short Tony has a fire on most nights, in most weathers, because he is a man and he has a fireplace. His dog lifts one eyelid to assess the situation before calculating that nothing needs to be done and that he can retreat back into the dreaminess of dogdom.

'I think they're Stevie's. And he's a mate,' I caution eventually, although there is an unconvincing note in my voice. I am not sure whether kidnapping a live sheep is made any worse whether you know its owner or not. But we have had quite a few swigs of red wine in the swigs before the recent swigs, and agree to explore the possibility a bit more over more swigs.

We agree that it would be possible to wait until the dead of night, leave the car parked on the corner where the public footpath starts, select a healthy-looking sheep, bundle it into the back of Short Tony's truck and smuggle it into the garden.

'How would we butcher it?' I ask. 'You'd have to be the one to shoot it. I only have a small air rifle. That would be no good. All we'd have would be a slightly bleeding and very annoyed sheep.'

Short Tony makes firm noises about the small-print conditions on his shotgun licence. Shooting it is not an option.

'According to Hugh Fearnley-Whittingstall,' pipes up the LTLP, 'meat is better if the animal is not stressed when it is slaughtered.'

We ponder this. 'We could take your Jag,' I moot. 'That would give it a smoother and more comfortable ride home.'

Short Tony is unenthusiastic about chauffeuring a sheep in his Jaguar. We swig some more red wine. I have a brainwave.

'Rohypnol!' I announce. 'That's the answer. I'm always getting emails trying to sell me Rohypnol. We get hold of some, find a sheep and doctor its grass. It will be dark, so the sheep will not notice that there is a blue tinge to it. Then we carry it into the truck and bring it back here. Len the Fish can then do the butchery bit if we slip him a chop or two.

'Additionally,' I continue, now enthused, 'there's another advantage. If we bottle out of the slaughtering bit and have to take the sheep back to the field, the Rohypnol will mean that it won't remember anything.'

There is a pause, before Short Tony pipes up. 'If you've given it Rohypnol, will you be . . .'

'No,' I state, firmly.

I pour some more wine to cover the silence.

'It would probably be better just to buy one like we normally do, wouldn't it?'

I nod slowly. The last sheep that I bought ended up going horribly, horribly wrong – although it is perhaps unfair to blame the sheep for this. The bottle is finished; the conversation moves on. Short Tony chucks another hunk of orchard on the fire.

We do so much of this sort of stuff together, Short Tony and I. Not necessarily stealing people's sheep, but nice neighbourly things like sharing a large meat order, rearing chickens, going to the village pub. It's the community spirit that you only find in villages. I do wish that he'd take up bowls once more – the team misses his perceptive forehand draws.

* * *

With temporarily not a lot else on my plate, I walked around the cottage, surveying my domain. And, as always, I paused in front of the single feature that everybody in the world loved and commented on. Something that I had wanted ever since I was a small child, and had fought for, and had achieved; something that even the massive time-pressures of my sabbatical had not prevented me from working to perfection; something so ludicrously desirable that I pointed and laughed whenever I saw it, which was lots of times as it was situated right smack-bang in front of the sofa in the living room. Something over which the posh and foxy Kirstie Allsopp from the property programmes would jump up and down squeaking in excitement.

A bookcase that opened on hinges to reveal a secret area beyond, like in the Scooby-Doo cartoons.

This was my intriguing artefact – constructed with my own hands, with a small amount of help from Iain the renovation man – my first ever foray into serious carpentry. People would gaze open-mouthed as I casually demonstrated its workings, the wall of books swinging away with a soft creak, exposing a dingy but substantial space beneath the props of the winding staircase. You could store all sorts of things in there – racks of wine, Hoovers, large guitar amplifiers – even, if you got the opportunity, posh and foxy Kirstie Allsopp. The architectural feature to end all architectural features. I had planned and built it in secret; the LTLP was amazed when she first saw it. 'Unbelievable!' she whispered, burying her head in her hands in excitement.

Anybody can walk out and purchase an Aston Martin, a Porsche. Get a trophy girlfriend, a vintage Gibson guitar, some Viagra, a pair of £300 shoes, membership of the Groucho Club, a special-edition set of Drake's Pride Professional Plus woods. But for the real man – especially in this post-Dibley world – there is nothing that has quite the 'wow' factor as a bookcase that opens on hinges to reveal a secret area beyond. Like in the Scooby-Doo cartoons.

God knows what the surveyor would have thought of it.

Advice: if you ever want to buy an old cottage then you should get a full structural survey done, and then completely ignore it. The reason to get it done is that otherwise everyone you know will shake their head and stroke their chin and mutter, 'Well I'd get a full structural survey done if I were you.' The reason to completely ignore it is that surveyors become negative and alarmed about everything. The path between mine and Short Tony's could lead to rights-of-way issues. The roof is of old construction, and not properly triangulated. The road sits slightly higher than the front door, which could provoke water ingress. Negative, negative, negative. I am surprised that anybody ever even gets as far as taking their surveying qualifications, due to the risk of shutting one's hand in the door on the way into the examination hall.

A Scooby-Doo bookcase would have given him cause to draw breath.

Intriguing artefacts aside, there were a few big decisions looming up at us at that particular point in our occupancy. I ambled around the building once more. There was no central heating. The second bedroom was a tiny attic area leading off the first. The floorboards seemed a bit erratic, and you could poke your finger through the wood that comprised the frame of the 'conservatory'. And most official conservatories, as far as I was aware, didn't feature an open foul drain in the middle of the floor.

At least I hadn't caught anthrax, which, according to Mr Cover-one's-arse Surveyor, may or may not have been contained in residual spores lurking in the horse-hair plaster on the walls. Horse-hair was all the rage in plaster circles in the eighteenth century. These walls are eighteen inches thick in places; they knew how to build walls then, even if they weren't that careful about the deadly germs they embedded therein.

And the rooms were very small. Perhaps we hadn't noticed this so much over our first summer, but as soon as the days drew shorter and the garden became inaccessible, the walls kind of closed in. There was no room for a large table to accommodate a dinner party, and the second bedroom was in a permanent state of indoor laundry-drying. Walking into it was like entering one of those 'amazing maize mazes' that have sprung up over Britain, but with my T-shirts and pants. An amazing pants maze.

It was a lovely little cottage – a perfect one. It was cosy and old, and had a secret Scooby-Doo bookcase. It just needed a few minor alterations to make it suitable for modern living.

*   *   *

It has taken me a while. But I am forced to accept that the chickens can probably fly.

They can fly. They can definitely fly. I watch one perching arrogantly on the higher extended escape-proof bit of fence that we have only just constructed with our expert gripping and twisting. I carefully tiptoe in through the gate in order to talk it down, like the chicken whisperer. My hangover shouts at me angrily.

A clinging air of foolishness seems to envelop me. 'Can chickens fly?' is one of those questions like 'Why are there seasons?' and 'How does electricity work?' You sort of think that you know the answer and that it is all very simple, but once you try explaining it to people then you realise that you are getting a bit bogged down. I know ducks and geese can fly, but I had sort of assumed that chickens had evolved out of it.

Studying the terrain, I find myself at a bit of a loss. I really do not want to resort to a chicken-wire roof, as I suspect it will make what is at present quite a pleasant environment into something a bit guantanamobayey. And then there is the issue of wing-clipping. I know Katie Thear says that it is what you should do – and why this didn't ring 'chickens can fly' bells with me I don't know – and she says that it doesn't hurt and it is just like having your toenails cut, but I have a small feeling that it is not like having your toenails cut at all, and more like having a tooth removed by a dentist who may or may not be slipping foreign bodies into your mouth whilst you mistakenly listen to Randy Newman records. Call me a townie animal-rights Linda-McCartney-eating *Guardian*-reading Pink-Floyd-*The-Wall*-listening soft-hearted milksop if you want, but I do not want to be the one to catch these free-rangers, to confine them in my arms, to contain their struggles whilst their wings are clipped, especially as they will probably peck me.

'Get down off there!' I shout.

It occurs to me, however, that we still have a full complement. The chickens can escape in theory, but they clearly choose not to. I am touched by this. It is a tribute to my chicken-rearing skills.

'Having a bit of trouble there?' calls Harold, smiling over the fence.

'Nonono,' I reassure him.

* * *

I tried over those subsequent few days to put the cleaner thing out of my mind, but the LTLP kept putting it back there again. Every speck of dust, every spillage, every microscopic worktop stain remnant of the previous night's chicken and a potato – all were thrown back at me, as if they wouldn't have been dealt with sooner or later. As I saw it, I could engage a cleaner or clean the house regularly to her standards, as demanded – but I was sure that there must be a simpler solution than that.

Some people have their flashes of inspiration at their desk; some say that the bath is the place to think. Some find inspiration by pottering in the shed or talking to their chickens; others stare for hours into space. As for me, I often find that exercise brings inspiration. So I went for a run.

Run! Run! Run! Len the Fish was cutting the grass on the verge in front of his cottage. He dropped his strimmer and started laughing as I huffed past. Down the hill to the dip past Big John's place and then a short but exerting slope that begins my longer circuit, bounding along in my *new branded running shoes*.

I don't think that I'd ever had cool branded trainers before. I had been a geeky unfashionable child before the band thing came along, with a mother who did not understand the sociological importance of youth culture.

Nikes! Nike trainers! I felt like the dog's very bollocks as I ran, and made urban street hand signals to a startled crow in the cornfield with my thumb and little finger. Run! Run! Run!

When I had bought these shoes, I had been torn between the allure of a cool brand and the sensible approach of specialist running footwear. Then I had found that Nike makes specialist running footwear and my problem had been solved. They also make specialist badminton footwear, volleyball footwear, basketball footwear, squash footwear, discus footwear and table-tennis footwear. It is important to buy the specific pair for each sport you do, otherwise you will not perform to your optimum.

I may be wrong, but I have never seen Nike bowls footwear. They are missing a key market there.

The point is that I had been after serious sports gear, not some namby-pamby fashion item. Run! Run! They were comfortable and bouncy, even wearing them for the first time.

Nagging concerns played on my mind about Nike's alleged reputation for exploiting a vulnerable workforce of orphans.

However, I had the bright idea of making the run 'ethics-neutral'. So, every ten paces, I made sure I thought a very liberal thought. That way, it would balance out. I also resolved to read the *Guardian* online website extra hard when I got home, especially the politics bits about the Middle East, etc.

Between these thoughts I pondered the cleaner difficulty.

I didn't want to get a cleaner. It would make my sabbatical position less sturdy. I didn't want my pants discussed. Run! Run! Run!

But cleaning the house wasn't much fun, and I had so many more important things to do with my day. Run! Run!

She thought that I was rubbish at cleaning; in fact, she thought that I was the worst cleaner in the world, which was both extremely unfair, an affront to my dignity and probably sexist, etc.

I was not going to win the argument anyway.

So I might as well get a cleaner.

That would mean that I wouldn't have to clean.

But it would mean that I would have failed.

It was the failure idea that I couldn't stand. I hate failing at things. I would rather not try – yet here I was, trying away. I turned into the lane that runs past the spooky disused church. Its enveloping ivy glowered at me as I trotted past, mocking my dilemma with the cruelty that only vegetation can.

Think of something else. New songs. I had been working on a couple of bits of material on the PC studio. One of them had a beat very much like the pounding of a runner's legs. Each beat landed on the very spot where my Nikes hit the pavement. Over and over again, thumping down.

Bom-bom-bom-bom-bom-bom-bom.

The extra oxygen to the brain; the increased blood flow – I don't know what caused that flash of inspiration. But suddenly, as I plodded past the duck pond, the cleaner thing miraculously became clear to me. And I realised that I had come up with a plan. An extremely, almightily, exceedingly, *alarmingly* cunning plan.

Surely it could not be as simple as this? I turned my plan over in my mind, trying to find flaws, examining it in atomic detail, like a pathologist sifting the burnt remains of a cat. But it was brilliant – surely brilliant. I leapt gracefully over some dog shit and read it back to myself in my mind.

- I would tell the LTLP that I had turned over a new leaf, seen the error of my ways, etc., and would now make a regular point of cleaning the house myself until it was as spotless as spotless can be, to the highest standards of professional cleanliness, and that therefore we would not require a cleaner;
- But I would secretly engage a cleaner to do this for me.

From every angle, my EAEA-cunning plan seemed foolproof.

i) I wasn't going to win the argument anyway.
ii) She would think that I had backed down whereas really I wouldn't
   have done and I would know this and would therefore win without
   any failure being involved.

I hoppity-skipped onwards, new horsepower to my stride.
Bombombombom. My revelation had given my legs a new lease
of life, and whilst heart and lungs were yet to catch up with events,
I felt like a grillion dollars.

I leapt into the shower singing a carefree song. Then glistening
and bubbly, I picked up the telephone to negotiate terms.

TWELVE

Everybody's got something to hide except me and my cleaner

'Right,' I order the LTLP. 'Have you got that?'

She gives me a look of blank incomprehension. For somebody with all the paper qualifications, sometimes she can be very dense. I explain once more.

'So you want,' she repeats, very slowly and carefully as if she is presenting the theory behind fluid dynamics to a classroom of bison, 'me to ring you.'

I nod vigorously.

'You want me to wait until you have finished bowls and have got to the pub. Then you want me to ring you on an empty premise, when I have nothing to say. So you can get your phone out.'

I pat the brand spanking new Sony Eriksson in my pocket. It has a camera, and games, and you can set the ring tones to be different things for different people.

'Yes. That's it,' I confirm.

She shakes her head slowly, and returns to her food magazine.

* * *

'We've worked out,' I remark to Nigel as we cross, 'that you play better under pressure. So we're trying to help you along, by playing shit.'

Big Andy says nothing, merely continuing to shake his head in trauma after his previous two woods failed to trouble the vicinity of the cott. But my words, as ever, contain wisdom. Nigel is playing like a dream, like a god, like a Sky TV bowls pro. We are well ahead against the villagers of Wolferton, and he has achieved this single-handedly. It would surprise me not if Barry Hearn should leap from the undergrowth waving a contract.

'This is not,' replies Nigel, stony-faced, 'the sort of pressure that I want.'

* * *

One man. One man who has moved to Norfolk to find himself, turning his back on the safety net of nine-to-five working for the Man, forsaking all material comforts but the LTLP and her highly paid executive job. Just a man, with a man's courage; nothing but a man who can never fail. I often wonder who would play me in a film of my life. Pitt or McGregor, perhaps, although an actor/musician would be nice, like Bowie, Collins or Sting. A rock biopic, especially if the producers had the budget to get hold of the original Sultans of Ping. Phil Collins would be best – after all, I was practically *in* Genesis.

Despite the temporary absence of any musical endeavours, the 'finding myself' sabbatical stuff was going quite well. I wanted to be quite sure that all this was done and dusted before I moved on to the next stage of my life, and interestingly each time I started to think that perhaps I ought to think about winding down the finding myself bit, I suddenly thought of a new place to look. I had found that I was a good cook, especially with things that went with a potato, and that I was not fazed by the gender-reassignment of househusbandry. I'd discovered interests: in bowls, in Solitaire, in daytime television, and despite leaving the big city and the mael-strom of office life, my problem-solving skills had not deserted me, viz. the cleaner scheme.

All well, then.

* * *

The LTLP frowned on her return home.

I watched her with delighted amusement. She blinked and looked confused, and took two or three unsteady steps around the kitchen. I could see her brain gradually registering that something was vaguely amiss, yet her conscious mind couldn't quite grasp the elusive amissness.

'Have you cleaned up in here?' she asked finally.

I nodded with a hugely modest shrug, and mixed her a strong gin and slimline. The initial reaction was promising. I had 'plans' for her that night of a man/woman nature, which, given the trouble that I'd gone to cleaning the house from top to bottom, seemed only fair.

'And the cooker as well,' she observed, cottoning on to my handiwork as she made further examinations.

'As you're home on time tonight,' I said, picking my words carefully, 'why don't we go out to eat? I'll drive, so you can have another drink or two.'

This was approved as a good idea. She made a short journey round the cottage, pointing out with some incredulity that I had hoovered and dusted also. I made a point of demonstrating the freshly changed sheets, the sweet smell and touch of Persil that nestles silkily on bare skin. But by this point, to be honest, I was a bit narked with her tone of constant surprise – it was as if I had never done any housework in my life at all, ever. Still, I had been working hard on arranging the cleaning all day. I would put her to work that night.

Ray Davies wrote of the Village Green Preservation Society – he really should do something about pubs. To be honest, village greens are two a penny in this part of the world – they're everywhere. I don't know whether Ray Davies hopelessly mistargeted the song or whether it was so successful that it became its own anachronism, like the one the Specials did about Nelson Mandela. But pubs are struggling. The economics of beer selling; drink-drive laws; communities fragmenting; people living miles from their work-place; the fall in fashion of live pub entertainment; DVDs, computer games; smoking; the remnants of pre-Dibley feminism dictating that blokes should not go to the pub every day; evil bureaucrats at the EU and their strangulating red tape. Villages that once had three pubs might now just have one; some villages do not have a pub at all. I am lucky.

Much as I try to support the village pub, I was not stupid enough to suggest that we dine there that night. If we dined at the village pub then the chances were that Terry would be in there, or John Twonil, and I would get a bit pissed and the romantic moment would be gone, or I might get into conversation with Len the Fish and Short Tony and agree to buy a quarter-share in a cow that Len had earmarked that was currently grazing out on the salt marshes near Brancaster, and the LTLP would hold her head and then start shouting at me. So we headed north out of the village and settled down in front of a crackling fire in one of our regular places on the coast.

My rare steak was delicious, and just the thing to keep my energy levels high for the night ahead. I nudged her attention towards the oysters on the menu but she chose cod, which I'm sure is just as arousing.

The evening was crisp on our return; the cottage was dark but promised warmth. I leapt round and opened the car door for the LTLP, stroking her hair gently as she stepped out. She looked at me as if I had started screaming passages from Karl Marx whilst hurling freshwater fish at the upstairs windows.

My seductive gesture was interrupted by the sudden realisation that I didn't have my front door key.

I always have my front door key. I carry my front door key

everywhere. I am utterly anal about having my front door key with me. In fact, I am always having a go at the LTLP for not having her front door key. Not having your front door key is just stupid.

Several rummages around my pockets later and my front door key was still most definitely not there.

The cleaner! The bloody cleaner. Skulking around, secretly cleaning things! She had clearly moved my key – cleaning it away from inside my pocket where it definitely was before. I explained the problem to the LTLP, not mentioning the cleaner bit and trying not to lose the charged romance of the situation.

'What's the problem?' she replied. 'I'll just grab the spare one.'

We keep a spare key in a private secret place. I don't know why we do this, as I always have my front door key. There is no reason to risk burglary or axemurderdom by hiding one away. But we do.

Or did. Because there was a problem with her 'What's the problem.' The problem being that I had given the spare key to the cleaner who did not exist.

*   *   *

Bowls works because the woods aren't perfectly round.

As they're not perfectly round, they travel in an arc rather than a straight line. This is the 'bias' of the wood – the shape and weight distribution that allows you to sneak behind, between and among things, to bypass short woods, to approach the cott in different directions. Some are heavily biased so they swing in dramatically at the finish; others follow a more gentle and predictable curve. The manufacturers have mathematical diagrams on their websites to help purchasers choose what's right for them.

It's a key part of the ritual of stepping up to bowl: foot on mat, stare at head, check bias. The manufacturer's badge or logo is generally smaller on one side of the wood than the other – this indicates the direction in which your shot will swing.

Getting that bit wrong is not advised.

'Wrong bias! He's got the wrong bias!' cries the opposing skipper as my wood starts out on the left and continues that way, hurtling further and further away towards the next rink. I hang my head in humiliation and shame. Getting the wrong bias is something that happens about once a year, and has no parallel in any sport. It is a relentless, slow-motion embarrassment that causes the game to stop whilst people stand, hands on hips, smirking. Hit wickets, own goals, double faults – all over in a trice. Getting the wrong bias is slow death, like starting a four-minute song before realising that it's in much too high a key for you and that there is a further octave leap in the final chorus coming up.

An elderly lady on the next rink scuttles over from their head to prevent my wood from crashing into their own game. She gives me a Look. Having crossed the markers that define a wood as out of bounds, mine is unceremoniously and brutally rolled into the ditch.

'You get the wrong bias, Alex?' yells Glen from about twenty-seven rinks away. His voice echoes around the green.

'Wrong bias?' asks Big Andy.

'Wrong bias,' I confirm.

'Drinks on you then, mate,' calls Nigel from the other end.

* * *

I checked the private secret place. I checked it as thoroughly as somebody who knew that there was nothing to find in there could.

'It's not there,' I stated.

'What do you mean: "It's not there"? You haven't even properly looked.'

'It's not . . . there.' And then – stroke of genius – 'I think a bird took it.'

Her mouth opened and she shook her head slowly from side to side. 'Don't be so stupid. I'm going to look for the spare key.'

'It's really, definitely not there,' I reported. 'I looked earlier as well, when it was light.' Honestly. I knew that she was desperate to get me into bed, but if she would just keep still for a moment and trust me. 'It happened before – remember? Because it's shiny. A bird took it.'

There was a short pause of derision.

Truth be told, my story wasn't really that implausible. Not really. The spare key had indeed been moved before, being discovered about four inches away in a bird's nest under construction. So it could have been a bird that moved it, not a man who needed to give it to a cleaner. There was an element of plausibility.

She paused once more, then dropped a bombshell. 'We'll go next door to Short Tony's.'

Short Tony also has a spare key. His lights were on; they were at home. Again, however, there was a problem. The Short Tonys would know very well why the spare key wasn't there – they also used the cleaner's services, although in a more vanilla fashion, and she would have told them about her new employment. But I hadn't quite had time to prime them about the small print regarding our arrangement. They would immediately let the cat out of the dustbag.

She headed off purposefully towards the secret path. My romantic evening was going, as they say, tits up. And not the type of tits up that I had been expecting.

'Hang on!' I cried.

The bathroom window was slightly ajar. I had forgotten my key, but had left a downstairs window open. It is just as they say: if you lead a truthful, blameless life then the gods will smile upon you.

'I can get through the window!'

She shot me a withering glance. 'Stop messing about. Just come next door with me.'

I examined the window frantically. Apart from a few tomato

135

plants it was accessible enough. It was quite tall, and about the width of an amorous and slightly overweight man; high enough off the ground to allow reasonable access in the 'head first' position.

'It's late and their kids will be in bed,' I said. 'Nothing for it. I'm going to try the window.'

'It's only just gone . . .'

The end of the LTLP's sentence retreated into a muffled mess as I yanked the window open as far as possible and launched myself through the opening. At least, I half launched myself through the opening. My front half emerged in the cottage, gazing wildly around the bathroom, my back half definitely did not. My belt was caught on the window fastening.

Some sort of poky thing was pressing into my stomach, making it difficult to breathe properly. Beneath me lay the bath, still slightly damp from my earlier careful sprucing, and a large fake olde-worlde painful-looking-to-land-on tap/shower combo.

Outside, my legs thrashed about helplessly, my shape and weight distribution all over the place.

'What the *fuck* are you doing?' I heard through the muffled-ness. I felt my ankles being grabbed, and then something tugging at my shoes. This pulled me back and forth across the fastening and poky thing, which dug in alternately to my stomach and penis. I cried out, knocking over some shampoo with a flailing arm.

'If you're going to fuck around jumping into the bath then you can at least take your shoes off,' came the explanation. I felt them wrenched from my feet and then – crash! – I was face down on the wet enamel.

I lay stunned for a second before rolling myself over with diffi-culty and pulling myself up to a kneeling position, gripping the taps for support. A face appeared at the window, which I blinked at ruefully.

'You really. Are. A. Cretin,' it said.

I blinked at it once more, too confused to reply.

'Now can you unlock the door, please? I've got a long day tomorrow.'

I unlocked the door. Britain these days has gone to the dogs. It is impossible to employ anybody without ridiculous complications and hurdles. The LTLP pushed past me into the cottage. My due credit for the private secret cleaner would have to wait.

* * *

Despite my humiliation, we take all eight points from the game.

A whitewash! Before this match we were fifth – level with the River Lane B team. These eight points will take us to the top of the table, assuming that everybody else in the entire league has forfeited their matches and has thus scored zero.

Am I chuffed at our victory? Yes. However, there are mixed feelings. I feel like a batsman who has seen his side romp home by ten wickets, having previously been bowled first ball, dropped a catch, fused the tea urn and been lightly sick over the ham sandwiches.

But bowls is a team game, and on another day it will be me who is the hero. I buy the beers cheerfully – it does not really mean anything, as Nigel will buy the next round, and then Big Andy, and then there will probably be three or four rounds after that.

I almost talk to the Chipper Barman as I wait for my phone to ring, but he is a bit busy with customers and I don't get the chance.

THIRTEEN

The lonesome life of Harry Leon

My piano has arrived!

Grandma always promised that I would have it one day. I think she identified me as a musician from an early age: I used to sit at the instrument for hours at half-term when I was very small, studiously working out 'Eye Level' by the Simon Park Orchestra with one finger.

'Eye Level' by the Simon Park Orchestra was the theme tune from the detective series *Van der Valk*, which starred Barry Foster as Dutch detective Commissaris Piet Van der Valk, fearlessly patrolling the underside of Amsterdam. The theme got to number one in the charts, which a lot of instrumentals did in the olden days. Simon Park was the Jean-Michel Jarre of his time.

I am as eager as that small child to see the piano again, and hurry to the window when a gravel-scrunching announces the arrival of a van. I have cleared a piano-shaped area in the back room. It is a bit tight, but a handy space exists against the party wall. The piano men huff and puff whilst I direct their efforts, the instrument balanced expertly on their specialist trolley. It ploughs through the shingle towards the French doors, as hefty and solid as I remember it. I scuttle back into the kitchen to put the kettle on – I haven't seen anybody all day, and a long chat with some piano removal men is just what I need to buck me up.

After the piano men have hurriedly drunk their coffee and left, I return to the back room to examine my new treasure. It looms up monolithically in the corner, a dark-brown edifice of pianodom. Visually, it seems to take up a quarter of the entire room; great dark shadows fall across the floor where the mahogany blocks out all light from the windows. No wonder John and Yoko needed such a large white living room.

I pull the stool out from under the keyboard. With that placed in the playing position, the piano/stool combination covers the entire floor area from one wall to the other. There is a nagging thought in my mind that I should have mentioned something to the LTLP about it, but she is a busy executive now and I try not to clutter her mind with unneeded trivia.

It is the beginning of a new solo piano career for me! I stride up to it in my Elton Johnness. Perching myself on the edge of the stool, I raise my index finger and daintily brush down on the middle C.

'Plink!' it goes. Wahay!

'Plink!'

'Plink, plink, plonk, plink, thud, plink, plonk, plink!'

Hmmm. 'Thud' is not good, but the note in question is an A flat, and throughout my pianoing career I have always tended to save the black notes for special occasions only. Using an A flat in normal circumstances is a ridiculous affectation. 'Plink, plink, thud.' A mixture of 'plinks' and 'plonks' for the foundation notes is satisfactory. At least there were no 'plunks'. That would be worrying.

'Plink, plink, plink, plonky plonk, plink plink.'

The 'soft' pedal does not appear to work – I give it a little kick, but it is dead to my foot. As with my thuddy A flat, I am not too bothered about this. I have never ever used the 'soft' pedal and do not mean to start this late in life. Admittedly the instrument does need a certain amount of tuning, but the sound has a charm about it which will do for my solo work in the meantime. I bash my way through 'Don't Let the Sun Go Down on Me' and 'Goodbye Yellow Brick Road' (verse only – the chorus has some tricky bits), before teasingly leaving myself wanting more by going for a quick game of Solitaire.

It's funny, but the arrival of the piano seems to perk me up enormously. No, I might not have got a record deal quite yet. No, or got that band together, although I will speak to the Chipper Barman again tonight and we will nail something down. But it inspires me. Sitting at the keyboard, idly stroking chords, I am struck by the beauty and simplicity of the situation. One man sitting at one instrument. The optional extra of a voice as well. This is all Burt Bacharach does, after all. And he's had years and years to practise, whereas I've only just begun. Perhaps I should do that sort of thing? I could conquer the world (starting with north-west Norfolk).

For old times' sake, I spend some time trying to remember 'Eye Level' by the Simon Park Orchestra. I had forgotten how simple it was. I play and I play and I play, getting the tune right, working on variations to the theme. The sound of 'Eye Level' by the Simon Park Orchestra fills the cottage, the notes falling out of the piano effortlessly and joyfully, resonating in sonic magnificence with the natural reverb of eighteen-inch-thick stone, overtones and undertones bringing the very essence of Amsterdam in the early 1970s into the small cottage. A shape looms up at the French windows – I spot its dim shadow out of the corner of my eye and turn my head, startled.

It is Barry Foster, original star of 1970s TV show *Van der Valk*! Oh.

No. It is Short Tony.

'It's arrived then?' he comments, having squeezed himself into the two square feet of room that do not contain piano or piano-related equipment.

'It has!'

A small concern crosses my mind.

'You can't hear it next door, can you?' I ask.

'Not at all,' he lies.

This is a relief.

'I thought you weren't bad, considering you say you haven't played for ages.'

I bask in this high praise.

'Anyway, my daughter's taking up violin lessons. I'll let you know when she starts.'

* * *

We waited patiently for the architect whilst he played with his computer-aided design machine.

This was a big moment for us. We had instructed the architect to come up with some ideas for changes, to use his expertise to maximise the space available to us, to help us replace some of the old rotten materials that had been making do for years, and to generally make the cottage suitable for modern living. And all this was happening on his computer right before our eyes!

'Do you want a coffee before we begin?' asked the architect.

He picked up his empty mug. 'I'll have to push past you again, I'm afraid,' he said, squeezing between our backs and the photo-copier. We stood awkwardly once more to let him past.

The outline of our cottage showed on the computer screen. I was going to press some buttons, as basically all software packages use the same sorts of keys to do the same sorts of things, but the LTLP slapped my hand. We waited for our drinks to arrive then stood again to let him through.

'You see the main thing that you need to do,' he began, once he'd taken a long swig, 'is to move the staircase. Part of the problem with the space is that the staircase – Hang on.'

His receptionist had poked her head around the office door. 'That man's here again about the windows,' she said.

'Just tell him that I'm not interested. Not interested!' he replied. He turned to us. 'You wouldn't dream how many people turn up cold-calling wanting me to replace those windows with uPVC,' he said, gesturing towards the rotten-looking wood windows. 'They've been perfectly good for decades. Where was I?'

'The staircase,' reminded the LTLP.

'Yes. Now. If you were to extend, as you're planning, there are a couple of options for the staircase. You could have it here,' he traced his finger around one area of the screen, 'or here.'

The LTLP was nodding thoughtfully, but I had already spotted a fundamental flaw in his scheme.

'The thing is,' I said slowly, 'moving the staircase will be a bit difficult, as there's a bookcase there.'

He looked at me blankly.

'Downstairs, under the stairs. You must have seen it when you came to do all the measuring and stuff. It's a bookcase that opens out.'

'Ah,' he nodded.

'Like in the Scooby-Doo cartoons,' I clarified.

'Are you completely and utterly barking mad?' she hissed at me, when we had negotiated the staircase and were standing post-architected in the street outside.

I blinked at her, confused. 'What?'

'We're thinking of spending tens of thousands of pounds of the bank's money on major alterations to the house, and the only thing that seems to cause you the remotest concern is your bloody bookcase!'

'Well . . .' I tailed off. There was the hidden space beyond, and the hinges, and the hand-planed side panel that fitted exactly against the ancient wooden upright beam that abutted the fireplace. There was the silent opening and the satisfying 'clunk' as the unit was moved back into place. There was the first glimpse of blackness beyond, the delighted look on the audience's face as they realised what was happening. But how could I say this? Scooby-Doo bookcases are like jazz – if people don't understand them then it is impossible to explain. I just shrugged in the end, which appeared to be a satisfactory response as she stopped shouting at me, and we walked in silence for a bit.

'I've got loads to do when I get back,' she said in the car on the way home. 'I shouldn't really have taken the morning off. What's for dinner tonight?'

'I was thinking of doing some chicken thighs,' I replied. 'And a potato.'

There was a long pause.

'I think we'd better have a chat about things,' she sighed.

* * *

In 1930s and 1940s London dwelt a songwriter called Harry Leon.

Harry Leon was a more successful musician than even I have been – more so even than the Sultans of Ping. In fact, he was billed on his sheet music as 'Britain's most prolific song writer'. It is common for people to refer to past musicians as 'The Beatles of their day' or 'The Jimi Hendrix of his day'. Harry Leon can probably be accurately described as the Westlife of his day, in that his songs were immensely popular among the undiscerning proletariat but have been almost completely forgotten because of their horrible sickly and saccharine nature.

'When the Blackbird Says Bye-Bye'. 'Down a Hazy Lazy Lane'. 'When the Robin Sings his Song Again'.

Like Bowie, Mercury and Richard went on to do in later decades,

Harry Leon chose a pseudonym under which he released his greatest hits. Thus, 'Art Noel' was born. It was a shrewd commercial move. And if I'd written a song called 'When the Blackbird Says Bye-Bye', I'd have changed my name as well. It was hardly Where's Johnny Christmas?.

Mrs Harry Leon was a music lover. So much so that, each morning, when Harry Leon woke up from his slumber and announced 'I am feeling creative today – in my role as popular 1930s songwriter I shall compose another sickly and saccharine tune on the piano, transcribing it onto sheet music in order to sell to the undiscerning proletariat', Mrs Harry Leon would physically kick him out of the house shouting 'Get out! Get out! Go get yourself a proper job!' So Harry Leon would hasten off into the North London streets.

Poor Harry Leon. It is a shame how some weak men are unable to fulfil the traditional upper-handed role in their relationships.

The piano dates from 1910 – a John Brinsmead, made by honest craftsmen in London. It is as heavy as you can possibly imagine a piano to be; solid mahogany and an iron frame. You would not wish it to fall on you from a great height. Even just as a piece of static furniture it is magnificent. You would have to be a Philistine to complain about it.

It stood in the same North London drawing room for decades until my grandmother sold up and moved to her bungalow. Such a heavy and bulky item required specialists to move it, but my grandmother was always careful with her money and thus engaged the specialist services of the men from the shop below, an Italian bakery. When I had turned up to help after a hard day's work typesetting advertisements for the Royal Philharmonic Orchestra, the piano was solidly wedged on the flight of stairs, jammed up in the corner between the risers, walls and banisters, not going up, not going down. White-coated Italian pastry chefs swarmed around it, scratching their heads, waving their arms in the continental fashion and wondering how to get the instrument free. I think at one point somebody might even have cried 'mama mia'.

Grandmother's staircase had a secret box room above it, suspended between the ground and the first floors, and accessible only by a tiny hatch in the ceiling just inside the front door. Just as Grandmother's piano playing was important to my genetic development as a musician, this secret box room was extremely influential in my subsequent bookcase design career. Having a secret box room on your staircase is brilliant, but even I could see that there were better places for upright pianos.

It somehow budged in the end; carried out at the stagger onto South End Road by a troupe of Mediterranean bakers. Carried away from its home for decades, from where it had formed the focal point of genteel drinks parties, away from the place at which Harry Leon had turned up regularly, bearing some blank music manuscript paper and a hangdog air, to say 'Hylda – I couldn't use your piano again, could I? She's chucked me out, and I need to write another tune of a sickly and saccharine nature, in order to pay the rent collector.'

'When the Blackbird Says Bye-Bye'. 'Down a Hazy Lazy Lane'. 'When the Robin Sings his Song Again'. All hit songs. All written on my grandmother's piano – the piano that now stands in my sun room. If that isn't a signal that things are looking up on the music front then I don't know what is.

* * *

Romance is in the air. The new piano will let me welcome the LTLP home with some love songs.

I've played her stuff on the guitar before, of course. 'Love of My Life' by Queen, 'I Can't Help Falling in Love with You', and an improvised one that I wrote myself called 'Won't You Please Unlock the Bathroom Door Now, I am Very Sorry for What I Said Oh Yes I am'. But these never quite work; guitars aren't about romance. Guitars are about fucking. The piano is different; it is a softly seductive instrument. With a gentle fire in the grate and flickering candles, it is a 'mood' instrument; some simple Cole Porter, light jazz, perhaps caressing improvisations on 'Eye Level' by the Simon Park Orchestra. If I set up the Telecaster and amplifier in the remaining square inch of the room, I will hopefully be able to gently tease out the last notes of 'Eye Level', letting the soft piano sounds dissipate dreamily away into the air, before leaping across, grabbing a plectrum, hitting the distortion pedal and launching into 'The Stripper'.

She is disappointingly tired when she finally wanders in through the door. It is not as if I have not had a hard day as well, liaising with piano men. Furthermore, there is a tense moment when she discovers that the internet DVD rental by post thing that has arrived is not a girl's film after all, but is another episode of eighties science fiction drama *Blake's 7*, set in space. I honestly don't know how that mistake occurred.

She paces round the kitchen, pulling off her scarf and coat. I decide to hold off on 'Eye Level' for the time being.

'All I want,' she protests, 'is to watch a nice fucking film, one of the ones that I put on the list. And every time we get something it's *Blake's* fucking *7*. I can't believe you – you must have moved my choices down on the list.'

She is being unfair. 'I didn't, honest,' I plead, cursing myself for forgetting to secrete the DVD away until such time as I could watch it, repackage it and send it back.

She gives a menacing harrumph, dumps her boots in the rack beside the front door and gusts through to the lounge. It is fully three minutes before she turns to see through the arch into the back room.

'*What the fuck's that?*' she howls.

FOURTEEN

Total eclipse of the heart

My vegetables have arrived!

Every week, I get a box of organic vegetables delivered direct from the farm in the next village. There are always potatoes and onions, then possibly carrots and other root veg, cabbage, tomatoes, leeks, squashes – whatever's in season; a selection of delights for the week. Except the squashes, which taste of warm water.

Pretty well everybody in the countryside eats organic vegetables direct from the farm, and for me there are two main reasons why I do this. First, aside from the variety and interest, and the feel-good factor of giving a farmer the whole revenue for his work, the produce is unbelievably, spectacularly tastier. This is not necessarily because organic tastes better per se, but is due to a combination of factors. It's far, far fresher for a start; the growers aren't obliged to concentrate on varieties that look pristine and have a long shelf life, and they can harvest when the crop itself is ready, not when the distributors demand it. This is absolutely key, especially with the non-root crops. By preserving and encouraging the growing of the traditional English varieties that have for so long been squeezed out by the demands of evil big business, we can all do our bit to act as custodians, not just of 'heritage food' but of food that has so much to offer us in the present day.

Second, the Vegetable Delivery Lady is quite fit.

I run to the kitchen in haste. Wearing my most 'come hither' wolfish grin, I adjust my hair and throw open the front door with panache.

Except it is not the Vegetable Delivery Lady. It is a man. With a beard.

This is not what I was expecting at all. I peer round him to see if the regular Vegetable Delivery Lady is perhaps hiding round the corner in order to spring out and shout 'Surprise!'

But it is not to be.

I am a bit disgruntled by this. When I signed up to the service it was on the basis that I would get my vegetables delivered by foxy Vegetable Delivery Lady and not by a man (with a beard). The organic farm is clearly not quite as it seems. Like many evil corporations, they treat their existing business like dirt whilst giving new customers all sorts of incentives to sign up. And people slag off Tesco! I take my box grumpily and bid him a good morning.

*　　*　　*

It turned out that the LTLP was getting a bit bored with things with a potato.

I mean to say, it wasn't that she phrased it exactly like that, but reading between the lines it was becoming more apparent that she didn't like potatoes as much as I did. It is funny. You can be with somebody for so many years and still learn intimate things about them that surprise you. Baked potatoes aren't quick, but they are easy, simple and nutritious, unless you do them in the microwave whereupon they are quick, easy, simple and nutritious.

But perhaps that is the problem. They say that the way to a man's heart is through his stomach, and this may or may not be true. But the way to a woman's foofoo is via her stomach as well, especially if you are starting at the face and working down. Those of us who are successful househusbands (or people on sabbatical who are temporarily fulfilling a househusband role) have come to know this.

If I have ever learnt anything about women it is that they are quite keen on you making an effort. You can be brilliant – quite exceptional – at something, but if you are able to do it just like that then they are not interested. It is their foreplay. The effort is what counts. And the attainment. The effort and the attainment. Leave the cave and go hunting for days for your woolly mammoth; return and provide. Effort, love. Reheat woolly mammoth: no effort, vague indifference and contempt.

I've found this on stage. The female-arousal effect of standing before a crowd of people singing and playing is all to do with the show. Nobody cares that you're not perfect, as long as most of the notes are in the right place. It's the fact that you do it that allows you to do it. And if I was going to be able to participate in the LTLP's own personal organic lurve box scheme I was going to have to raise my game.

Norfolk is the place for food. There are dressed crabs, of course, and samphire, and vegetables. Then there are the Pie Lady's delicious pork pies, and Len the Fish's home-made sausages and Tham's Chinese takeaway. There is nothing better than settling down for the evening with a Tham's, except possibly settling down for the evening with a Tham's and a Pie Lady pork pie on the side.

It occurred to me that getting a Tham's would not qualify as the requisite amount of effort.

We have cookbooks like anybody else. Delias and Nigels and Nigellas and Jamies. We started off with just a few, but they have been breeding on the shelf and now spill over onto random piles. They are all pristine with disuse.

And I do cook, in my own style. In many ways, I model myself on Hugh Fearnley-Whittingstall. He is a genuine countryman from

Gloucestershire who produces simple yet delicious meals from the best the land has to offer – nothing pretentious, nothing over-complicated. He respects the chicken community and is not afraid of criticising Tesco. Delia Smith is, of course, a Norfolk heroine, and baked the cake that adorned the cover of the Stones' *Let it Bleed*. Slater, Oliver – I admire their talents.

Yet the book that has intrigued me most was by none of these people. It was a birthday gift from somebody optimistic, and is called *Nose to Tail Eating*.

Nose to Tail Eating is by a chef called Fergus Henderson, and his thesis is that you should cook every single bit of an animal that you kill, or otherwise you are evil. 'There is a set of delights, textural and flavoursome,' he promises in his introduction, 'which lie beyond the fillet.' Bits of a sheep, for instance. You know, bits. Not just chops and shanks and roasts. Ears. And eyes. And colon. And bits.

His philosophy did strike a chord with me. Trying very very hard to be a responsible country-dweller whilst maintaining a touch of rough primitive man about me, I resolved to follow Fergus Henderson's example. All I needed to do now was to wait for my special delivery.

* * *

I'd been put off overambitious cooking before.

Very early on in our relationship, I made the LTLP a coq au vin. I followed the recipe exactly, but unfortunately made a small mistake with the ingredients: instead of the required bouquet garni – a sort of teabag filled with herbs and stuff – I absent-mindedly picked up instead some wine-mulling spices that she'd been given for Christmas two or three years previously. We sat down later to an awkward meal of coq au mulled vin for two.

She was sympathetic; when you have just met and are trying to make a nice impression on each other you do not like to say anything too critical in situations like this.

That was ages ago. This night would be different.

A while later, her mother and father came to dinner. A double-booking had meant that she had to entrust me to source ingredients and make the chicken dish. The chicken seemed outrageously expensive in Sainsbury's, but they were selling whole turkey legs at ninety-nine pence each, and we sat down later to an awkward meal of Thai green turkey leg curry for four. I was still new to her mother and father, and they were ever so good about it.

Her mother and father would not be present this time round. Yes, this night would be different.

No bowls game; I didn't have a gig arranged.

This night would be different.

* * *

'And there will be a special romantic dinner waiting for you tonight when you get home,' I purred in conclusion. 'Honestly – you're going to love it.'

A Noise of Suspicion travelled down the telephone wire to me. But she did not know what I knew, I smiled to myself in an understated and yet endearingly rapacious manner. We assured each other of our mutual love and I replaced the receiver.

'Feeeel like maa-kin' lurve!' I sang tunefully to my tea, doing pelvic motions in time with Mick Ralph's guitar. I had a bit of work that I should be getting on with, but I had just twigged the technique of counting cards, and was aiming to get the Solitaire score to above minus one hundred and forty dollars.

A scrunch of gravel; there was a loud knock! I hurried through to the kitchen and threw open the front door in enthusiasm, to find a large Highlander beaming down at me.

'How ye doing?' he said, in Scottish.

Stevie is the village miller, another soul from elsewhere in these isles who has made this small corner of England his home. I saunter over to his windmill each summer's day to buy my bread. Going to the village windmill each day to buy bread is one of my top pleasures in life, even if it does prompt a constant nagging doubt that my life might be some bizarre *Truman Show/Matrix* hybrid, but with stop-motion puppet characters and narrated by Oliver Postgate. Its sails rise above the low-lying cottages, panning out over the fields and countryside and screaming 'Tourist attraction! Tourist attraction!' far and wide. Brown road signs nudge you towards it from the main road; leaflets bulge from the racks in local shops and pubs.

I am constantly being stopped on my journey by pensioners with caravans asking where it is.

'You've got it!' I exclaimed in excitement.

Stevie nodded, and began unloading pieces of sheep. The sheep that I mentioned earlier.

Legitimate Sheep. It was legitimate sheep, I hasten to add. Ordered via the medium of telephone, paid for, and set to be split between me and Short Tony. This is what Stevie and Mrs Stevie do whilst the tourists hibernate for the winter – genuine real-life shepherding. I had bought a real sheep from a real shepherd! Truly there was no better country-dweller than me. He checked the freezer bags as he went along – chops, shoulders, half-legs. As an animal, it was definitely beyond revival.

When the joints had all been counted out he paused.

'D'ye want the heart and stuff?' he asked, in Scottish.

'Oh yes,' I nod.

I can't remember where I read that stuffed heart was an olde English lovers' meal; I think it was in the sophisticated food section of a Sunday newspaper supplement from the village shop. Whatever – it makes sense, what with the heart/love and fertile spring lamb gambolling away connection – and the aura of heart is somewhat more meaningful than the crude cock symbolism of the alleged aphrodisiacs rhino horn or tiger penis. There was a recipe in the Fergus Henderson book that would sweep her off her feet, that would overwhelm her with its imagination, its effort, its intense sensations, its erotic potential. Even I have to admit that you do not get erotic potential by cooking potatoes, unless, perhaps, you do two smaller ones and lay them on a plate with a courgette placed between them.

I slipped the quivering heart from its bag and plopped it down onto a large wooden block; it studied me balefully whilst I rinsed my hands in order to dig out the instructions.

Examining the heart carefully, I was struck with wonder about the ingenuity of the professional chef. What to a layperson might just be a quivering mound of ventricles and aortae, a useless blob of muscle once parted from the sheep that once hosted it, is, in the right hands, a delicious and promising lovers' meal for two, a perfect accompaniment to clean sheets and champagne. The concept was both impressive and daunting. But I skimmed the recipe once more, and before too long I had snipped bits off, mashed up all sorts of ingredients – bread, onion, garlic, stuff – into a pappy paste and was stuffing heart cavities with carefree abandon.

Stuff! Stuff! Stuff! I pushed the mixture deep and down into the warm hollows of the organ as instructed, probing and pressing tightly to fill every inch, small spurts of blood and heart juice squelching back out over my wrist. It was funny how the chambers fitted like a glove puppet; my fingers sliding in and out cosily. I played with it a bit, holding it up beside my head.

'Hellooooo, Mr Heart!' I said in a funny squeaky voice.

'Hellooooo my friend!' it replied, whispering in my ear.

I could have done that all afternoon, but there was work to be done. I removed my hand and continued with the preparation phase. 'If you fail to prepare then you are preparing to fail' runs the mantra used by, among others, purveyors of Strategic

HR Initiatives. But it is good advice. I prepared and prepared. It was a special occasion, after all.

Heart takes hours and hours to cook in the oven; there would be time for a run and perhaps a bit of light work in the mean-time. Then I planned to take a bath, making sure to wash my bits really really carefully. In the glossy newspaper supplement magazines from the village shop there are always women complaining that their partner is an inconsiderate lover. Nobody could ever say that of me. I washed the blood and bits of heart pap off my hands, trying to get most of it out from under my nails.

'I feeeeel like mayy-king lurrrrrve,' I trilled to the taps.

The bathroom mirror held my attention for ages – I had around two days' growth of stubble. I debated whether to shave or not. I have never quite worked this one out – I certainly looked extra manly with my two days' growth of stubble, and I am sure that this rough look appeals to the women of the species, whatever Dawn French might do next. But then again, and going back to the considerate lover bit, I did not want to scratch her face too much during my animal passion. I find these sorts of dilemmas recurring in my life. In the end I picked up the razor and shaved the lot off, doing the chin, neck and sides first so I could check again what I would look like with one of those seventies David Bedford moustaches.

I decided to hold off on the seventies David Bedford mous-tache for the time being.

The water sploshed over my face, the final glob of foam gone, I pronounced myself pleased with the results, which compromised nicely. I was clean shaven and smooth-skinned (considerate lover, see above), and my neck was pitted with bleeding cuts (rough, manly). A fresh and rather fetching T-shirt and trouser combo later and I was ready, if not for the kill, certainly for the picking off of the weak member of the herd.

The aroma of slowly baking sheep's heart was starting to fill the cottage; I noted that it did not smell quite as expected. Sometimes food in the oven takes a while to settle down, due to the molecules rearranging themselves as they cook.

Romantic music. I would need romantic music.

Like every couple, we operate a Venn Diagram system of musical taste. The things I like are in the left-hand circle (good music), whereas her tastes are in the right-hand circle (chart stuff; women's music, although she is reassuringly anti-Dido). In the middle overlapping bit is one chill-out CD that had been taped as a free gift to the front of the *Observer*, and the track 'Wish You Were Here' by Pink Floyd, written about legendary former frontman Syd Barrett's descent into madness and subsequent retreat from swinging London to insular obscurity in the east of England.

I don't think that I can bear to listen to the chill-out CD once more this week, month or lifetime. It is enjoyable, but too missionary position. 'Wish You Were Here' is a great track, which blends the wistfulness of loss with the joyousness of remembering good times. But it would probably be pushing things to stick it on repeat for two hours. I rootled through the CD shelves, which are always set up in strict alphabetical order, trying to find something that would relax her.

Cardiacs. ('Do you actually *enjoy* this?')

Leonard Cohen. ('Are you trying to get me to slit my wrists?')

Fairport Convention. ('Is there any chance of listening to something from, like, recent years?')

Mercury Rev. ('But not that.')

The Proclaimers. We do, actually, both like The Proclaimers, and I once took her to see them play as a special secret surprise romantic birthday present. But it is not the sort of soft ambient gentle seduction music that I am after.

Jethro Tull. ('What is *this* shit?')

A CD of banjo music, purchased on a whim some time back. I quite like banjo music, although I am aware that I lay myself open to 'haha – move to Norfolk, take up the banjo' gibes. Banjo music is maligned, and is perfectly OK in its place.

I decided that banjo music was probably not appropriate in the circumstances.

Finally selecting a CD, I carried it over to the mini system that is apparently all we have space for. Before putting the case away I paused – something had been bugging me about this particular one for ages. Picking away with my fingernails, I finally managed to peel off the last remaining piece of sticky tape that had been obscuring the track listing under an annoying small torn bit of the *Observer*.

After which point I opened the oven to discover that the evening had gone totally, horribly, desperately wrong.

Even the addition of a delicious bag of salad could not rescue it. I glared at the heart furiously, trying to resist the urge to start shouting. I was sure that it was clever cooking and all that. But as a meal it was shit. It was shit. It was shit! Shit!

I fought to quell a rising tide of panic. Dinner smelt like sick, looked like a defecation and – what is more – was already stuck fast to the plate, presumably due to the puddle of gelatin that had oozed from the organ. I know, because I turned the plate completely upside-down to check, and nothing fell off, except the delicious salad. My eyes were fixed upon dinner in horror and revulsion and disgust; I clutched my temples, muttering 'What am I going to do? What am I going to do?' out loud whilst pacing back and forth gripping a fork. I had not done a Fearnley-Whittingstall or a Slater or an Oliver. I'd produced a Bentos.

Booooooooooooooo.

* * *

The car trundled mournfully past the deer park, down towards the old common and past a housing estate of pigs. Exotic smells arose from the bag in the footwell, but it was not these that assailed my senses. The sense-assail receptor part of my brain was occupied with the struggle to work out how it was possible for such dead silence to exist when she was shouting at me so much.

'All I want,' she pleaded, almost in tears by this point, 'is a reasonable meal when I get home from work. Just a . . .'

'But . . .'

'Just something nice! Something ordinary and nice! Why can you never do the basics? Why does it have to be one-off stunts all the time? Stunt cooking – four nights out of five you've made no effort whatsoever and on the fifth you've used every single fucking pot and pan to make me some fucking . . . Oh don't worry about it.'

The thought crossed my mind that when she was saying 'don't worry about it', what she was actually meaning was 'worry about it very much'. A small rabbit dashed across the road in front of me; the Tham's lurched alarmingly in the paper bag wedged between her ankles. She was going to mention the cleaning now.

'Stunt housework! You make a big thing about doing your big Wednesday morning clean-up – which is great and all wonderful and thank you, but when was the last time that I got home on a normal day to find that you'd wiped off the work surfaces or washed anything up? When?'

I was pleased that she was pleased with the big effort that I was making each week on Wednesday mornings, but something told me that it would be a mistake to explore this avenue further.

'There was that time when . . .'

'I *knew* you were going to bring that up! You can *remember* a *specific time*! This is *what* I am *saying*!'

I pulled up at the T-junction opposite the village pub. The lights in the window looked welcoming and unattainable.

'Any traffic coming from your way?' I asked, in what seemed to be a natural way of changing the subject. I yield to no man in my admiration of the great chefs who have put English cooking on the map recently. But the fact is that people ate peasant food in the past because they were peasants. Boiled pig's cock and the like were the only options available for the poor downtrodden masses in Merrie England, and reviving them as gourmet is the affectation of an idiot.

FIFTEEN

2 4 6 8 power play

I switch on the Sky box.

I feel that getting Sky TV was some sort of watershed in my life. Once, when I was little, before Dibley and before drum machines, before 'the kids' was spelt with a 'z', I was abreast of all the new technologies that were sweeping the globe in the wake of the integrated circuit. I not only knew of their existence, but I was excited about each one and would take to them instinctively when they finally arrived in our house. Now, I am hopelessly out of touch with everything electronic. I was comfortable with the ZX Spectrum and video recorders; the Sinclair QL and DVD menus lost me completely. Gradually, I forgot about technology and the zeitgeist and all stuff like that, and discovered beer and music and chickens and girls, or at least pictures of them on the internet.

But I have Sky TV now. Admittedly I mainly use it to get a better reception for the BBC, and I still haven't got round to adding my 'favourites'. But who can say that I am not down with ze kids now?

I settle down to watch the bowls.

Alex Marshall is the world number one bowls player, according to the commentator. There is something exciting about being the near-namesake of a legend, although physically we are very different. A shaven-headed bull of a man, he looks like he could hold his own should there be any conflict about the positioning of the mat. His opponent is Robert Chisholm, who is a young lad from Newcastle.

Barry Hearn knows what he's doing. There is constant reference by the commentators to the players' 'Premier League dreams'; the coverage is sponsored by a dynamic poker website; players wear personalised glossy sports shirts, in colours that are co-ordinated with their woods – speckledy for Marshall and a bright yellow for Chisholm. The graphics whiz around the screen football-style; advertising hoardings line the bright blue carpet-green: PartyPoker dot com, Premier League Bowls, Potters Leisure Resort. The last, the venue for the Premier League itself, is in Norfolk. Of course.

There is no 'We Are the Champions', or 'Simply the Best' or the woman who sings repeatedly that she is ready to go. But the players walk on to loud rock, waving slightly sheepishly at the audience and cameras. They don't have to keep their own score.

I lean forward on my sofa as Alex Marshall draws gently in on the backhand. There's no denying it – the standard is excellent. The players have got themselves into the Zone, and are treating the audience to a masterclass of their craft. The woods are retrieved for the next end.

Suddenly the lights go out in the auditorium. '*Power play!*' booms a pre-recorded voice over the PA. '*Power play!*' Immense spotlights machine-gun crazy zigzag patterns on the mat. I involuntarily jolt backwards in alarm.

There is a momentary pause, before a spontaneous and rising 'Oooooh!' erupts from the audience. I have never heard such an 'Oooooh' before. It is voluminous, and laced with heavy irony, but is somehow not unkind – like the response from an audience at a game show when the top prize is revealed to be a jug kettle. The

'Oooooh' comforts me, although I suspect it might not be what Barry Hearn exactly had in mind.

'He's taking his power play!' announces the commentator, excitedly.

It is reassuring that such a quintessentially English tinkering to such a quintessentially English sport gets such a quintessentially English reaction. I hope Barry Hearn and the Sky people don't mind too much. You can love something and still take the piss out of it. In fact, that sometimes means that you actually really really *do* love it, or that is what I tell the LTLP anyway.

Anyway. A power play. It's gripping stuff.

* * *

It's a slog when you're in a young band, paying your dues. 'Paying your dues' is what all bands have to do to be successful, although after a while with Where's Johnny Christmas? it did seem that we'd built up quite a bit of credit on the dues front and were awaiting an opportunity to trade them in for some money and adulation tokens. Writing songs, practising, writing more songs, practising some more, promoting our own show at the church hall – it wasn't enough. Getting better gigs was a problem – I wanted a bigger audience, a booming PA, crazily zigzagging spotlights.

Little squabbles started breaking out. I, for example, was fed up with the transport situation. Iain drove a 125cc motorbike, which got him to his job as a postman and back but wasn't particularly appropriate for transporting a drum kit around. I had a large old car with a fabric sunroof and it was possible to squeeze the bass drum and floor tom through this and onto the back seats, each time knocking off one more small piece of trim from the interior. Iain's assurances that he was all set to take his test and could then upgrade to a 250cc model seemed tokenistic at best.

I exasperatedly pointed out the key role of transport in rock music. Led Zeppelin, with their personalised Boeing 747; the convoys of tour buses that criss-crossed the States carrying Emerson in one, Lake in another and Palmer in the third. Even, it seemed, the itsiest, bitsiest band had at least a large van with their name in writing on the side.

We agreed that something needed to be done.

'There's Almost Grown,' said Iain, referring to a band from Basildon who we were on friendly terms with. 'They've got their own proper transport – remember, their guitarist has that Mark 2 Escort estate, with "Almost Grown" across the windscreen; the "Almost" above the driver and "Grown" on the passenger side. Like, you know, Kevin and Tracey.'

I did not consider this to be a proper long-term solution.

In contrast to Iain, who hated being a postman and who was all set to give up and go professional, Dave was pessimistic about our prospects. He'd missed several rehearsals because he had been hospitalised twice – once after falling onto some spiky railings, and then again with a broken foot. I had taken him out for a drink after his recovery from the foot thing, to talk about things and to generally cheer him up, but unfortunately when I had dropped him off at home late in the evening, I had proceeded to pull away too quickly in my large old car with the fabric sunroof and had run over his foot once more.

So we bickered, like bands do: about transport, about gigs, about money, about the songs. About the name Where's Johnny Christmas?, which suddenly didn't feel quite that perfectly right.

We weren't pulling together as a block. Looking back with hindsight, it was all a bit shambolic. Kudos to Simon for doing something about it.

Simon's mother worked in the post office. I would see her quite often – it was a small branch situated in the corner of the newsagents that I frequented for my *New Musical Express*. She was always friendly and supportive.

'I want a word with you!' she screamed at me as I walked in one morning.

I have always been very perceptive in reading subtle signs from the opposite sex, and knew enough to turn one hundred and eighty degrees and hastily exit the shop.

'I want that thing out of my drive by –' she shouted after me, before her words were cut off by the closing door.

'What do you think?' asked our singer, proudly, when I'd hastened round to his place to see why his mother had shouted at me in the post office.

I goggled at the enormous Luton van that filled his parents' driveway, spilling out over the kerb and onto the street.

'Simon, could I have a word, please?' called a measured voice from inside the house.

'In a minute, Dad.'

'Christ, it's very . . . big,' I breathed.

'Dad's going off on one a bit,' he admitted.

I caught sight of something, and walked round to look at the writing, expertly stencilled on the side of the van. A logo! A proper logo!

'I am not,' I said, very, very firmly, 'changing our name to "Geoff Skinner Removals".'

'Now, please, Simon,' came the voice from the house.

* * *

It's a singles match, which entails four woods each. Instead of our 'first to twenty-one ends' system, the games are a sprint – two 'sets' of five ends each. There is no room for a gentle warm-up on

Sky TV; no 'getting used to the green' over the first three or four ends; no possibility of relaxing a little once a lead is established. It's Twenty20 bowls; punk to our prog.

Robert Chisholm's power play begins uncomfortably – Marshall's first wood comes to rest absolutely adjacent to the cott, slightly to the front. Chisholm counters by bowling his own slightly behind – if the first wood is knocked at any point, the cott will cannon forwards towards his.

Marshall's second is extremely close once more; Chisholm tries to follow this and just fails – although his effort draws appreciative claps from the audience. Marshall changes tack with his next wood, putting it in long with the same idea in mind – insurance should the cott move. It's slightly awry, however, and this gives Chisholm the opportunity to hit the head hard with his next attempt – the pack of woods is disturbed; Marshall's are moved, and Chisholm goes one-up.

Alex Marshall takes a stroll up the green towards the pack, and stands, mulling over the situation, for a good while. This is allowed in singles – Alex Marshall doesn't have Nigel to shout instructions and explanations to him. The power play apparently means that his opponent gets double points in this end should he win – so being one shot down is not a disaster for him. The final two woods change nothing – two points to Chisholm. The players share a joke, and Marshall picks up the mat to hand to the other man. It is exciting.

There is an intermission, whilst the Geordie is interviewed to a backdrop of him racing a go-cart accompanied by more loud rock music. Marshall wins the next end, meaning that the first set is tied, and Sky goes to an ad break. The ads are all aimed at young men like me: shaving equipment, Wickes builders' merchants and vans.

* * *

Having a band van with 'Geoff Skinner Removals' on the side lifted our spirits a lot, and we started to move on, recording a proper demo tape and getting some positive gigging offers on the strength of our edgy sound and impressive-looking van. And suddenly something cropped up that would give us some invaluable experience: a residency; the chance to become a professional house band. It was unpaid, but before large audiences and in return for free rehearsal facilities.

'The junior school want us to do the music for *Bugsy Malone*,' announced Simon. 'It's their summer end-of-term show. They say that if we do the music we can carry on practising there.'

I was taken aback by this.

'*Bugsy* fucking *Malone*?' retorted Dave.

'Yes. The film.'

I thought for a bit. 'I actually really like the film,' I said. 'And I quite fancy Jodie Foster in it.'

Dave turned on me. 'Jodie Foster won't be there,' he said. 'And she was like – eleven? And actually – isn't it a boys' school?'

'What do you think, Iain?' asked Simon.

Iain pondered hard. 'It's not very rock and roll,' he concluded. 'But I suppose it might be a laugh.'

We signed up for our third gig: *Bugsy Malone* at Brentwood Prep School.

* * *

Alex Marshall is brilliant. I am drawn to the screen in utter appreciation of his art, as if I am at the London Palladium back in 1994 and watching the Richard Thompson band – the best gig that I have ever been to that didn't have me playing at it. His woods gently ease through the narrowest of gaps; his body language is utterly confident even when he falls behind or is seemingly faced with an impossible shot.

The younger man, on the other hand, appears understandably nervous. You can see his relief when he takes points, sense his anxiety as his woods travel towards the cott. This belies the fact that he's pulling slightly ahead, even though he has once more to resort to firing at the pack to try to make something happen.

There is another ad break. Wickes again, Compare the Meerkat, Churchill Insurance. A car advert, backed by Blur's 'Song 2' – not the quiet verse, just the loud, loud chorus. 'Woooooo-hoooooo!' it goes. 'Woooooo-hoooooooooooo!' as the distorted bass guitars scream grunge from the television set before we cut back to the bowls.

Alex Marshall is interviewed as he strolls along a sandy Norfolk beach. He is pleased to be the world champion and excited about being in the Barry Hearn league. He then goes on to level the second set by completely taking out Chisholm's closest. It's three points each going into the final end; the first set being a tie means that this is effectively sudden death.

And then Marshall cracks a little. It's his turn to roll the cott – he'd like a short one, but it doesn't even reach the marker that indicates the minimum distance for it – meaning that it's then returned to his opponent to place where he wishes. Even the best players can hit a bum note or forget the words. Chisholm is ruthless – he sends it as far as possible down the green, and Marshall's first wood is a good yard too soft to reach it.

By now, I am sitting right on the edge of the sofa. It's scenarios like this that will surely draw the millions of viewers that these men deserve.

Chisholm draws in right next to the cott, but the lapse seems to have jolted the champion into a further Zone of Higher Determination. He brutally fires his next wood directly at his opponent's, sending it flying to one side; the cott shoots off, coming to rest in the ditch. From this moment, the result is never in doubt. Marshall's next wood lands three inches away at most – the crowd applauds his brilliance. Chisholm has put in a great effort but it is not enough – Marshall takes two and wins the match. Even the great champion himself looks relieved at this, but mixed with this relief is the look of adrenaline, of power, of everything having come together in the wonderful physics that is wood on green on cott. He turns to shake his opponent's hand, the glow of the winning bowls player about him.

It is the big piano chord feeling.

* * *

There is a specifically magical moment when you play the electric guitar. When you have your backline set up, when all the plugs are in, all the effects pedals set, when you've been through your last act of tuning. When everything's ready, you flick the switch on the amplifier and electricity surges through the system – not an immediate rush, but a very short delay as the valves heat and start to glow.

At that moment, the guitar transforms from a dead thing in your hand, from a piece of wood on a strap with six inert lengths of wire, to a living being, at one with you. A low hum, and every shift of your hand, every touch of your fingers carries a power of immense wattage, a note, a chord, the scrape of palm on string, carried through the leads, through the electronics and amplified a millionfold. It's the intoxicating power of being able to shift an immense musical boulder with the lightest brush from the tip of your index finger.

I hit a couple of chords, sending them through the air to infinity.

'My name is Tallulah . . .' began the ten-year-old boy in a squeaky falsetto.

'That's it, I'm leaving the band,' said Dave.

And so that was it for Where's Johnny Christmas?. It was demoralising. We borrowed a bass player to honour the commitment, but after a three-day run that was the end.

A parent approached us as we were packing away after the final show.

'We're having a barbecue next week for the boys' birthdays,' she said. 'I don't suppose you would be interested in playing for us?'

I stared at her.

'What day is it on?' Simon asked brightly.

I gave him a look before turning to her. 'We'll let you know,' I replied politely.

Two bands; two false starts: many people would have given up.

But even then, I knew that the music business isn't a knockout cup. One loss doesn't mean you're out. Instead, it's a long Premier League. You can pick yourself up, start again, and as long as you're able to grind out some results you have every chance of being in contention for a trophy at the end of the season, perhaps presented at the annual dinner.

We were very down at the time. All our work seemed to have come to nothing, we'd argued with a friend, and even the spiritual presence of road manager Geoff Skinner hadn't been able to stop things falling to pieces.

But although we knew that things weren't hopeless, we certainly weren't expecting what came next. The woods all fell into place, and lasting success was just round the corner.

SIXTEEN

Living in a piano paradise

I go for a run.

Run! Run! Run! Across the road and up the hill towards the village shop; steady strides and deliberately concentrated breaths within the athletic splendour of my Matalan tracksuit. The motivational 'I go for a run' MP3 playlist music spurs me on at the correct pace.

'Turn around and life's passed you by . . . look to ones you love to ask them why . . .' sings the man from the Doves.

My body is responding well to this exercise, and it is not until I pass Eddie's house that I find myself gaspingly short of puff. Unfortunately Eddie lives about a hundred yards away. I am already yearning for the safety of my warm, armchair-filled cottage.

I shrug my shoulders, or at least I do in my mind, as moving a shoulder muscle would use up half my available energy reserve. A few minutes later I have run the length of his bungalow and am on my way up towards the small patch of grass that houses memorial benches and the village sign.

Run! Run! Run! It is important that I maintain a sensible pace, as I do not want to be foolish and cause a pulled or strained Thing. I turn down the hill at the green lane, gracefully evading some dog shit.

'Theregoesthefearagain . . .'

My legs are holding up. I'd had an inkling on the preliminary warm-up jog towards the gate that they might be in danger of dropping off, but they are still very much trotting away, albeit somewhat independently from the rest of my body. I can't find any brain impulse that is making them move – they just seem to want to do their own thing. That is fine by me. Carry on, legs. If my legs, on their own initiative, can get me at least back to the main road then they will have served their purpose.

Kate Bush introduces herself to my ears. I cannot fully interact with her under current circumstances, and it occurs to me that I am the only person in the world ever to listen to this particular song and not do the arm movements. The duck pond passes, like a speeding glacier. Wowww oh woww oh wow oh wow oh wow oh wowwwwowwwww!

Unbelievable.

* * *

Steerpike.

A completely fresh start, with a completely fresh line-up. I auditioned new musicians, and, alongside a new bass player named Ken, settled on me, Simon and Iain to complete the fully revamped quartet.

Steerpike. Anti-hero turned villain of the classic Mervyn Peake Gormenghast trilogy, youthful renegade, Machiavellian plotter, false lover, killer, ugly slightly deformed man who had suffered horrible burns in a murdering accident. What a name for a band!

'It's all right, I suppose,' agreed Ken.

Simon and Iain were enthusiastic. It turns out that none of us really liked Where's Johnny Christmas?. Getting the right name for the band was vital, and Where's Johnny Christmas? just wasn't quite there. I mean – it was all right, but it didn't trip off the tongue as well as it could, and there was a danger that *New Musical Express* would run a headline like 'A Dog is For Christmas' or 'Where's Johnny

Christmas? He's down the Toilet' or 'Where's Johnny Bollocks?' more like. This was the nadir of the music press, when they were more interested in trying to be funny and clever and making cheap gags than telling you anything particularly deep about music.

Steerpike. A single explosive word, like many of the bands of the time – modern, timeless, unique, aggressive. Yes, a completely fresh start. But sometimes to succeed you have to have the courage to make changes. And this was when things started to happen for us.

* * *

The piano has become a valued member of our household, even if the LTLP has yet to embrace it with her full bosom. There is something about having an old piano in an old house – it just feels right. I feel like we should sit round it every night, making our own entertainment with songs like 'When the Blackbird Says Bye-Bye', like they did in the days before the likes of the *Vicar of Dibley* took over our leisure time as well as our sexual politics. I have been trying to get some songs together, in the spare time I have between sabbaticalising, househusbanding and thinking that I really must nail down the Chipper Barman on the band front.

I settle myself down on the stool and play an expansive chord.

'Hey . . . Jude,' I begin from memory, trying to balance the singing part with the complicated piano arrangement that I have worked out myself.

Something immediately does not feel right.

I hit the notes again, without the singing bit. There is a complete gap in the middle of the chord. The 'G' has broken, right in the centre of the keyboard.

I am a bit aghast at this. I try the song again. It goes:

'Plink plinnnnk, plonk plink thud plinnnnnk, [gap] plink plonk plink, thud plink plink plo-o-onk plink.'

This is horribly annoying. The broken A flat is one thing, but pretty well every song that's ever been written has a G in it somewhere. On exploring the keyboard further, I find that other notes appear to be coming out in sympathy. There is the occasional 'bofff' and the odd ' '.

'Hey Jude, don't be a ' '; you were made to go out and bofff her; remember to get her into your ' '; then you begin to thud bofff bofff her.' I grit my teeth in frustration.

I open the case at the top to see if I can effect some running repairs. Dust billows out at me, but through the caked-on grime of decades of Grandma the piano mechanism is just about visible. The sound is clearly made by those wooden hammers, surrounded by tons of strings and felts and levers and springs. It is terrifically complicated, and, despite being a man who has crafted a secret Scooby-Doo bookcase *and* mastered the traditional art of gripping and twisting chicken wire, I do think that it is one step removed from a DIY job.

My eye alights on a business card for 'general piano repairs and tuning' that's been Sellotaped to the underside of the wood. Rescue! There is an expert general piano repairer and tuner available, one who has mastered this particular instrument and who knows it inside out and who will come to my aid!

I grab the cordless phone and read off the telephone number. 'Edgware 6421.'

Oh.

My professional life after the accident with the Royal Philharmonic Orchestra's telephone number found me at the very genesis of the internet. From bulletin boards to Compuserve, from web 1.0 to web 1.0.1, web 1.0.2, web 2.0 and beyond – I was there. The web was small then; it is huge now – and to find what you are looking for without wasting vast chunks of your life, you need to be fairly canny. From Altavista, Dogpile to Yahoo! and Google and Bing – search engines may have improved over the years, but so has the need to cut through the chaff of irrelevance, spam and useless information. That's where experience comes in, and why the human element will always be paramount. If you know how to use your search engines properly – and I mean really properly – then you can dismiss all the crud and locate what you want in a whisker.

I type 'piano repair man' into Google and find somebody on about page 17. Time to get a professional in.

* * *

If you're ambitious in the music business, sooner or later you're going to need to get a professional in.

Bands have on occasions managed themselves – the Smiths spring to mind immediately, and in many ways Steerpike were the Billericay Smiths. But these are the exceptions. At that time we didn't know when the band was going to break, but we wanted to be prepared and were determined to be a bit more focused, following our fresh start. Just as Howard picks the team and goes to the league meetings, and Nigel collects the subs, we needed someone to look after all our non-musical activities: bookings and finance to begin with then travel, merchandising, licensing and deals.

Enter, Mike.

Whilst it was not exactly the case that Mike was given the manager's job because he knew girls, his CV did fit in with the section of our job description that read 'desirable – knows girls'. The point was that he was a player, a networker, a ducker-and-a-diver, an enthusiast, someone who was in with the players on the scene. And he knew girls. He brought some to the rehearsal where he first met us, and they stood there listening – genuine girls, all soft-skinned in their girlness.

We didn't have much of a chat – he just watched us play and nodded a lot. But suddenly Steerpike was a professional, managed band. In a way, he was our Barry Hearn figure.

I saw Mike again the day after that rehearsal. It was pouring with rain – relentless, teeming – and I was trudging home from the station, drenched, after a long hard day placing advertising for the Royal Philharmonic Orchestra. A car drew up beside me. So much of the music business is about the image you project, and Mike's Vauxhall Chevette was clean and well turned out although it seemed to have a problem with a bellowing exhaust. He reached over and wound down the passenger side window in his managerial capacity. 'You're wet through! Do you want a lift?'

This was a lucky break. Not only was I cold and wet, but a short car journey would give me the chance to have a proper talk with him. I was excited that we had somebody on board who would bring us the sort of professional approach that we'd been lacking.

'Oh thank you so much, young man,' said a voice from behind me.

I turned round in confusion. An elderly lady pushed past me, opened the car door and sat in Mike's passenger seat.

Our new manager gave her a startled look and stammered something inconclusive.

'That's so kind of you,' she said.

I shrugged, opened the back door and climbed in; we had a proper talk about the sort of professional approach that he would bring us – a proper talk that entailed me shouting over his shoulder and an old lady sitting wetly in the front seat.

* * *

The Piano Man is dapper and well presented; he sports a dark blue suit and immaculately brushed hair. Impeccably well spoken, he introduces himself at the door with the flourish of a man to whom flourishy introductions come with ease. I sort of say 'hullo' in return, and we have one of those awkward 'waiting for the kettle to boil'-type chats.

His manner puts me at my ease – you can never be sure with piano men. The GIF image of a piano on his website seemed authentic enough, but there is no substitute for examining somebody's piano credentials in the flesh. We proceed through to the back room, and the pianistic object of his assignation.

'This is . . .' I begin.

'Oh my goodness, what a simply wonderful piano!' he exclaims, striding into the room.

'Yes, I . . .'

'Wonderful! Beautiful!'

'It's been in my family for . . .'

'Let's look inside. Oh! Gracious! This is marvellous!' He runs his finger over the mahogany in a teasing caress.

'Yes, it's . . .'

But my words disappear into air. He is transfixed and lost in pianoland. I watch as he removes some tools from his briefcase and undresses the pliant instrument of its panelling, disrobing it of swathes of wood until its innards are exposed and vulnerable. With expertly probing fingers he works gently away at its strings, feeling its felts, squeezing the dampers, uttering small cries of satisfaction and pleasure at each little discovery.

After a tactful period, I decide to speak once more.

'So how much do you reckon?' I ask, cutting straight to the chase.

He looks up at me, disappointed at the interruption. 'Ah – well it's in beautiful, beautiful condition. Beautiful. But – there are things that are wrong and that need a complete overhaul or replacing.'

There are clearly some detailed points of historical and mechanical interest that it would be worthwhile to investigate further with the man. 'So how much do you reckon?' I ask instead.

'But on the whole, a beautiful instrument. It's so rare to find one like this.'

'So how much do you reckon?' I ask.

'Well,' he ponders. 'You could skimp slightly on one or two things. But some aspects do need addressing urgently.'

177

'Like what?' I enquire.

There is a game called 'I went to the supermarket and I bought . . .' that we used to play as children to while away long car journeys. The first person says: 'I went to the supermarket and I bought . . .' and then names something beginning with the letter 'A', like 'Apples' or 'Apricot Yoghurt'. The second person then says: 'I went to the supermarket and I bought . . .' and then names something that begins with the letter 'B', like 'Bananas' or 'Beans' – but then has to say 'and' and name all the things that have been mentioned pertaining to previous letters of the alphabet, like 'Almonds' or 'Anusol'. It is a memory game, essentially.

His answer is a bit like when you get up to the letter 'M' of that 'I went to the supermarket and I bought . . .' game, but with things that can go wrong with a piano.

'So how much do you reckon?' I ask.

'Hmmmm . . .' he mulls.

'Yes . . .?' I ask.

'Well, you have to take transport into account,' he warns. 'That will bump up the price a bit, as you're quite a way away. I would guess that the transport from here will be . . . well, golly, I'm going to have to give you a really rough estimate here . . . around sixty pounds.' He pulls an apologetic face. 'You really do need expert men to move such an instrument. So yes, I would say sixty pounds, I'm afraid.'

I am relieved at finally dragging a figure from him, even one just for the transport. And, truth be told, I am not of the mind that sixty pounds is an excessive amount to transport a piano, even if you don't get a swarm of Italian bakers thrown in. But being a good negotiator I try not to reveal this. If he's concerned about sixty pounds for transport then he's speaking my kind of figures – i.e. low ones.

'I'll try to get it cheaper for you, but let's allow about sixty pounds,' he continues, 'just to be safe. So that's' – he draws breath, frowns, thinks, uses his fingers as a counting device – 'mutter mutter sixty pounds mutter mutter possibly cheaper mutter no sixty pounds, just to be on the safe side mutter mutter . . .'

'Around five thousand pounds,' he concludes.

Five thousand pounds.

As the Piano Man re-dresses the instrument, I do some small sums in my head. I often don't read the newspaper on Tuesdays or Wednesdays – that would save about one pound eighty a week. Some utilities give you a discount of 50p if you switch to direct debit, which I surely could, and I always ask for extra mushrooms in my bacon sandwich when I drop in at Barney's food van – do I really need those?

I cannot say that I am terribly optimistic about all these savings adding up to five thousand pounds, however. That is, five thousand pounds of disposable income, rather than just five thousand pounds. Five thousand pounds that I can spare to mend an admittedly old and historic piano, rather than five thousand pounds that we might otherwise spend on food and heating and lighting and for the LTLP to build a new life with Mrs Harry Leon after I have been found at the bottom of the Wash with an old and historic piano tied to my ankles.

When he has left, I sit at my piano, sadly.

'Hey Jude, don't be a " "; you were made to go out and bofff her; remember to get her into your " "; then you begin to thud bofff bofff her.'

Perhaps it sounds all right. Five thousand pounds says it sounds all right.

* * *

Mike and I sat and chatted for a while outside the sheltered housing where we'd dropped the old lady.

Mike had plans. Bigger gigs, better venues, support slots. A mailing list and a PR campaign; a strategy to get the band's finances on a more even level. It was great to hear somebody talk like this. Our sound followed that of seminal breakthrough bands like Blur, Flowered Up and the Soup Dragons: an ultra-happening blend of jangly indie music played over a dance/rock beat, and he would be the man to take us into the first division of jangly indie bands who played their music over a dance/rock beat.

'On the music front . . .' he began.

I sat up straight and alert, keen to hear what he had to say.

He pulled out a tape from the pocket in the driver's side door: Nirvana, an American band.

'They play their verses really quietly,' he began. 'And then they play the choruses really loud. So it goes quiet, loud, quiet, loud. And then,' he concluded, waving the tape at me, 'they finish off really loud.

'It's the future,' he added.

There was a short pause. I had a huge respect for Mike's managerial abilities, but his knowledge of songwriting and the history and popular context of music was next to zero. Despite rock and roll being an American thing, Britain has always been an exporter, not an importer. Success would lie not in following some minor American band's simple stabs at punk. It would be refining, embellishing upon and taking out to America and the world the new and future sound of England – jangly indie music played over a dance/rock beat, the sort of sound that Blur was perfecting. Forget the Yankee quiet/loud shouty stuff.

It wasn't the time, but sooner or later we would have to tell Mike to stick to his brief of financial and commercial management, and knowing girls.

'Right,' I said, determined to humour him for a bit.

SEVENTEEN

Short Tony's 115th dream

My bowls playing doesn't seem to be improving.

I have to be realistic. I am a great musician, fantastic house-husband, good cook, considerate lover and promising chicken-rearer, but modesty forces me to admit that I am not getting much better at bowls. I turn up and I enjoy myself – but it looks as though I will never play Sky Premier League Barry Hearn standard. They switched the blocks around and put me with Huey the other night – he's new to the team and looks quite promising. I was determined to make him feel confident that he had joined the right club.

I kept missing by miles, constantly knocked the opposition's woods into advantageous positions, and split my trousers whilst switching to forehand on end twelve.

Perhaps I was the wrong person to make him feel confident that he had joined the right club. For me, it's the dynamics of the settled block that makes it work. We know each other; we chip in. At every point in the game, one of us – be it me, Big Andy or Nigel – will be going through a good patch. That is why keeping a regular threesome together is so important. Like the Beatles' solo careers, the sum is greater than the parts.

*　　*　　*

'We arrived in hope, we depart in . . .'

Big Andy miserably tails off. There is nothing that immediately springs to mind that can describe it.

'Hope,' I admit with shame, had almost morphed into 'Expectation'. Less than an hour ago we had seen the *Lynn News* – fourth in the table, with the famous victory from the previous week still to be registered. We had fielded the regular line-up – Nigel, Big Andy and me – fired up from early-season success. We had found the bar, a proper bar that had beer and everything, and the trays that would allow us to take the pints out onto the green. I sat contentedly on a plastic chair, my deeply, deeply unfashionable shoes yet to be laced, drawing deeply from a driver's lager shandy.

'Lovely evening,' I had remarked to nobody in particular.

An opposition bowler had plonked himself down next to me, reaching into his bag for woods, measure and deeply, deeply unfashionable shoes.

'Ha! That's Orrie!' he had chuckled as a man shambled into view from the side of the clubhouse. 'You all right, Orrie?'

Orrie was all right.

'He's a one, he is,' my new friend had revealed. 'All over the place. You know, I was playing last week, and he's on the next rink, and I'm just placing the cott down, and suddenly there's a wood appears by my feet, and it's his! He'd seen me put the cott down and had gone for it, even though he was playing on a completely different rink! Thought it was his cott! But he's a good old boy. And he tries hard.'

'We haven't had a headline yet,' I had complained to Nigel as we had congregated around rink number two. 'It's mid-season – about time we got ourselves one.' The *Lynn News* tries to portion headlines equitably, so that all clubs can share in the excitement of large, bold type. 'Have a good game.'

'Have a good game.'

'Have a good game,' I had said to Orrie, against whom we had, of course, been drawn.

The opposition skipper had then taken Big Andy aside and asked him if he'd mind keeping an extra eye on the scorecard, as Orrie could occasionally get confused.

'We depart in . . .' tries Big Andy again. But even this is premature. We are nowhere near the conclusion of the match, although our chances of victory have departed several ends ago. I start laughing, a nervous, involuntary, slightly hysterical laugh, as their skipper once more draws in to take the points.

Orrie has turned out to be some form of genius. He has a strange, slippery action that involves placing most of his entire right leg flat on the mat and propelling the wood from a low, almost prone position; half his shots either pull up short or head alarmingly out towards the other rinks, usually accompanied by a cry of 'Oh bloody hell, that one's gone again!' But he also has flashes of brilliance, his woods swinging in and nestling in and around the head, next to the cott, pushing ours out of the way. Cleverly, they have paired Orrie with what appear to be the two best and most consistent players in their club, meaning that we are almost twenty points behind before you can say 'we depart in'. Meanwhile, Big Andy has forgotten to score an entire end, and has to ask for Orrie's help in revising his card.

'One down,' I yelp at Nigel.

'In humiliation . . .?' asks Big Andy. 'Come on. It would be nice to at least get to double figures.'

'We're going to get a headline all right following this,' I say, after my two woods have failed to trouble the measuring device.

'In a bloodied mess . . .?'

'I'll have a word with Howard,' I say. 'It might be possible to submit the cards to the newspaper with the scores blacked out, like MPs' expenses.'

On the next rink, Karen spots the numbers on our scoreboard, catches my eye, points and laughs. Any more games like this, and our Albert Victor League dream will really be over.

* * *

'*What* are my Denby plates doing in there?' snarls the LTLP.

I shrug my shoulders and make vague noises, which is what I generally do when I'm trying to avoid answering a question. She is as unimpressed with this tactic as she was all those years ago in the registry office.

The shortfall in egg production has been disappointing. The chicken book all but promised us an egg per chicken per day, and we are nowhere near this target. Dimly, I wonder if we have definitely been sold actual chickens. The LTLP picks up a rake.

'I thought perhaps that some nice crockery would make a difference,' I mumble, hiding a Le Creuset casserole behind my back. She gives me an incredulous look, as if I have suggested inviting the reclusive Barclay brothers for dinner, but only on condition that they offer to wash up and dress as comedy rabbis.

Short Tony is stomping around in the chicken enclosure. 'I'm getting my gun out if it carries on like this,' he warns. The chickens back off in alarm.

'How many did you get yesterday?' I ask him.

'One. Just one.'

Something occurs to me. I cast him a funny and askance look. We have an 'every other day' arrangement, by which I take the eggs on Tuesdays, Thursdays and Saturdays, he takes them on Mondays, Wednesdays and Fridays, and there is a free-for-all on Sundays. A grave and uncharitable thought is forming in my mind that Short Tony might be pretending that his yield is down, in order to cover up the fact that he is swiping production on Days That He Is Not Allowed. I stroke my chin thoughtfully.

'Here you go,' I tell the chickens, setting down their hummus salad, and immediately regretting my suspicious nature.

'We'll see how it goes today,' I sigh. As I open the gate to make my way back to the cottage, I notice Short Tony casting me a funny and askance look. I haven't a clue what that is all about. I collect the empty plates, ready for the dishwasher.

'Yew all right then, boy?' calls Harold from over the fence.

I give him a sheepish nod. As my other neighbour, I feel a bit bad that I have not yet gone round to Harold's bearing gifts of eggs. He's a very kind old boy, and always been generous with produce from his back garden; if anybody deserves some free eggs it is him. And as somebody who's lived in the countryside all his life, I'll wager that he'll be pretty impressed with my chicken-rearing achievements.

'Them chickens of yours doing well?' he asks.

'Absolutely fine,' I boast. 'I've just been feeding them. One of the things when you have chickens is to make sure that you get their diet right.'

Harold looks at the Denby china with a raised eyebrow. 'Well, I did have two hundred when I was farm manager up the road,' he says.

I had no idea that Harold was an amateur chicken enthusiast as well! I rest my elbows on the fence to talk to him.

'I'm surprised you haven't got any now,' I say. 'You've got loads of room for them – you could get two or three – keep you supplied with eggs?'

He looks at me and shakes his wise countryside head. 'Damn sight easier to buy your eggs from Morrisons,' he says.

* * *

Big Andy's coop is now occupied.

'My chickens have arrived!' he exclaims on the telephone line from his house, all of one hundred yards away.

Despite him essentially having stolen my chicken idea, I am pleased for him.

'Have they had any mail yet?' I reply.

'Ha!' he says, in the way people often say 'Ha!' if they don't find something funny.

'What are they like?' I ask. I have never seen a rescued battery chicken. Despite being a hardened country-dweller, I've never liked the idea of battery hens, and I admire him for his charitable act.

A note of doubt creeps into his voice. 'Well – they *look* like chickens,' he ponders. 'Sort of.'

Another man with chicken doubts.

'Anyway, I need some advice from the expert,' he continues. 'What time should I be putting them to bed?'

I am an expert. An expert! The words resound with me resoundingly. For ten, almost twenty years I have been hanging on to old, obsolete expertises – the computerised typesetting mark-up systems, the local newspaper directories – but now, in one telephone call, I have moved on. I am so proud of my chickens. They have given me love, and eggs, and the status of an expert. Although I wouldn't mind a few more eggs. Yes, truly, these chickens have changed my life.

'Well, I try not to keep them up too late,' I caution. 'Although on special occasions I do allow them to stay up to watch *The Wire*.'

There is a bemused pause. I am not sure that he knows that I am joking. They would not be interested in *The Wire* – they are chickens. That is the thing with being an expert – you have to watch what you say as people will take you at your word.

'Thanks,' he replies.

'I'll pop over.'

They do look like chickens. Just.

I have never seen battery hens before. Just looking at them, stumbling around Big Andy's enclosure, released into their first ever taste of the open air, shell-shocked and frightened, is a sobering experience. I want to add a sombre voiceover, perhaps accompanying it with 'Drive' by The Cars. Animals should not live like this.

All are thin, painfully, unbearably thin. They walk uncertainly and none have proper feathering. One has a massive sort of growth on her arse. 'We've called that one "J Lo",' says Big Andy.

I regret looking down on his choice of chickens now. He has done a very good thing by homing them, and any petty competition between us is dead. They look at us through the wire: the tiny one, the one who is almost bald on one side, the one with a bad leg, the one with the arse protrusion.

'I'm sorry that I was a bit rude about your chickens,' I say. 'They'll be great.'

We discuss the logistics of shutting them away at night, with or without glossy American TV shows. I slip off home to clean out my coop.

*   *   *

There was one other project that Short Tony undertook when he renovated his cottage.

It was based around the centrepiece – a feature that Mrs Short Tony had always wanted. This centrepiece consisted of a large dining room with a lovely, spacious farmhouse-style table. Its distressed pine sat comfortably at home within the eighteenth-century walls, the sort of setting that would make even the meanest of feasts seem lush and homely.

Two weeks later he invited me in for a quick coffee. I stepped through the door into this dining room and boggled in astonishment.

A dartboard was on the wall, with its own electronic scoring system. Beer towels and mats were carefully positioned around the room. Signs indicated opening hours and directions to the toilet. And, most noticeably of all, the dining table had been adapted into providing the supporting base of a four- by six-foot snooker table.

Essentially he had converted the dining room into his own private pub, whilst his wife was at Morrisons.

Having a secret Scooby-Doo bookcase was one thing. But this was a whole new level of ambition. I have been in awe of him ever since.

'Thud, thud, thud.' Twenty-six again. It was twenty-six every time. I have always been rubbish at darts. The LTLP and Mrs Short Tony chatted in the sitting room.

There is a definite gender divide in the village. If I want to do something (for instance, to take something absolutely and completely at random out of my multitude of hobbies and interests, go to the village pub), I will generally go with Short Tony and Big Andy, and we will often meet Terry, and Len the Fish, and perhaps John Twonil or Glen up there. If the LTLP fancies going out she will contact Mrs Short Tony and Mrs Big Andy, and perhaps some other village ladies. There is nothing sinister or sexist in this. It is just how it pans out.

Listening in whilst awaiting my next turn at the oche, I realised that Mrs Short Tony was trying to persuade the LTLP to join the village book group.

I had almost joined the book group. Before I decided that I would become a musician, I thought that I might be a literary type. I devoured books as a child. But my reading slipped when I stopped commuting, when I ceased to need to lose myself for a half-hour from Harringay Station. Whereas I once used my free time to maintain my literacy, I now used it to improve my numeracy, via the medium of Solitaire on the PC.

Mrs Short Tony had approached me with her list, and I had even got as far as choosing a book for the group to discuss. *The Time Traveler's Wife.* I had heard of it, and I reasoned that it was probably about space, like *Blake's 7.*

'Who else is in the book group?' I had asked Mrs Short Tony, almost as an afterthought.

'Well – there's me, Mrs Eddie, Mrs Len the Fish, Mrs John Twonil, Mrs Glen, Mrs The Chipper Barman, Mrs Martin The Bloke From Up The Road That Works In IT, three other ladies from my previous book group in the next village – and you,' she replied.

I backed away from joining the village book group.

Don't get me wrong – I am perfectly happy in the social company of the fairer sex. But it had seemed too terrifying – especially as they planned to meet in the private room of the village pub. All those hormones plus white wine. I would not get out alive. But seeing that it is always the males that organise things, I couldn't help but be pleased that the ladies had got a book group together with Mrs Short Tony, Mrs Eddie, Mrs Len the Fish, Mrs John Twonil, Mrs Glen, Mrs The Chipper Barman and Mrs Martin The Bloke From Up The Road That Works In IT. It would give them all more of an identity in their own right.

I won the darts; I lost the snooker – despite Short Tony having given me the best cue (an Argos 'Jimmy White' signed one). I have always admired Jimmy White, and feel a natural affinity with him, neither of us having ever won the World Championship snooker. It is even amazing that Jimmy does as well as he does, using such lightweight plasticky equipment. When he retires from snooker I bet he will be a brilliant cleaner and househusband as well, whilst his wife carries on with her secretarial work or whatever it is she does. It is not fair.

Jimmy White is a legend the world over. He has trophies, pots of money, the respect of the public and his peers. But when a man sits down alone to contemplate his life, he has to ask himself this: did I achieve everything that I could have, as a man? Winning, losing; triumph and disaster – I may well have confronted those impostors. But did I have a bookcase that opened on hinges to reveal a secret area beyond, like on the Scooby-Doo cartoons? Did I have my own personal pub, created from the remnants of a dining room whilst my wife was at Morrisons? Did I have chickens?

Red wine, a fire, comfy sofas – the four of us settled down at the end of the Saturday evening. Nothing pressing to do; no particular reason to get up the following morning – a blissful opportunity to hang out and chill. Is there anything nicer than settling down with friends in front of a log fire with a bottle of wine? (Aside from beating Alex Marshall at the Potters Leisure Resort, before being asked if you'd join Joe Jackson for a quick impromptu performance of 'Is She Really Going Out With Him' between power plays.) I sank into the upholstery feeling like this had been the nicest evening ever.

'By the way,' remarked the LTLP sweetly. 'I found some ladies' glasses in a case beside the bed. Whose are they, please?'

Joe Jackson quietly packed his guitar away in its case, slipping out of the back door in embarrassment. The 'power play' spotlights all turned to face me and there was a big 'Ooooooh!' from the audience. It took me all of 0.0000001 seconds to work out the answer to the LTLP's question, and I suspected that it was one that wouldn't go down particularly well. So to try to cover, I cleverly blinked at her several times before trying to put her mind at rest by going red, stammering and looking shifty whilst making weak protestations.

'Perhaps they're the Vegetable Delivery Lady's?' offered Short Tony.

I did appreciate his attempt to be helpful, but Short Tony's conciliatory interventions at times like this are generally less like pouring petrol on the flames than chucking the petrol, the flames, a box of fireworks, a British seaside pier and Richard Reid the Shoe Bomber into a large hadron collider and switching it on to see what happens.

Nevertheless, this did give me the opportunity to change the subject neatly, so that the LTLP would probably forget about the actual topic of conversation.

'I doubt they're the Vegetable Delivery Lady's,' I said. 'Besides, it was not the Vegetable Delivery Lady last week. It was a man. With a beard.'

I was quite pleased with my 'man with a beard' explanation, and thought hard about how to follow it up. Perhaps with a general discussion about beards and their place in society. One glance at the LTLP, however, revealed that she had not been sent off-track. Perhaps it would have been better to simply point out that the Vegetable Delivery Lady had never been up to my bedroom, whether for an act that involved removing her glasses or not. Why must I always overelaborate?

'Search a bit harder,' suggested Short Tony, continuing in his unhelpful vein. 'You might find a discarded brassiere.'

I was not at all thrown by the fact that the last time anybody used the word 'brassiere' was in 1952. 'No . . .' I replied with rapier wit. '. . . she only ever leaves brassica.'

The room echoed with laughter at my clever joke. When I had wiped the tears from my eyes I looked round to find that, in fact, it had only been me laughing, and that it was just a very echoey room.

'Well?' asked the LTLP.

There was a silence. I looked round from face to face. It was time to explain about the cleaner.

'What I don't understand,' she spat, for the fifteenth time since a sheepish trudge back along the secret path that had been punctuated by vicious pokes to the back, 'is why? I mean? For God's sake – why?'

I tried to start explaining again, but to be honest by this point the explanation was confusing even me.

'I thought you'd be pleased! You were always going on about how the house wasn't clean, and how you thought it was a shithole, and now it's all clean and lovely every week!'

Her eyes widened quite alarmingly. 'No,' she countered. 'No. What I am asking you is: why did you get a cleaner without telling me?'

'Because you told me to get a cleaner!'

'No,' her voice became more patient. 'What I am asking you, again, is this. Let's be very clear. I am not asking you: why did you get a cleaner? I am asking you: why did you get a cleaner but pretend that you had not got a cleaner?'

'Because . . .' I tailed off. I was not sure myself any more.

'I mean – did you not think that I would find out? That I wouldn't suspect something after you miraculously did some reasonable cleaning job every week at the same time? Did you?'

'I . . .'

'I don't understand! I just don't understand! I asked you to get a cleaner. I wanted a cleaner. You didn't want to clean. I would be paying for the cleaner to do your cleaning for you, because I have a fucking proper job. But instead of getting a cleaner, which was what I wanted and you wanted, you refused to get a cleaner. Then, because you were so shit at cleaning, you got a cleaner but pretended you hadn't. But *why didn't you tell me*? What was the point? I don't get it. I just don't get it.'

She paused for breath before her face lit up.

'Was that what the ridiculous charade when you locked yourself out was about?'

I didn't know what to say. I could tell her of the fear of failure and the redundancy stuff, and talk to her about the need, as a man, to be in control of things, even things that I am not much good at. She poked me again. I couldn't really see that this would be a very good conversation to have at that particular moment in time, so I mumbled something stupid instead.

'I suppose I just thought it would be funny.'

There was a long, incredulous pause.

'Funny? Because you thought it would be funny?' She put her face in her hands and gave a deep, deep sigh. 'Have you thought – has the idea crossed your mind – that you have too much time on your hands?'

EIGHTEEN

Exit music (for a chicken)

'We're in the *Lynn News*!' announces Big Andy.

We cluster round him, excited. The *Lynn News* prints the bowls results and tables for the entire West Norfolk area, as well as running detailed match reviews by their legendary pseudonymous bowls correspondent 'Roving Jack'.

'Where?'

'Here. Halfway down. Blah blah blah "... drew with Albert Victor with all of the blocks drawing for the first time in many years".'

'And?'

'That's it.'

'No headline?'

'No headline.'

We are scandalised that our historic 'all of the blocks drawing' result doesn't even merit a headline. With everybody else having finished and tied, we had been a single shot down on the final end. Nigel's wood had slowed and slowed, it had crept and crept, it had lolled in towards the cott before it had expired on its final roll just within the required range. A huge cheer had rung out from the assembled me and Big Andy. Bowls can be a disappointment or it can be a triumph – and this had been punch the air time, hugs of delight, real *Pensioners' Own* stuff. A tie in sport is a wonderful thing – the Albert Victor are a very friendly bunch, and they took us into their small clubhouse, which has a bar, and gave us sandwiches and sausage rolls. It was a perfect evening in every way, although admittedly they did not lay on any strippers. Hopefully next year there will be exactly the same scenario, except that we will win it, and there will be strippers. But you can't have everything.

It surely deserved a headline.

'We ought to get moving,' says Nigel.

I take a hefty swig of my London Pride. 'Don't worry,' I say. 'We still have time to finish these pints and to thrash River Lane (B) too.'

Everybody looks at me oddly.

'Never mind,' I say, finishing the dregs of my pint.

* * *

Egg production is still down.

The chickens seem to have been enjoying our hospitality for some time, without having thought to contribute their side of the bargain. I stand with Short Tony watching them; we discuss the situation. There is still a nagging doubt that we may have been sold short by the chicken lady.

'No – they're definitely chickens,' insists Short Tony as we stand watching them aimlessly scratch around in the dust. Once more I regret being foisted off with this silly breed rather than pure-bred Transylvanian Naked Necks.

The slow laying is one thing, but there is another worry forming in our minds. Chicken One is a happy chicken. She pecks around contentedly, clearly overjoyed to have found a good place to make her nest. Chicken Two also carries this air – wandering in and out of the hen house in amusement. Likewise, Chicken Three, Chicken Five and Anne Robinson seem utterly at home in the comfy enclosure, at peace with themselves and the world.

We are concerned about Chicken Four.

Chicken Four is the smallest of the flock, and has always seemed fragile compared to her sisters. But she has now gone a bit peculiar. At first, we thought there was a particularly large egg on the way; the hen was sitting down a lot, and then sort of bouncing awkwardly on both legs as if she were on an invisible chicken space hopper that was ever so slightly too big for comfort. However, no egg subsequently appeared and now Chicken Four does not seem to be able to stand or move at all. Her eyes are bright, and she is pecking around encouragingly – but her legs don't work. Perhaps she has had some form of chicken stroke, perhaps she is just being lazy. Either way, we have confined her in the emergency isolation ward (Short Tony's conservatory).

She clucks at us. 'Chicken problems,' she seems to be saying.

'I'll give Len the Fish a ring,' sighs Short Tony. 'See if he has any ideas.'

'I'll leave it with you,' I reply. I have arranged to visit my parents for the day. This will subsequently prove to be a very, very timely thing to do.

* * *

I don't know where the LTLP gets the idea that I have too much time on my hands. Cooking, looking after the chickens, sorting out the money for the cleaner – it all mounts up. Add these sabbatical time pressures to the cost of petrol and the threat of *The Thin Blue Line* repeats on DVD, and it means that I don't visit my parents as much as I should. Booooooo – I am a terrible son, selfish and wastrel, I reflect for about 0.0000001 seconds before Ken Bruce starts up with 'PopMaster'. Leaving the motorway, I drive down through Ongar, past the old, old cottage where my grandmother grew up; and then on, through the Essex towns, skirting the Brentwood headquarters of Barry Hearn's Matchroom

Sport organisation, past the places where I first made my name in the big time.

'We're in the *Scene*!' announced Mike, bursting in breathlessly to the rehearsal session.

The band clustered around him, excited. The *Scene* carried all the local music news, as well as running gig reviews by a variety of legendary anonymous authors. Mike had promised us PR, and he had got us PR. He waved the fanzine around triumphantly.

'Give it here!' Simon ordered, grabbing it from Mike's hands.

He scanned through the article in question.

'Where?' he demanded.

'Here. Look – halfway down, after the bit about the opening act. Blah blah blah. "I was in the toilet when Steerpike were playing, but I did manage to catch the headliners who blah blah blah."'

There was a short silence.

'Is that it? Is this your PR? "I was in the toilet when Steerpike were playing"?'

It was a blow, as Steerpike rocked. Ken had turned out to be a solid bass player, and possessed rock and roll hair, and Simon was writing brilliant songs. Although his initial publicity attempts had been disappointing, Mike was working flat out getting us good gigs and knowing girls. And I was the well-respected lead guitarist in a band, playing the most prestigious pubs and clubs across the county.

'How are we all going to fit on there?'

The sound man shrugged. 'Well that's the stage.'

We trooped up onto the tiny stage, to organise ourselves for the soundcheck.

'Where are you going?'

'I'm not going on that side. Nobody can see me behind the pillar.'

'But you always go on that side.'

'If anybody should go behind the pillar then it should be Alex. There's no point anybody looking at him.'

'What do you mean "there's no point anybody looking at me?"'

'Well you never move or dance or anything – you just stand totally still, staring at your fret board. You may as well be behind a pillar.'

'That's a bit unfair – I . . . '

'He's right. Alex – behind the pillar.'

The enormous van with 'Geoff Skinner Removals' imprinted on the side had been traded in for a more sensible option – a VW Camper with a fridge for beer and beds for women groupies. We'd built up a local following, we'd laid down some tracks in the recording studio, we'd been featured in the music press.

'You just need to crack the publicity angle,' we told Mike. 'You know – do something outrageous and newsworthy.'

* * *

'You have to put olive oil on your finger and stick it up her jacksy.'

'I've got a really bad line. Can you repeat that?'

Short Tony repeats himself, sounding aggrieved.

It appears that Chicken Four is an 'egg bound hen'. I dimly remember the term from one of the chapters in the Katie Thear book, but I'd hurriedly skimmed those pages and moved on to reading about something nice, like cuddly feathers. 'Egg bound hen' is a condition that is very rare and unlikely to happen, but involves the egg getting stuck on the way out. Clearly its rarity works proportionately to the fuckwitteddom of the person to which the chicken belongs. I try to envisage what the symptoms would be if I had an egg stuck on the way out, using role play, and it seems to fit the chicken's behaviour.

'I won't be back until very late,' I reply, in answer to his next question.

Beep beep. I have an SMS message! I pull out my new phone, proudly.

'Done olive oil finger thing' it reads.

'Success?' I reply.

'No egg' comes the response.

I spend some time on the internet, looking through chicken forums for ideas and advice. I find lots. The chicken community is clearly full of wonderful, supportive people.

'Try feeding it olive oil' I text.

'Different olive oil' I add, a few seconds later.

We have another short telephone conversation, mainly about what Short Tony could feel when he pushed his finger up her jacksy. My mother and father look on, with raised eyebrows.

* * *

'Excuse me?'

There was a voice. Simon and I set down our menus to discover its source.

The waitress was young, and blonde, and well spoken; her make-up understated, her breasts gently yet firmly packed into her Pizza Hut uniform, like a calzone. Our surprise was less to do with the fact that a Pizza Hut waitress had appeared, given that we were in Pizza Hut, but everything to do with the fact that we'd literally just been sat down and given menus, and that she was looking at Simon in an enquiring way.

'Weren't you playing at the Castle last night?' she asked Simon.

'I was!' replied Simon.

'I was as well,' I interjected.

'I really enjoyed it,' she told Simon.

'It was a good gig,' replied Simon.

'I thought it went well,' I interjected.

'Are you playing there again?' she asked Simon.

'We should be soon,' replied Simon.

'We could let you know,' I interjected.

'Will you let me know?' she asked Simon.

'Yes definitely. I'd like to,' said Simon.

She turned to me. 'He's got a great band,' she said. 'Are you ready to order now?'

I guess that this was the first time that I was recognised and approached by a member of the public. I'm sure every musician, every celebrity, remembers their first time: from the simple 'aren't you . . .?'s and the 'I saw you on the telly!'s to the detailed and obsessive fan questions: Jeff Beck being asked about chord shapes; Alex Marshall being interrogated on his drawing technique; Dawn French engaged in conversation about late twentieth-century gender politics.

It's nice to begin with, but could soon become annoying.

Simon and I discussed the mechanics of autographs. This was in the days when autograph requests were genuine – not a way of making a quick buck on eBay – and we wanted to give the fans value. But we quickly realised the drawback, as we practised our signatures on the menu as our pizzas were cooking.

Even after three or four scribbles, a painful wrist-ache was emerging. Simon and I wrote line after line of names – but it was bloody hard work. God knows what it would be like at the Brit Awards. We discussed developing simpler signatures to make the process more efficient. If, for instance, I just signed 'AM', then it would take a mere two-ninths of the time that it would to sign my whole name. Perhaps with a little picture of a smiley face or a guitar afterwards, just to show willing.

We settled on this. The only exception, we figured, would be when the women groupies appeared and asked us to sign their breasts. Women groupies who asked us to sign their breasts would deserve a full and considered signature. Plus a little picture, whether of a smiley face or a guitar, or both.

*   *   *

I arrive back in the village early in the evening, and immediately hasten to Short Tony's, via the secret path. But there is no positive news.

'I've given her a hot bath,' he says. 'And some nice corn. But . . .'

He has no need to expand upon the pause.

'She just can't move at all, can she?' I observe.

Short Tony thinks for a bit. 'We've got an old remote-controlled toy car somewhere. I guess we could try to rig something up to help her get about?'

'Like a chicken Ironside,' I ponder. 'But obviously without the ability to solve crimes.'

We reject the suggestion as impractical and stand around for a while, watching a motionless chicken.

'Give me a shout if there are any developments,' I say eventually. 'I'll be round first thing in the morning to see how things are.'

*   *   *

Saks. The YMCA. The Pink Toothbrush, the Castle, the Essex Arms. A proper demo tape, from a proper recording studio; mentions in the press; blonde waitresses offering extra toppings for free. A manager with an entourage of girls; gigs when we wanted them; other musicians paying tribute. There is no doubt that – on a local level – this could be called 'success'.

But there was a flip side. With success comes expectation and ambition. When you are young and hungry, sometimes you can get frustrated when you feel that somebody is holding you back from getting a small bite to eat. And if you are in a hurry, it is understandable that instead of waiting patiently whilst that person dithers about in front of the larder, you want to gently nudge them aside, politely yet firmly, so that you can realise your dreams by reaching in and grabbing some biscuits or, perhaps, a packet of crisps.

Iain was struggling. I had always liked his drumming style, but he had been having difficulty with the more complex arrangements that we were exploring, and the council's Environmental Health Protection Team had served him with a notice that he was to cease practising them in his bedroom. That was a moot point, however, as he'd been run over and had broken both legs.

We went to see him as a band, and rallied round in support by asking if he knew of any other drummers. And he did, and we got a very good temporary drummer out of it. And when he was better . . .

There is no need to expand upon that. Dave and now Iain. They were my best friends. We'd been together for years – from being kids in the corner of a garage messing about and not liking motor racing, to being in a bona fide real deal band. We'd shared the laughs and the arguments, the stage fright, the stress, the applause, the indifference, the fun, the dreams. And now they were both gone. My best friends, cast aside to further my own career.

And the worst bit? We got Mike to break the news. I didn't even have the guts to talk to Iain myself – we got our manager to ring him, and then I spent the rest of my life avoiding my old friend. Ambition and ego are the dark interlopers that poison success – I know that much now that I am older, now that I have turned my back on the big time to live a more honest life here in Norfolk. But I knew it then as well, deep, deep in my heart. Mike called me to say that he'd done the deed. I thanked him. And I resolved never, ever to ask somebody else to do my dirty jobs ever again.

* * *

'I think you should be the one to shoot the chicken,' I tell Short Tony.

We stand in silence for a while. There are a million reasons why he would be the best person to shoot the paralysed chicken, not least of which is the fact that I would probably miss.

He nods, sadly. 'I'll get the gun.'

Despite being a country-dweller, I don't really know much about shooting. I've shot clays, and I've shot tin cans, and I've taken on the role of beater during an organised shoot in Big Andy's back garden when he thought that they might have a rat in the compost heap. But nothing more than that. The closest I've come to actually shooting anything living was when we thought that there was a prowler in the village, and even then I had second thoughts and replaced my air rifle in the cottage before bravely going unarmed to investigate. Crashing around in the dark waving an air rifle is always a bad idea when there are policemen crouching in the foliage.

Ironically, having not located a prowler in the vicinity, I returned to the cottage to find that I had left the front door wide open with an air rifle propped up by it. I kicked myself for my stupidity – I would have felt very foolish if a homicidal maniac had walked into the house and murdered the LTLP! The Tony Martin case was still big news; Mr John Redwood had been on *Question Time* only the previous week complaining that law-abiding householders were still unsure of what they could do should they walk into the sitting room to find themselves confronted by a swivel-eyed maniac loon.

Fortunately, I had been aware of my rights, and had slowly and calmly switched off the TV.

I wouldn't have a clue what to do with a dying chicken. But Short Tony is a shooter; a responsible one, who knows the ways of the land.

I look at the patient – her eyes don't have the brightness that had given us hope for her recovery. Just a few hours before she had been resolutely cheerful as I had popped in to chat to her and to stroke her little head. But this morning, Chicken Four has already fallen out of her box, shat all over Short Tony's conservatory and started making piteous noises. She is unable to move and is in terrible distress, the sort of distress that you can't leave an animal in.

Jeremy Kyle is in his mid-forties. Chicken Four lived for only a few weeks. Care to explain that one, religious fundamentalists? I turn away as the clucks cease.

'I'll sort out the carcass from here,' mutters Short Tony.

We are both sombre and upset. Poor Chicken Four; I am more personally affected than I'd anticipated – I *knew* that we should not have given them names. Booooooo, boooooo and triple boooooo. I have only been chickening for a few weeks and already I have lost around seventeen per cent of the livestock. Perhaps this is another thing that I am not cut out to do; perhaps poultry-rearing is the formulation of Strategic HR Initiatives of the countryside. I hope that the other five understand. I would be miserable if I thought that they hated me.

NINETEEN

A little man and a house and a hole for a window

'We're not ahead by enough,' hisses Big Andy nervously, as we cross over in the penultimate end. I know what he means. Four points is never a comfortable margin, and our opponents have been unlucky. Their skipper, in particular, has the air of a man who has been playing beneath his ability; all three wear the regulation whites and greys that indicate their participation in the more serious leagues.

Three minutes later and we are but two points in credit.

Their skip and lead confer, before the mat goes down and the latter, a big avuncular man from somewhere up north, grasps the cott within massive sausagey fingers before sending it far down the green. A long one – a very long one. He takes his first wood and stares, stares hard and unflinchingly at the stationary cott as if the blameless white ball had just spilt his lager and gone on to feel his wife's buttock during the clear-up operation. Still staring, he swings his arm back with grim intent.

His wood heads off far too short and straight.

'Oh . . . *bollocks!*' he explodes.

The green falls silent.

'Erm – sorry, everybody,' he ventures.

We win by five.

I don't know where loud swearing comes on the disciplinary code. It is certainly less serious than not wearing the requisite deeply, deeply unfashionable shoes.

'Weren't you once banned from the league for something?' I ask Rod, as we settle down on the benches to watch the last game conclude. I grasp the lettuce and bag of new potatoes that he's sold me from his allotment. They will make an excellent meal of something and salad and potatoes.

'No – that was Frank,' he replies, taking a swig from his tin of John Smith's. 'Farting. Persistent farting. God, that boy could play a symphony orchestra on his arse if he wanted, he could.'

I try to envisage having this talent. Frankly, I can't see it being as handy as, say, being able to build a fence – although having it in reserve would be at least as useful as knowing about computerised type mark-up systems. Rod shakes his head, sadly.

'We were crossing between ends, right in the middle of the park and he let one fly. Echoed all round the rinks, it did. The Chairman got a letter. Referring to "flatulence on the greens". Two years they banned him for.'

'Two years?'

'Didn't pick him for two years,' insists Rod.

We finish our beer in thoughtful silence.

∗　∗　∗

The Downs form my favourite walk. They're a bit of a drive away, but worth it.

This is Norfolk, so they aren't the downiest Downs in Britain, but they suit me down to the ground. I amble along the path, trampling dirt into the small valley where dirt has been trampled for thousands of years.

I overtake a lady on the inside. She has grey hair tied back into a bun, like witches do in children's picture books, and a small terrier which, although not actually yapping, has the air of one that might spend a high proportion of the day being yappy.

'Beautiful day,' I remark as I pass.

'It's wonderful, isn't it?' she replies.

'Bit of cloud up ahead, though,' I caution. The weather. It is important to have conversation to hand about the weather.

The path cuts a shallow valley through the landscape, grassland easing up the slopes on either side. It meanders such that I suppose it was probably once a river, or an inlet from the Wash up past the ancient barns of the farm and into the village. I try to form a picture of history in my mind – the Romans walked this road once, but before them must have been the true Ancient Britons, settlers and farmers; then Neoliths or Palaeoliths or whatever type of Liths were around at that point. Afterwards, the people of the Dark Ages and medieval era, trudging the meadowland as I do now; the farmhands and workers and squires of days gone by; the sons of Albion, the men of all our pasts, the very seed of All England. Right up to the hikers, birdwatchers and strollers of the present day, with their Ordnance Survey maps and ham sandwiches. A clear timeline: thousands of years of Norfolk, England on this very soil. Breathless, I stop walking for a moment and hold my arms out wide; I feel the history of the moment surge up from the earth beneath my feet; the people, the races, the wars, the work; the life and the achievements; the very essence of my ancestors flowing like electricity into every nerve ending in my body.

'Excuse me,' says the sinister old lady from the children's picture book, trying to get past. I blink. There is a disappointing absence of tingly nerves. All this history electricity stuff is rubbish – no ancestral mysterious forces for me. That is typical of the ghostly spirits of Norfolk's ten-thousand-year history. Even after ten thousand years, they will never accept you as one of their own.

I am just an idiot in the way. Mrs Witchety Witch's yappy dog looks at me suspiciously.

The landscape passes through a short semi-gorge then opens out to the right in rolling hillside as the path turns a corner. The view from here on is wonderful. Norfolk can be a bit like funny comedy actress Tamsin Greig: perhaps not what some people would consider conventionally beautiful, but the more you explore around and about, the more you are likely to find an interesting or unusual bit that is nourishing to the eye. A young couple cycle tentatively towards me, in single file.

For some reason, the meadow contains a field-within-a-field enclosed in wire fencing. Its grass is a deep, deep green: lush – almost artificially so – in comparison with the rest of the landscape. It's like no other green I've ever seen in nature before. Felt-tip pen green. As green as green can be. As the cyclists approach, I feel that I should say something about it. It truly is remarkably remarkable.

'Lovely day,' I remark.

'Beautiful!' replies the lead cyclist.

I do not mention the grass. It would be wrong, somehow. If I deviate in topic from the weather they may think me eccentric. I wait until they are safely round the corner then mention it to myself.

The weather. What *is* it about the weather? I read once that the British are obsessed by the weather because we were once essentially either seafarers or farmers. Everything we had or did depended on the weather. Cutting corn, landing pilchards, getting in a quick game of bowls before attacking the Spanish – 'looks like it might be nice today' really *meant* something. And now all we have is some sort of race memory – a nervous tic that is perpetuated by the worry that you might get a bit wet during bowls or that your outdoor gig will be a washout.

Some cows graze in the shadow of a copse. There are only around seven of them – surely too few to warrant the descriptive extravagance of a 'herd' – but they are perfect picture-book Friesians, immaculately clean Atom Heart Mother cows with that agriculturally friendly air that the black-and-white ones possess in droves. One glances at me in passing. She is the epitome of cowdom. It occurs to me that if I'd been commissioned to shoot a front cover for *Cow World* magazine, I'd have found my muse.

I say nothing about the cow to the man who overtakes us at this point. Green, green grass is one thing, but if I approached the topic of cows he would surely call the police. He nods towards the sky and makes a sort of happy grunting noise. We both know what he means.

There is a solicitor's letter waiting for me on my return. I have never received a solicitor's letter in my life, despite everything. I look at it carefully before tearing it open in some puzzlement. It will presumably cost me money and make me annoyed to read it, just taking a wild stab in the dark.

'Dear Mr Marsh.' The opening is clear enough. Frankly I am impressed with the clear directness of his opening. He will be chucked out of the Law Society if he continues in this vein.

'As you will doubtless be aware, you were a beneficiary of your late grandmother's will.'

Gosh.

'Blah, blah, blah, cheque . . .' (I paraphrase).

'A substantial four-figure sum.'

A substantial four-figure sum.

I have been left a substantial four-figure sum. This sort of thing just doesn't happen to me. I sit down heavily on the sofa, stunned. To say that the news has hit me like a football-sized chunk of uranium contained in a safe that has then been placed in an iron-framed piano and sent plummeting from the fifteenth-floor window of the Institute of High Gravity Studies with a member of sixties hippie combo The Mamas and the Papas tied to each leg (John Phillips having a large quantity of loose change in his pocket) followed by an antelope, a large bag of ball bearings and a parcel marked 'DANGER OF INJURY! Do Not Attempt To Lift This' would be an understatement.

It is a lot of money. I mean, in the big scheme of things it might not be – it wouldn't buy a dialysis machine for the hospital or rescue the Edinburgh Woollen Mill shops, and you'd probably get paid that for a mere couple of months' work coming up with Strategic HR Initiatives for a living. But as an out-of-the-blue, arriving-in-the-post-one-morning, totally unexpected windfall . . . It's . . . it's . . .

It's a lot of money.

I sit down and try to turn things over in my mind. Despite the odd little bits of work I am starting to pick up, and the potential revenue from any band I might start with the Chipper Barman, it would be fair to say that the LTLP is still somewhat the main wage earner. The merchandising, licensing and deals that Mike had negotiated for Steerpike have proved disappointing in the long term, not providing me with any income to speak of. That is the unfairness of the music business for you.

I need to use this money wisely. It can't get pulled into the morass of household bills, everyday expenditure, bar tab. I don't generally read the money section of the newspaper, but I've heard of ISAs and funds and stuff – somewhere where I can wisely invest. Stocks and shares are a bit dodgy these days – how about a small business? Something that I can get my teeth into, that can get me started again. What about the LTLP? She deserves a real holiday, a proper one, something to show my love and gratitude.

What could I do?

'Oh absolutely wonderful. I'm so wonderfully pleased that you've changed your mind,' says the Piano Man. 'When can we come and pick it up?'

* * *

It had been several months since our meeting with the architect, but the remainder of the inheritance and the fact that we had been able to secure temporary accommodation in a small nearby terraced house owned by Narcoleptic Dave had spurred us into building action. Narcoleptic Dave's place was cosy and warm, and the rent was very reasonable – but it was sad to be away for a while and returning home to the cottage was a bit of a shock. The grounds were a quagmire, the conservatory had been demolished, foundations had been marked out. Half the cottage still stood, but where the seventies bathroom, unusable attic room and drippy roof had previously lain unmolested, sat a great big gap. Nobody had yet gone down with anthrax.

Resting up against a tree, ripped out from its hinges beneath the now-gone winding staircase, stood an ex-Scooby-Doo bookcase. I looked at it sadly. No more would it open, close, open, close to the wonder of all who beheld it. No more would I walk past it, touch it, gaze at it enraptured that I had the best thing – the very best thing – that a man could possibly have: a bookcase that opened on hinges to reveal a secret area beyond, like in the Scooby-Doo cartoons.

I clasped the forlorn pine and lifted it sorrowfully, carting it with some effort across the mud to the shed. It could still serve some purpose in there, although it would never be the same again. I was sure that there would have been some way that I could have kept the artefact, could have routed the building work around it, could have made it a centrepiece. The LTLP, perhaps, would not have been too happy, but it could have worked. And I would have got away with it if it wasn't for that pesky architect.

213

If you are going to make changes to your house, to make it suitable for modern living, it is important to employ good craftsmen. People who understand the history of the area; who can be sympathetic to the context of your work. Above all, people who won't rip you off, unlike builders in cities, who are always pretending to fix your roof and boasting about their appearances on *Watchdog*.

The Reliable Local Builder was enthusiastic and experienced. When I met him on site for the first time it was to hand over a down payment and talk about bricks.

Honestly – I had no idea that bricks came in such varieties. There were red bricks and yellow bricks and grey bricks and black bricks. There were bricks that were mixtures of colours. There were smooth bricks and rough bricks and new-looking bricks and artificially aged bricks, and reclaimed bricks and English bricks and foreign bricks and . . .

Choosing the bricks had proved difficult. It seemed to me that it would be a good idea to get bricks that matched the existing remaining bricks, as much as possible. But we couldn't really tell in the catalogues, and we certainly couldn't tell on the internet. I had to physically look at bricks by viewing the samples that the Reliable Local Builder had brought to show me.

These were a mixed bunch, and after a cursory inspection, I decided that I didn't like them. This seemed to disappoint him immensely. He then showed me some more bricks. I didn't like those bricks either, and what's more there was a slight suspicion in my mind that they were the same bricks as previously demonstrated.

He pointed out politely that, like teenagers, bricks change their character immensely once they're laid. I pointed out politely that in that case there wasn't much point in him pointing out non-laid bricks to me, if they were going to be completely different once they were pointed. He took my point and we went to visit a wall together. It's on this sort of give and take discussion that successful building projects are based.

The bricks in the wall seemed hauntingly familiar. I asked the Reliable Local Builder if they might be the same bricks that I had previously rejected on site, and he hummed and hawed for a bit and conceded that they might be. I confirmed that I didn't like these bricks, so we moved on to a large builders' merchants to see some more examples.

'These ones are pretty good,' he offered, indicating a sample board that was mounted on the wall in the extensive brick department. Once more, on examination, I found myself with a creeping sense of recognition, which was confirmed by a brief cross-referencing of the information on the label. I made terribly English noises about not wanting to be a difficult customer and all that, but explained that I would much rather have some different bricks, which I subsequently chose.

Later on, he telephoned me to double-double check that the bricks that I had chosen were definitely, definitely the ones that I wanted, in case he had made a mistake and not heard correctly. It is always best to check. I was pleased with his Reliable Local manner – it's a shame that the common fallacy of 'never go with the cheapest quote' has gained such widespread acceptance. This all boded well for the future.

* * *

Alex Marshall is struggling in the Sky Premier League Bowls. 'Every point is precious if these bowlers can keep alive their Premier League dream,' urges the announcer. The reigning champion, Billy Jackson, seems an amiable man – he shares a joke with Marshall and the technical officials as the specially made Thomas Taylor woods are being cleared for the next end.

Billy Jackson wins the match on an absolute fluke. He holds

his hand up sheepishly to acknowledge the fact; Alex Marshall returns a rueful smile. Alex Marshall is now sixth in a league of six. I do hope that this is not an omen.

'Sixty pounds please.'

I hand over the money willingly, the first sixty of the five thousand to go. You can call me stupid, you can call me sentimental, you can call me financially suicidal – but what else would I spend the money on? I've got my health, I've got my music, I've got my bowls, I've got some chickens. I've got so many things that my life is almost one big Nina Simone song. It was my grandmother's piano and my grandmother's money – and who am I but a custodian of our shared past? 'When the Blackbird Says Bye-Bye', 'When the Robin Sings his Song Again' – I have a responsibility to this. If they can put a blue plaque on the wall of Paul McCartney's old ex-council house then the least I can do is to mend a few hammers to preserve the history of ornithological song.

I try to explain all this to the piano removal men, but they are a bit pushed for time, drink their coffee and hurriedly leave.

Wandering back into the ex-piano room, I am struck by the space that's been freed up. If you could put a piano in every room and then remove it, you'd suddenly and magically have a huge house, mightily suitable for modern-day living. No worries, no hassles, just like that. The piano method of extending your property. Far easier than using a builder. No matter how Reliable. Or Local.

*   *   *

A few weeks later, I met up with my Reliable Local Builder once more.

He was nervous and ill at ease for some reason. Having taken a quick look at the situation myself earlier, I strongly suspected that I knew what this some reason might be. We walked through the earthworks, around the rubble, past my nice hedge, which now looked like it had been dragged through a human backwards, to the back garden – or the patch of mud where the back garden used to be.

The cottage was coming along nicely. This was the great thing about getting a Reliable Local Builder. The small rooms were opening out into large ones; the place was becoming nicely suitable for modern-day living – which was fortunate, as Narcoleptic Dave wanted his house back, and we were due to be moving back in.

I was particularly pleased with the walls. There was a big wall that contained what we called 'Bedroom 3'. It was a well-constructed wall made of bricks and period breeze-block. The bricks were exactly as chosen and were laid as straight as straight can be, in an attractive Flemish bond. The mortar-work was excellent, as was the pointing. I could not criticise the wall in any way.

We examined the wall together.

'Where,' I asked in a very calm and considered and keeping-a-lid-on-it way, 'is the window?'

'Yes,' replied the Reliable Local Builder.

I looked harder at the wall. Not being a technical type, I had imagined that a gap would need to be left in advance for the window, rather than some retrospective hollowing-out process being necessary.

'I think the brickie had a bit of an off day,' he offered.

'An off day.'

'Either that, or he was looking at a different version of the plans.'

My mind searched in vain for any memory of these mysterious second windowless plans. 'It's just that I was rather hoping to use it,' I mused, 'for looking out of.'

'Mmmmm.'

There was a long silence. I looked at him. He looked at me. A feeling of unease was rising up my body, pawing at me with needy claws. I blinked and shook my head, but it did not want to go away.

TWENTY

Who draws the crowd and plays so loud, baby it's the guitar man

'Can you turn that off, please?'

I look at the LTLP in surprise. She is making annoyed gestures towards my laptop.

'But it's Jethro Tull!' I protest.

'That,' she replies, narrowing her eyes, 'is my point.'

I have discovered Spotify – the website that basically lets you listen to any music you can possibly think of, all for free. Granted, it hasn't got stuff like the Beatles or Pink Floyd yet, Madness and King Crimson are noticeable by their absence, and Mike seems to have been a bit slow in contacting them to license Steerpike, but otherwise it is brilliant. Just search, click, listen, and that's it.

One of the great things that I have discovered about the service is that it contains loads of progressive rock. There is not much progressive rock on iTunes, as it generally goes on too long for it to be worth them offering it for under a pound, whereas with Spotify it is almost as if your computer has bought a Mellotron and grown a beard. Therefore I have been catching up on all the immense works of metaphysical sophistication that I remember from vinyl. Once, when I was very young, I closed my mind to stuff like this – I was too self-consciously 'cool' to appreciate my music being compared to the likes of the Tull. But I'm a proper, rounded musician now. Labels in music are ludicrous, anyway. There is only good music, bad music, and Dido.

The LTLP does not appreciate this. I am a bit cross with her dismissive attitude.

'I think you should give it more of a chance,' I protest, as a flute solo climaxes and guitarist Martin Barre leads a call-and-response blues riff repeated thirty-eight times. I shrug. 'I know progressive rock does have a bit of a bad reputation, but the interesting thing is that the best, most well-regarded stuff – your Genesises, your Tulls, even something like Tubular Bells – essentially consists of a series of cracking tunes linked by short musical bridges. So whilst it's the existence of those bridges that defines the genre, if you like, really it just goes back to those cracking tunes – which are the essence of pop music anyway.'

'Aside from Yes, that is, who sound like an explosion in a wank factory.'

I warm to my theme. 'So whilst many people have likened progressive rock to classical music, I'd say that it's more to do with the traditions of opera – big numbers with a theme and links. You know?'

I am pleased with my analysis. Sometimes I think that I should have gone into teaching; perhaps I might retrain one day. As Kevin – my tutor from bowls – once discovered, there is nothing quite as satisfying as imparting learning to people.

'I think it's shit,' she replies.

I am annoyed once more. The problem with being a teacher in the twenty-first century is that trendy teaching theories have made it all but impossible to exclude pupils.

'Can you turn it off now, please?' she adds.

I sigh, and close the website down. There is uncomfortable silence. Walking across the sitting room, I turn the television on.

* * *

'How did you get on last night then?'

Big Andy snorts.

'We got hammered,' he mutters.

It transpires that a mix-up had occurred, and only two players had turned up for Big Andy's block.

It happens. People have to drop out at the last minute, or get the wrong venue, or so-and-so thinks that so-and-so-other has spoken to so-and-so-somebody-else, but, in fact, so-and-so-somebody-else hasn't been spoken to and has no idea that they're down to play. Alex Marshall and the Sky Premier League players presumably have rafts of secretaries and officials to ensure that everybody turns up on time; we rely on the odd phone call, a quick word after the previous game and just generally *knowing*.

We've been short a few too many times now, however. We're struggling for people.

It's virtually impossible to win if you have only two players – the odds and percentages are so heavily against you. The emphasis is therefore on playing defensively, on damage limitation. If you can avoid losing by too many then the two bonus points – that go to the team with the most points across all the blocks – might be saved. In its way, it's an interesting challenge.

'I have to say – when I've been in a block of two, I've quite enjoyed it in a perverse way,' I reflect, as the car pulls out of the village. 'It focuses the mind. Gets the adrenaline pumping.'

'We played bloody well when there was just me and you last year, over at Terrington St Clement,' agrees Nigel. 'We only lost by a few.'

'It can even be an advantage,' I reply. 'I mean – that was the night of Eddie's party. And as we only had two people, we managed to get back there before the food had run out.'

'Which was an advantage,' concurs Nigel.

'And in the cup last year,' I continue, 'I was playing with Short

Tony, and Mrs Martin The Bloke From Up The Road That Works In IT – and she'd never played before, never even picked up a wood. So that was effectively a block of two. I played really well, and did a pretty good coaching job on her.'

Mrs Martin The Bloke From Up The Road That Works In IT inexplicably never played bowls again after that one game. I never found out why. It is a shame – she was ever so enthusiastic beforehand.

'Anyway, we got hammered,' repeats Big Andy.

We park the car where we can and make the rest of the journey on foot, traipsing along the dirty pavement beside the main road, out of place in the metropolitan setting; deeply, deeply unfashionable shoes safely hidden within our bowls bags from potential mugging hoodies. A group of four teenagers eyes us coolly from where they are mucking about on a bench. Exhaust fumes and cars, none stopping, all looking to speed quickly out of, or into, the centre of town; all looking for that little advantage over the other guy at the lights. Litter blowing about in the street – new, fresh litter; old, faded litter. Shop fronts that could do with care and attention; fast-food outlet after fast-food outlet. This is the gritty urban reality of bowls: the lie to the cliché of old men, tea and scones; bowls in a dystopian twenty-first-century society, like a sort of Rollerball version of bowls; bowlsageddon. If Terry Hall and the Specials wanted to zig-zag past in an old car singing about bowls then this would be a good enough time as any to do so.

Past some more exhaust-stained buildings, past the side of a pub into a gloomy alley passing under a red-brick arch and then . . . and then the vista opens out. The traffic noise abruptly disappears; an expanse of trees and grass; lovingly tended allotments, a pavilion and a green that's beautifully cut and cared for. I am taken aback and rue my shallow prejudices. I have been living in the countryside too long and have turned into some sort of rural snob. The revelation of the green beyond the alley is not just the bowls equivalent of a motorcyclist removing their helmet to reveal a beautiful woman shaking down her long red hair. It is the bowls equivalent of a motorcyclist removing their helmet to reveal a beautiful woman shaking down her long red hair, offering you a pint and asking politely if she can leave her long leather boots on whilst you have sex with her across her Yamaha, as she has to get away quickly to meet her father, who owns the Gibson guitar company.

It is nice.

* * *

The Pink Toothbrush club was the Potters Leisure Resort of alternative music. Every major band from the pages of the *New Musical Express* played there, as a step on the ladder to stardom and fame. Blur, Ocean Colour Scene, Spiritualized, Bad Manners – they all passed through what had become our home venue.

It was nothing much to look at – a rough, slightly piss-stained doorway in a rundown shopping street. But once through that and the short and dark corridor beyond, the vista opened out. The noise of indie music, an expanse of stage and dance floor, a cheerfully tended bar and a sea of live music fans, half-cut on Newcastle Brown.

The Sultans of Ping were in the charts.

The real charts, not just the indie charts, or the *New Musical Express* charts, or the Pepsi chart or whatever – the charts that were on Radio 1 and *Top of the Pops*. Clearly they had been booked months beforehand, when they were just nobodies – but I don't suppose there was a person alive in 1992 who didn't have their no. 67 smash 'Where's Me Jumper' going around and around their heads.

Dancing at the disco, bumper to bumper.
Wait a minute – where's me jumper?
Where's me jumper?

Being with musicians like that was intimidating. I was glad that we had moved on from the motor racing song.

* * *

Even though I've not visited this particular green before, I recognise a few people in the opposition – a friendly and genial bunch, many with interesting tattoos.

'We're still waiting for one player,' somebody informs us. 'He should be here by now.'

We change into our deeply, deeply unfashionable shoes and wait for a short while, chatting away on the edge of the green. Nigel, Big Andy and me – warming up, soundchecking.

'Looks like he's not coming,' their skipper eventually concedes. 'We'll have to play with two. Sorry about that.'

Big Andy shrugs. 'We're quite happy to wait a bit longer if he's on his way,' he says. And we are, of course. They are good lads, and we have no wish to gain an unfair advantage, although if their third player does not turn up then we are quite looking forward to hammering them into the green with our overwhelming bowls superiority.

'Don't worry mate, we can't keep you waiting any longer.'

'Have a good game.'

Big Andy shakes his head at the irony of the deeply, deeply unfashionable shoes being on the other foot. I lay down the mat at the correct position and cast the cott – it speeds off, far further than I'd anticipated, across the hard and even surface. I adjust the strength of my opening wood accordingly.

The tactic for playing with one extra man is, of course, to win big – taking the pressure off your other blocks by guaranteeing those two bonus points. The sun still radiates hot beats as it hovers low over the town centre; Big Andy is in his shorts whilst I leave my shades on for the first time this year. 'Bit quicker than you think,' I warn Nigel as we cross on the first end.

* * *

'I'm sorry we're late,' said the singer from the Sultans of Ping. 'We missed the junction and ending up getting lost in some fucking place. Where were we?'

'Canvey Island,' interjected another Sultan of Ping.

'Canvey Island. Stuck in a broken down van in fucking Canvey Island. I'm sorry.'

It was good of them to talk to us. They were genuine people, with no 'we're no. 67 in the charts and you're just the support band' airs. Obviously it made sense for them to be pleasant to up-and-coming bands that would probably one day be in a position to do *them* favours, but some headliners would not have taken this attitude. We chatted for a bit, but they were tired.

A third Sultan of Ping appeared. He looked miserable and slightly bedraggled. In fact, on a closer examination, they were all looking grim. Here was the reality of life on the road – from gig, to gig, to gig, living on burgers and lager, sleeping in the van, washing occasionally. An unscheduled tour of Canvey Island had been like lifting a big bale of straw up to a respectable height before dropping it smartly on an elderly camel suffering from a chronic calcium deficiency.

For the first time in my life I had a smidgen of doubt about the path that I had chosen.

* * *

There is an enormous crash from the next rink.

Glen has fired hard and missed his target completely, his wood careering on to ram into the low wooden gate in front of the pavilion.

225

A lady scuttles over to check for damage. Glen looks bashful.

'Funnily enough,' he ruminates, 'I took a row of potatoes out here once.' He nods his head towards the allotments. 'Fired, missed the target, knocked down a whole row of 'em.' He smiles and shakes his head. 'That was in 1974. I was younger then.'

I would ask him more about the great King's Lynn potato massacre, but our block has problems of its own, and I do not need to get distracted.

Satisfied that the gate has suffered no critical structural failure, the lady returns to her game.

'Two down,' calls Big Andy as Nigel's shoulders sag.

We are not doing well. Nigel, in particular, is playing as if he is head of the government agency tasked with redistributing bowls points to teams forced to play with a numerical disadvantage. Nigel is a true sportsman. He used to be a top-class club cricketer and a decent footballer – and he has transferred his natural aptitude to bowls. But tonight, everything he tries seems to go wrong – he knocks our woods out of contention, he knocks their woods into contention; he hits the cott but hits it too hard and springs it out of range of our scoring shots. I run off to fetch him an emergency isotonic tin of Old Speckled Hen from my bag, but even that does not change our luck.

'Come on *bend*! *Bennnd!*' I scream, as my wood fails to bend. I have taken to shouting at my woods lately – I'm sure that this is a sign of stress. Big Andy is quieter; Nigel just stands with hands on hips.

'One down.'

* * *

'Where'sJohnnyChristmas? – you'llneverfindhim – where'sJohnny-Christmas? – you'llneverfindhim – wooooo hoooooooooooo.'

Waves of light played on the dry ice that swirled around me during my guitar solo. Andy – our new drummer – whirled his arms around the kit, Ken paced the stage throwing his head back and forth in time with the bass guitar, Simon snarled into the mic as he improvised the last lines, ready to cue the final bars. I stood and concentrated very hard on my fretboard. It is important not to play wrong notes during a climactic guitar bit.

'Thanks very much,' announced Simon.

As we trooped off the stage, I left the guitar plugged in and switched on, squealing and howling in a torrent of sonic rage as it fed back through the PA, carefully propped up against the amplifier so it wouldn't fall over and chip the paintwork. Pumped up, we jogged down the stairs to the small backstage area – the stairs that had been trod by Blur, Ocean Colour Scene and – shortly to come – the Sultans of Ping. The noise from the club, the howl of the guitar – there was no doubt as to the path that I had chosen.

Although it would have helped if we'd not split up a short while later.

I suppose that once you've supported the Sultans of Ping, it's difficult to keep motivating yourself to get bigger and bigger highs. There was no animosity, no personal or musical differences – just . . . the end. Ken and Andy melted off to do their own thing; I moved to London and eventually started the band that would have broken through globally, had I not selflessly given it all up to leave for Norfolk to support the LTLP.

And as for Simon – we'd spent the most exciting part of our teenage years playing and writing songs together, my lead to his skip. We'd shared good times, bad times, triumph and disaster; we'd blown the church hall apart, we'd moved people with intimate gigs and heartfelt songs. We were going to spend the next few years touring, and releasing albums, and expanding our art, and signing women's breasts. But having triumphed at one of the biggest live concerts of 1992 – the Sultans of Ping at the Pink

Toothbrush club, having wowed an audience that doubtless included representatives of all the major labels and international concert promoters, we somehow managed to snatch defeat from the jaws of victory.

So that was it for Steerpike. And I never saw Simon again.

* * *

We avoid eye contact and shuffle our feet as we pack our woods away at the end of the game. The rest of the team is tactful. Losing to a block of two is shameful, is embarrassing, is a humiliation of Maxmosleyesque proportions. Rod's block has won by seven, securing us the bonus points anyway – but having our skin saved in such a manner just adds to our discomfort.

Four points all – a draw – which solidifies our low/mid-table position. Early talk of bowls trophies and presentations seems ridiculous – a fiasco like this, some close games and a single storming victory is not the stuff of champions. One-hit wonders, more like. The Norman Greenbaums of bowls. The Simon Park Orchestra of the greens. I zip up the burgundy bag morosely.

It is getting chilly as we return through the red-brick alley. The wall on the left-hand side belongs to a public house; grilles and air vents let loose an enormous thumping and screaming noise that perhaps would have made it through the bricks anyway.

'What the bloody hell is that racket?' asks Nigel.

From somewhere inside, a girl vocalist is yelling away in angry competition with a drummer and a guitarist who is playing very simple power chords very loudly. The words are muffled, but the impression is that it is very unlikely to be a love song of romantic and tender yearning or a Miles Davis cover.

'Good God,' he continues.

'It sounds all right to me,' Big Andy replies, surprisingly. 'I mean – once upon a time, I'd have gone in there and had a listen.'

I nod. I think of the places that I used to listen to music in, and the skanky pubs that we used to play in. The Essex Arms. The Castle. A small raised stage in a black-painted room; the smell of spilt beer and the crunch of glass beneath your feet. And I am filled with the urge to say 'Shall we?' and drop in for a lukewarm bottle of Newcastle Brown in a plastic glass, and listen to a girl vocalist shouting about how she hates something muffled, and then maybe have a chat to her afterwards about sharing gigs and equipment.

We pack the bowls bags in the car and drive off to the village pub.

TWENTY-ONE

Look what they've done to my sink, ma

Short Tony stomps to my front door.

'Have you been in all day?' he demands.

I know to what he is referring. Short Tony is a man of enthusiasms. Whereas I have had a fairly steady and constant desire to build my life around music and bowls, he flits from one interest to another, like a butterfly with a hobbies catalogue. Running, playing tennis, playing snooker, karaoke, bowls . . . I admire his enquiring mind. As it is, he has been waiting for the object of his new interest to arrive: a device that will allow him to make his own sausages.

He has been anticipating this delivery for days now. Each time, the parcel people cunningly thwart him with 'we called' leaflets and/or phantom door-knocks in the lightest way possible with the very tips of their fingers. I give him a weak shrug. 'They haven't left it here.'

He has an explosive look on his face; a combination of frustration and dangerously low blood-sausage levels. I trot after him as he storms back along the secret path. Scrawled 'If I am Out . . .' instruction posters are Sellotaped up on every possible piece of his house that a parcel man might conceive of as being a delivery point.

Curse evil Parcelforce! It might be Short Tony's immediate problem, but I have been quite looking forward to coming in to some home-made sausages. Len the Fish has promised to teach him the basics, and then use his machine and my kitchen to give a full formal sausage-making demonstration to the ladies of the village one afternoon.

Because we have no great live music scene.

Returning to the aforementioned kitchen, I shut the door and put the kettle on. I will drink my tea at the enormous new farmhouse table that now dominates the room. There is nothing quite like having an enormous table – I give it a hearty and affectionate thump with my fist. The country units and oiled worktop, the aged stone tiles, the wood-clad steel beam that supports the new ceiling: this is a place that's truly suitable for modern-day living. I don't know why I got so wound up by a few minor delays in the building work.

* * *

Barney's had not been busy.

Everybody likes Barney's. The place is legendary among foodies for miles around. This part of Norfolk is jam-packed with good places to eat, whether upmarket or cheap and cheerful, but Barney's is something special. There is cheerful service, and there is atmosphere, and there is alfresco seating in its lay-by on the A148. I leant up against the counter and ordered my bacon and mushroom sandwich reflectively. I had a horrible sinking feeling in my stomach about the building work, and the only thing that I could think of to make things better was to eat comfort food served from a van.

There was a new notice taped to the counter.

'Following advice from the Environmental Health Inspector,' it informed, 'we will be cooking our yolks hard. If you would prefer a soft yolk please ask.'

There was a man whose job it was to advise roadside trailer cafés how to cook their yolks! But we were not obliged to take his advice. It must be frustrating for him, having all that responsibility but no real power.

I took my bacon and mushroom sandwich and drove off. Next time, I resolved, I would get something with a soft yolk, to stick it to the man. I sat parked up on the Common for some time. It would save me getting cross with builders for another twenty minutes.

'What do you mean you're fucking *colour blind*?!' I had shrieked at the Reliable Local Tiler, losing my rag with him like I'd done with the other builders, and thus treating him with equal dignity and respect as a less abled person.

He shrugged. 'I just don't distinguish some colours very well.'

I gritted my teeth and went through the tiles with him, explaining each of the delicate and subtle green hues that the LTLP had chosen in order to create an intricate and tasteful pattern in the shower.

'Have you got that?' I asked.

He nodded. I left him, pointed out to the Replacement Reliable Local Carpenter that he appeared to have accidentally nailed the dishwasher shut, and wandered back through the kitchen, past the newly installed cooker, newly disinstalled by the official CORGI gas inspector who was using phrases like 'unbelievably shoddy' and 'disgraceful work'.

Out in the garden, I gazed at the bricks that had arrived to complete the garden wall. Something about them nagged at me. I looked at the rest of the wall, then I looked at the bricks, then I looked at the wall again, and then I remembered the bricks that I'd originally been shown, all those months before.

'I'm around all day if you need a coffee and a chat,' offered Short Tony, kindly. For the previous few weeks he had been tactful but attentive, knowing that I had reached a Low Ebb.

I muttered some words of ingratitude and returned to my Ebb.

Later on, I took him up on his offer and parked myself morosely in his lounge. He told me that he was always around if I fancied a pint, which was true, and put *Neighbours* on the television to cheer me up. It didn't cheer me up. The fact is that Ebbs are by definition reasonably low, so my specifically low one was an especial downer.

The Reliable Local Builder was still building. He had been building for ages and ages. I was bored with his building. Our lease on Narcoleptic Dave's place had expired, and having moved back into the cottage, it was the 'sharing personal space' bit that was most distressing: I am a natural loner and when it comes down to it, I absolutely refuse to share my personal space, unless I have to go into a small space with some people. Hence my Ebb.

I had my doubts about the Reliable Local Electrician, and the Replacement Reliable Local Carpenter had been working in the kitchen for so long that it had ceased to be a commercial transaction and had morphed into some kind of hostage situation. Oh yes – and the stairs had disappeared.

It had seemed a perfectly simple concept. The original stairs, which were perfectly good stairs, stairs that one could use to journey from the ground floor to the first floor and back again, were in the wrong place. Despite the devastating loss of the unique bookcase that opened out to reveal a secret chamber like in the Scooby-Doo cartoons, these stairs were to be removed.

Some new stairs were to be constructed as a replacement. These stairs would not provide a unique Scooby-Doo-type bookcase, but would still facilitate movement between floors – a gap in the ceiling was left, specifically to accommodate them. I am not an architect or a builder, so I had to piece together the gist of the subsequent problem myself, but it seemed to be something to do with it being a lot easier to demolish some stairs and to put them in a skip, than it was to build new ones. Whatever the cause, I seemed to have become the long-term owner of Norfolk's most inappropriate atrium.

Johnny Cash lived on a cotton farm during the American depression; many of the significant black artists of the sixties came from extreme poverty. Heavy metal was born in the factories of the West Midlands; great music emerged from the urban jungle of Coventry. If there was one benefit about the stairs situation, it was perhaps it would make me a better musician. You cannot be a creative artiste until you have a certain amount of life experience, and that includes suffering.

'I'm off for the night,' called the Replacement Reliable Local Carpenter.

'Bye,' I replied, waving through the aluminium ladder that comprised the trendily minimalist form of ascent from my kitchen. 'Do you have any idea when . . .'

* * *

'Well my view is that bowls is essentially a simple game,' insists the commentator.

The Sky commentators are rebelling. Apparently there is some new jargon that has been introduced into the sport by the authorities and this is providing a source of complaint and confusion among the bowlserati. I have no idea who these shadowy authorities are – they are possibly related to the soft egg people – but I am relieved that they haven't yet addressed our own club vocabulary, be it 'Roll it out! Roll it out!' or merely a loud cry of '*Bollocks!*' Meanwhile, the state of the head is resolved to Greg Harlow's satisfaction, and he strides back to the mat for his final shot.

Greg Harlow is my wildcard for the tournament. He has slightly bigger ears than the other players, and appears to have a fan club of female groupies who cheer him on whilst wearing 'Greg Harlow' T-shirts. His colour is bright green; his opponent Alex Marshall, who again needs to win this one to keep his Premier League dream alive. This is one of the final group stage matches – the stakes are getting higher and the power play 'ooooohs' getting shriller.

'And Alex has promised that he's prepared to get his heavy artillery out for this game,' assures the commentator.

And he does. He pummels Greg Harlow – who does not play at all badly. He gut-punches him with the gentle draw; he bitch-slaps repeatedly at his face with weighty forehands; he springs the cott into Harlow's goolies before treading on his head and stamping down with a well-directed fire. It is frightening to watch, even on the television. The shell-shocked audience there have witnessed a man fighting for his life, fighting for his Premier League dream, a man who started the morning at the foot of the table and will end it in contention for the semi-finals. It is a heroic feat that they have witnessed.

Later, fancied prospect Billy Jackson loses to young Robert Chisholm, and is the first person to be eliminated. He puts a brave face on it – but his Premier League dream is over. He has played well, but the rub of the green hasn't been with him. For every Elbow there has to be a Steerpike.

* * *

I spot a parcel van.

It sits on the road outside the cottages, its diesel engine at a slow throaty late-period Leonard Cohen idle. I have just returned from the farmers' market, and dash down the secret path, clutching my bacon.

I pass a new sign, taped to Short Tony's front window. 'If out, RING ME or LEAVE NEXT DOOR!' It flaps in the wind, like a piece of paper that has been taped to a window. The Parcel Man is consulting his clipboard; I can see his bulky figure through the glass in the cabin of his van.

Scooting round the corner, I screech to a halt at Short Tony's front door. No parcel has been left on the step. Another huge sign is affixed to the woodwork. 'RING ME if out or LEAVE NEXT DOOR!' The anger and rage that any amateur graphologist could spot in the handwriting has made it superfluous for him to append 'YOU FUCKERS'. I look at the sign. I look at the empty, parcelless doorstep. I look at the sign. I look at the doorstep.

The engine revs up behind me. I turn and sprint towards the van, shouting and waving my bacon angrily. '*Oy! Oy! Hang on!*' I can see Mr Parcel shift his body as he engages a gear. I jump up and down to get his attention.

The window winds down and a querulous face glares at me. I explain, politely but firmly, that he was meant to leave the parcel with me or to ring should nobody be at home, as clearly explained on the signs. I try not to sound too angry or sarcastic, but some of that slips through. (I do not mention that his delivery is an important sausage machine, as that would be complicating the matter.)

'But he is at home. I've just delivered it.'

'Oh.'

I am deflated and sheathe my bacon. 'Sorry,' I mutter, limply.

I retreat down the driveway in order to have a go at Short Tony for not taking down his signs immediately. But not too much, in case he doesn't give me any sausages.

* * *

'Krrrikkwhoshhhhhhttt!' exploded the Alarming Noise.

I tied my shoelaces hurriedly. It was fairly clear what had happened. After protests, representations and a lot of swearing, the Replacement Reliable Local Carpenter had constructed some temporary stairs, stairs through which the LTLP had clearly fallen.

The noise of a woman falling through some stairs is one of those unmistakable sounds. It's something totally and utterly distinctive, like a Routemaster bus, for instance, or a vicar falling out of a tree. I rushed into the kitchen. She was sat on the floor amidst a pile of wood, a bemused look etched into her features. 'Fuck!' she breathed.

We had been due at Short Tony's for some dinner, so I pulled her up and sent her next door for a stiff drink. I then commenced my Accident Investigator's role, before carpenteering some temporary stairs by balancing a plank on top of a wooden crate. I was pleased with my efforts. I don't know why carpenters make such a fuss and take so long about everything. This would allow us to reach the top half of the flight (which still stood, seemingly unaffected by the cataclysm) with a small amount of effort.

Despite my satisfaction at the temporary solution, the saga of my stairs was threatening to cause me some form of breakdown. I had wondered before we started the project whether we should apply to be on the *Grand Designs* TV programme; little did I realise that Channel 4 might one day be interested for *Bodyshock: The Woman with a Riser up her Arse*.

I double-checked that the plank was holding reasonably well then zipped next door for some roast beef and a calming glass of wine. I did not see the Replacement Reliable Local Carpenter again for some time. The LTLP was OK in the big scheme of things. Building sites are dangerous places, and it is not as if she had been gassed or electrocuted.

The LTLP was electrocuted.

A short cry followed by silence from the refurbished scullery had announced this fact. I looked up from the TV in astonishment.

'Would you come here a minute?' demanded a voice – a familiar voice, but expressed in a weaker-than-usual timbre.

We met in the connecting corridor where she claimed that she had received a large electric shock from the sink. Even though I was sceptical – I have watched enough *Tom and Jerry* to know that 'being electrocuted' entails contracting a blackened face and sticking-up hair – I pushed past her and poked my head round the scullery door to investigate. The sink was there, an innocuous look on its face.

The short cry had been real enough. I realised that I would have to perform some tests. Not having much electrician's gear in the shed, I was nevertheless able to locate a diagnostic tool which consisted of five long strips of bone, each sleeved in a layer of skin, connected to the end of my arm.

The sink smiled coyly at me.

I placed my hand close to the stainless steel surface, slowly moving it closer, inching millimetre by millimetre. Everybody knows that electric things hurt less if you approach them like this – it is probably the mix of metric and imperial units. I touched the sink and nothing happened. I grinned, reassured. Silly woman.

Recklessly, I removed my shoes and went through the same process.

'Oooaarghhhhyoooy!!' I shouted.

There was a sort of noise, which I took to be the insolent laughter of a domestic fitting.

Bough's Law states that when something surprising or un-expected happens as a consequence of a repeatable action then you shall mindlessly repeat the action to make sure, no matter how unpleasant the previous consequence.

'Oooaarghhhhyoooy!!' I reaffirmed.

'The sink is live,' I carefully explained to the LTLP, whose prac-tical knowledge of wiring etc. is weak. I had an idea, and switched off the lights in the back room, which had been behaving oddly. I returned to the scullery in order to touch the sink again. It was pitifully impotent.

'That is interesting,' I mused. 'When the lights in the other room are switched off, the sink is normal. But when they're switched on, it gets all electric.'

There was a silence.

'That could be useful,' I continued.

The LTLP glared at me. I trotted off to the telephone. I did not see the Reliable Local Electrician again for some time.

* * *

Actually, I do know why I got so wound up by a few delays in the building work.

Having builders is hell. Even Reliable, Local ones. They invade your house and knock down your stairs and rip out your Scooby-Doo bookcase and electrocute your LTLP and bamboozle you with their ideas and promises and use of the obsolete Julian calendar. And for what? A couple more bedrooms, a big kitchen, some central heating, a shower room and a small alcove above the stairs designed specially in which to hang a Fender Telecaster guitar. Apart from that, they are useless.

If I ever have my life again, I would choose Strategic HR Initiatives over being a builder any time. Strategic HR Initiatives are useless to man, but they don't cause man any actual physical pain. I finish my tea at the enormous new farmhouse table with one final slurp, take to my feet and lob the mug in the dishwasher. The fascia board beneath the appliance falls over.

'Now would anyone like some potted head?' asks Len the Fish, clamping the sausage machine firmly to the side of the table. The ladies of the village look on eagerly as he prepares his demonstration. Eddie, Short Tony and I sort of lurk in the background.

Short Tony has brought a crate of Adnams Broadside with him. I wave away the opportunity for a refill. Somebody will probably ask me to play the guitar later, and I will need a clear head. Len the Fish passes round the plate. 'Potted head, anyone? It's just the head boiled up then formed into cubes.'

I take a piece of potted head on a cocktail stick and smother it in English mustard. It is very nice; in fact, it is the best potted head that I have ever tasted. The remainder of pig rests glumly on the table whilst the audience looks on fascinated.

'It's good,' I offer, munching on my head. I take back all the nasty things I said about Fergus Henderson. Perhaps I am just not a great offal chef. He is probably a lousy bowls player.

Eddie fires up the great cogs and pistons of the sausage machine as directed, whilst Len the Fish starts making incisions in the slab of meat. Meanwhile Short Tony is instructed to start skinning in order to produce some crackling for a starter. A hundredweight of potatoes go into a stockpot ready for boiling. Len's sausage-making demonstration is brilliant. You would not believe how interesting it is watching a man make some sausages. Meat goes in, followed by lots of fat, followed by seasoning, then you sort of mix it up and chuck it in the machine and sausages come out! It is hypnotic. Several tourist attractions offer far less.

Three hours later, I have turned off the gas at the hob and we are all tucking into the most home-made meal of bangers and mash that you can possibly think of. There are rolled joints from the remainder of the meat, and a bag of sausages for everybody to take home. We chink glasses and make fascinating conversation about the provenance of the food on our table.

I cast my eyes across my friends in the room, and smile in utter satisfaction at the dinner party scene. It seems as if a weight has lifted, as if I have crossed a line or reached the brow of a hill. The world of living with builders and of Strategic HR Initiatives seems so far gone; my whole life is ahead of me, in my place in the countryside, with my new friends, the cottage a perfect balance between olde-worlde charm and suitability for modern-day living.

And yet as I sit back in my chair it dawns, the smile freezing on my face as the horror reveals itself, the Satanic, dreadful bargain exposed; the quivering, icy fingers of Maxdom digging away at my collar in their awful grip.

Perhaps we all turn into Max. Perhaps it is impossible to grow up in a town and then move to the country without some Maxification process going on. I take a good hard look at myself in the bathroom mirror after excusing myself for a couple of minutes. Delighted laughter can be heard from the kitchen.

I do not think I am too Maxy. We are just having a dinner party, that's all. That does not make me a Max. I am being ridiculously oversensitive. Max is a cock, a twat, a fool. He would not appreciate good music, or play bowls. Above all, Max is never a sympathetic character. And nobody could ever accuse me of that.

Returning to the kitchen, there are two pieces of head left. I offer them round; there are no takers, so I bung them in the fridge. I drop various hints, but nobody asks me if I would play the guitar. Having finished the entire crate of Broadside we thank Len the Fish for his demonstration and decide to go to the village pub. I would stay for the LTLP's tidying-up demonstration, but there is nothing worse than people looking over your shoulder when you work.

TWENTY-TWO

I get sales talk from sales assistants when all I want to do girl is lower your resistance

If the train journey from King's Lynn to Ely is one of the great railway journeys of the world, the café at Lynn Station is one of the seven modern wonders. The man serves hearty breakfasts, cheap mugs of tea and bacon rolls; he is friendly, flexible, genial and helpful. Railtrack will catch him one day and punish him. Catch him, inject him with Costa Coffee, beat him to death with laminated menus, bury him in chilled pre-packed sandwiches, erect him a tombstone reading 'Meal deal to go – just add £1.50'. I settle down in the carriage with tea and a sausage sandwich. If there are two things that you want when you're heading for the land of Strategic HR Initiatives, it's a nice polystyrene mug of tea and a hand-made sausage sandwich.

I am going to London. The LTLP has to work there for two days, and has suggested that it would be nice for me to join her. So here I am. Across the savage and mysterious windsweptness of the fens; past the beautiful marina at Ely, the moorings lazing in the shadow of one of England's greatest cathedrals, the vista the boating leisure pursuit equivalent of the Sandringham Bowls Green.

The LTLP does this journey every morning. She must be the luckiest woman in the world.

From Ely, the train continues south to Cambridge, birthplace of the Pink Floyd, then on through the commuter towns and northern suburbs: Ray Davies, Fairport Convention; Alexandra Palace, Hornsey, Harringay Station – home of train delays and of funny electric rain. King's Cross and the capital.

I pause and take a deep breath as I step from the train.

I'm back.

'Scuse me, mate.'

I am delaying the other passengers from getting off by pausing and taking deep breaths and thinking that I am back. I mumble an apology and head off down the platform.

* * *

'Thanks a lot. This is our last song.'

My guitar was still feeding back slightly, adding an extra magnificence to our cavernous sound. Looking out from the stage I could just pick out the faces of a couple of people – Unlucky John and the LTLP. I gave them a cool nod.

The Bull and Gate in Kentish Town, North London. A famous old place, of world renown. The Venue of Legends. The rest of the Precious Things awaited my guitar introduction for the final song. I held off for an extra few seconds, toying with the crowd like a small child with a musical Play-doh fun factory.

This was years later. The band in London – the one where it finally clicked. We played immense, towering pieces, tapping into the zeitgeist by lashing on huge amounts of swampy overdrive and reverb, whilst not including much in the way of stuff that you could actually hum. I hit a G chord and it crashed around the space like an elephant; then followed it with the C and B flat like a pursuing herd of antelope.

It sounded fantastic. I didn't know then that I would turn my back on this, that I would take a deep breath and walk away with open eyes from the explosion of success, interest and acclaim that was swelling up around me, the culmination of every dream I'd had since my early teens. That after everything that I had got wrong, I would finally say 'no' when things finally went right. That I would do this to move to Norfolk in order to play bowls and to have some chickens.

The bass and drums joined in and we played our finale, about a woman who was trapped in some rubble after a remarkably severe earthquake.

*   *   *

I have forgotten so many things about living in town: that to cross the road you have to just cross it rather than wait for a gap in the traffic; that you do not try to pass the time of day with shop assistants; that people no longer pay bus drivers. Visiting London as a tourist is fun, it is energising; it has none of the horror that once associated it with Strategic HR Initiatives.

I usually stay with Unlucky John, although he has inconveniently moved now – too far from the centre to be particularly useful; or take a short train ride out to visit my mum and dad, *The Thin Blue Line* notwithstanding. But this time is different.

We have a hotel room. We have a central location, we have fresh sheets and lovely towels, we have the sexually charged aura of a hotel bed, we have toilet paper that is folded twice at the end to create a little triangle.

'Meet me in Selfridges,' demands the LTLP by text message. 'And don't be late.'

Selfridges! My heart beats slightly faster. She probably wants to buy special lingerie, I would imagine – perhaps something romantic in red and black. Selfridges! I bet it will be expensive. Perhaps it will have little patterns down the legs.

With a little time to kill, I take a short stroll down Charing

Cross Road and Denmark Street, to look at the guitar shops. The instruments – both new and vintage – beckon to me tantalisingly from behind the glass, drawing me in like six-string crack 'ho's. There is a small nagging feeling at the back of my mind that the LTLP will be cross should I purchase a vintage guitar on the joint Tesco credit card, even though it will earn us Clubcard points. You need a range of guitars if you've got a wide repertoire. A Gibson Les Paul, bashed around but radiating the spirit of rock, catches my eye from the corner of a window.

'Hey bud,' whispers the Gibson Les Paul. 'You wanna fuck?'

I had bought the Telecaster from here.

A Fender Telecaster guitar! King of guitars. A god among six strings, and a great god at that. The light from the ceiling fitting had danced on its sunburst body, sparkled on the immaculate chrome of its fittings. It was, and still is, my pride and joy. To plug it into a screaming amplifier and to pick out a mere handful of notes is to be connected on a direct line to the absolute primal excitement of blues, country and rock and roll. Its body was smooth, its design flawless, like a really smooth and well-designed flawless woman. It cost more money than I've ever spent on a present for myself ever, ever. But it was there. In the shop. Willing me to buy.

I didn't have a screaming amplifier to hand when I got the guitar back home, but no matter. I strapped it on and played regardless; hitting the strings unamplified, entranced by the song of the vibrating steel, the ever so faint hum of the resonating maple. I stroked the wood with my hands back and front, with my chin and the side of my face – as smooth as smooth. I smelt it. It even smelt beautiful: wood, varnish, metal, polish, grease. I could well have had sex with it if it wasn't for the danger of steel string lacerations to my penis. I loved the guitar, but I did not want to attend Accident and Emergency with steel string lacerations to my penis. For all I knew the people there were not musicians and would have got the wrong idea.

You would get thousands of Clubcard points for a vintage Gibson Les Paul. Thousands. And you could use those to save money on your shopping, or to get air miles, or discounted membership of the RAC. I look at the price label again. You see – the economics of buying it wouldn't be as black and white as all that.

I drag myself away, up the street, heading reluctantly then purposefully towards the lingerie department of Selfridges.

* * *

A sunburst Fender Telecaster is why I have to finally nail down the Chipper Barman.

We've been circling each other for months now. 'We must sort something out.' 'Yes, we must sort something out.' 'Well, the next time you come in, we'll sort something out.' Yet we have not sorted anything out.

Elton John once said that, for the remaining members of Queen, having the band on ice after Freddie Mercury's death was like keeping a Ferrari in the garage but not being able to drive. Elton John knows his stuff. Having a Fender Telecaster lying dormant whilst the Chipper Barman works shifts is a very similar situation. Guitars, for all their smoothity and smell and sexual allure, are made to be played.

'You are *not* buying that!'

I blink. 'What? Why?'

'Put it back,' she insists. 'No.'

'What?' I stare at her, baffled.

We have split up to look around Selfridges. I have been idly browsing the menswear floor whilst she has disappeared off, doubtless to find something enticing for the night that might be easily removed with tongues and teeth. Now she has returned and is criticising the garment that I've found.

'But it's really good,' I insist.

'Put it back.'

The T-shirt is bright red, and boasts a print depicting two women engaged in what looks like a lesbian leather bondage session. One is certainly tied to something, anyway – you can tell if you hold the shirt upside-down and take a step back. The other one clasps what looks like some form of dong.

Her eyes roll, like heavily-biased woods. I try to explain that this sort of design stems from the original ethos of punk, that these are all the rage, that Selfridges is a very trendy shop indeed and would only ever sell artistic stuff and nothing tacky. Indeed, what a reflection on post-Dibley Britain it is that women are empowered to be featured on T-shirts, one tied up, one with some form of dong, and are not forced to conceal their practices underground. Frankly, I am both surprised and disappointed by her homophobia. We are still arguing as we approach the till.

'But . . .!'

'You're not buying it.'

'But . . .'

'Where, precisely, would you wear it? To the village shop?'

I halt in my tracks, just short of the pay point, and smile the broadest of broad grins. All has become clear – she hasn't caught on to my reasoning.

'No, stupid. It'll be brilliant for wearing onstage.'

There is a long, long silence, and then, as if from the far corner of the shoe department, comes the distant rumble, the steady crescendo and then the almighty whoosh of an approaching tirade.

'What do you mean: "onstage"? When, precisely, are you next going to be "onstage"?'

'Well –'

The shop assistant has been waiting to see whether we are going to take the final steps to the counter and pay. I shoot her an apologetic glance.

'You haven't been "onstage" since that crappy dirgey depressing thing at that shithole pub when about ten people turned up! You –'

'That was the Bull and Gate! In Kentish Town,' I interrupt. I do not get a chance to explain to her that it is the Venue of Legends, or that we hadn't quite got our publicity machine going that night, but that the eighteen people – and it was at least eighteen people – who had turned up had all really enjoyed it, especially the song about the earthquake.

She is shouting at me now.

'Then what – fifteen years ago when you were pissing around trying to play guitar with Simon and your mates, or that embarrassing time when we first met when you played at a party with John and everybody went to stand outside? You don't go "onstage", Alex. You sit around trying to write songs with your Pink Floyd fixation, pretending to yourself that you're going to be a rock star one day.'

'Oh.'

'Now are you going to buy that, or not?'

'Have you bought anything?'

'No. I tried on a shirt, but it was too small.'

I cast my eyes downwards and return the T-shirt to the rail.

*   *   *

That was unfair.

There were definitely eighteen people at the Bull and Gate gig, because I counted. And at least seven of those eighteen weren't connected in any way with the band itself.

But . . .

*   *   *

The train out of King's Cross is busy – very busy. I put my bag on the seat next to me, open a broadsheet newspaper wide, place a smelly-looking sandwich on the table in front and adopt the facial expression of a yob. I want to be alone with my own thoughts on the return journey.

A man in an enormous cowboy hat walks into the carriage, asking me politely if the seat is taken. Americans! They have no idea of our customs, which he proves by introducing himself.

I am taken aback. Not wishing to appear rude, I do likewise, before furiously studying the newspaper to make the conversation go away.

'Is there a washroom on the train?' persists my new companion. 'I've literally just made it from the airport.'

I lower my hands and struggle with forming a proper reply, before settling on the only honourable one in the circumstances. 'If you've just come from Heathrow,' I advise, 'I would hate for the first impression of our country's sanitation to be a train toilet in the late afternoon.'

Once more I lift my newspaper, hoping that my concession has satisfied his pathological need to confer. I adopt an exaggerated 'look, I am reading my newspaper'-type pose. On the other side of the aisle, a man sniggers. I am sure that he is sniggering at me.

But it is pointless to resist. The man is too excited, having just arrived in England and caught a passenger train, a mode of transport which, he will later tell me at length, is unheard of in many parts of the USA. I fold my newspaper, slightly shamefacedly. I have been in London for a day and a half, and I have turned back into one of them! We make conversation.

He is from Arizona, which makes him a proper American, American to the core. I tell him that I have always wanted to visit Arizona, and that our equivalent places, Devizes and Ashby-de-la-Zouch, are not nearly so exciting. He asks about train timetables and frequencies to try to get a handle on the general public transportation situation, and nods in wonder at my answers. He looks enthusiastically out of the window as only somebody from a desert state could.

'Are we still in London, or is that an English village?' he enquires as we speed through Knebworth.

'And what are those? That's a nice bit of growing land.'

I spend ten minutes giving my interesting historical perspectives on the English allotment movement, from wartime to present day.

'And that? Wow, that square; that is lush.'

I realise to what he's referring, and glow with pride.

'It's a bowling green.'

'A what?'

'A bowling green. Do you not play bowls in America? Like . . . lawn bowls? Where you have to get each bowling ball closest to the white ball?'

'Oh! Like a game the old folk play!' he laughs.

'Right,' I say, in a very small voice.

TWENTY-THREE

101,374,539th nervous breakdown

My *ham* has disappeared!

I went to the village shop. I didn't buy many things at all, but I know I bought some ham. I know I bought some ham in particular because it was to be the centrepiece ingredient for my lunch (a ham sandwich), but now I am home and there is no ham.

I sift through the shopping bag about twenty-seven times, then go and search the boot of the car – but there is still no ham. It has gone missing in mysterious circumstances and whilst it might seem a trivial thing to some people, it is quite important to me. I slump into an armchair in chagrin and bewilderment.

This has a last-strawness air about it; my life at present does not need complications such as missing ham. I am a failed musician with no job on my own in an empty cottage, and I'm sure the toothache is coming back on. A creep of despair starts crawling up my back. I have this immense and overwhelming urge to run out into the road and shout 'Help! Help! Help!'

I worry about this. The thing about running into the road and shouting 'Help! Help! Help!' is that essentially it is a cry for help. Trying to pull myself together, I attempt to think logically. There is clearly a simple explanation. I search the shopping bag again, but the ham is still not to be found. I've not put it in the fridge; I've not put it in the bread bin, or on the mantelpiece.

At this point I decide that I had better retreat back into the living room and resume the sitting down for some time. Life is quite difficult at the moment, and I do not need extra things to make it more so, viz. missing ham.

And so I hit a Crisis of Confidence.

I am a thirty-thing man who plays bowls and is not a rock star. I have a genuine hundred per cent American Fender Telecaster guitar sitting in its own specially made alcove at home – which is lucky, as it LIVES THERE ALL THE TIME what with NOT BEING A ROCK STAR an' all because I am a nobody WITH A PINK FLOYD FIXATION who SITS AROUND writing crap SONGS.

Boooooooooooooooo.

I do not have a proper job. I mess around doing the odd bit of freelance work, but essentially I rely on the LTLP for money, as I am a househusband who is pretending to be on sabbatical. In return, I look after her, keep the house clean and cook her meals. Except that I do not keep the house clean as I was SHIT AT THAT and we now have a cleaner, and my meals are SHIT AS WELL and EVERYTHING IS GOING WRONG.

In capital letters as well. This is serious. A faint yet familiar 'thud thud thud' starts from next door. I need to get myself together. I seem to have sent my life down in the wrong bias.

Crises of Confidence. They're like the worry that a man is going to shout at you, except that it feels like the whole world is shouting at you, perhaps following it up with a strongly worded letter. They have been a feature of my life ever since I can remember. Like many people who suffer from such an affliction, I do my best to disguise things, but unfortunately I tend to disguise them in those cheap 'disguise sets' that you have when you're a child, with ridiculous thick black glasses and eyebrows, and a puffy plastic nose.

Crises of Confidence do not necessarily mix well with Time on My Hands.

One of the problems is the silence. When you've been a thrusting executive used to the buzz and vibrancy of businesspeople in wanky spectacles taking helicopter views and formulating smart strategies about the outcomes of Strategic HR Initiatives, an empty cottage tends to seem very . . . empty. When you've been in a rehearsal studio with four people all competing to play as loud as possible each in a different key, a quiet moment seems very . . . quiet. But when you are on your own apart from some chickens and the odd visit from the Vegetable Delivery Lady, things can get a bit – on top of you. It's the motivation to do things. It's the most difficult thing about being at home all day. No wonder housewives are always boffing the milkman.

'Thud thud thud.' Perhaps I should talk to somebody. Ring Unlucky John, or pop next door down the secret path to Short Tony's. But it would be unfair to burden either of my friends with all my concerns about the rest of my life. And I have always been very careful not to accept life advice from people who convert their dining rooms into pubs whilst their wife is at Morrisons.

I clear my throat.

I am not particularly good at the confessional stuff. Frankly, I would always prefer to keep things to myself. I internalise, like a lot of creative people. Although psychologists would probably recommend it, I have never been a big fan of exposing yourself by being all open and shouting stuff from rooftops. That is what Neville Chamberlain did, and he never quite got the same level of respect again.

I stand silently, taking some moments' thought before speaking.

'I am a bit stressed, that's all,' I mumble, going a bit red. 'I've just got loads and loads of things on my mind, and I'm finding it all a bit – well, you know. So I'm sorry if I've been a bit – well, you know. I just feel that I've been a bit unfairly treated.' I pause for a second. 'I'm sorry. You've all got your own problems, I know.'

'Cluck,' reply the chickens.

I set down their bacon and beans, which they seem extremely pleased with. Honestly, even if I am a bit miserable, there is nothing better than an appreciative audience for a nice meal that you've cooked. As I understand it.

'Anyway. I think I need to make a couple of positive decisions,' I announce. 'Sort of sit down and work out what's important to me and what – are you ignoring me?'

The chickens peck frantically at their lunch. A couple have already grabbed bits of bacon rind and are running off to the other side of their area to eat it on their own. I gaze over at them in dismay before stomping out through the gate.

'You're just fucking rude!' I shout.

I don't know what to do. It is a bit like being at a crossroads. You can either turn left, or you can turn right, or you can go straight on, being careful to give way to the traffic from the left or right (unless you are on the major road and have priority). The problem is that if you stop to think too much at the junction, the man in the lorry behind you will start hooting, and after a while perhaps get out and punch you in the face.

We have given up bothering to shut the gate, and a couple of chickens follow me down the path. They are simple creatures. It must be lovely to be a chicken – no worries, no cares, meals provided. Ooooh – dilemma! Shall I take a sip of water from the trough or scrape a small hole in the ground? A sip of water, I think. The hole can wait until later.

I think that it might be time to move on. Even though my sabbatical has been a roaring success in every way, the man in the lorry is hooting and I can see an angry face in my wing mirror. And what of the LTLP? She works hard, very hard, and deserves more of a contribution from me.

'I would do anything to make the LTLP's life a bit easier,' I think, as I scrunch across the gravel.

Smoke starts curling up around me from my pants.

But yes, I think it is probably time to move on.

'Tell me, John,' I ask, having plucked up the courage to pick up the phone and speak to a soulmate of a non-avian nature. 'You heard all the bands that I was in. What were we like?'

He thinks about this. 'Mate – you were legends,' he concludes, impressing me with his simple honesty. 'I still have a tape of the Pike somewhere.'

So it wasn't just me. There *was* something there.

'Although that band in London you were in was a bit depressing. And I remember early on you went through that Jethro Tull phase.'

Jethro Tull! It is a fucking insult. Fucking beardie weirdy flutey progressive hey nonny nonny crap!

A chicken wanders right up to the French windows, and stops for a bit. She lifts her head and seems to see me there on the telephone; we lock eyes for a moment. 'Get on with something,' she seems to say. 'Stop pissing about watching us chickens, *house-husband*.' And then she catches sight of a tasty bit of grass or a grub, or something, and trots off once more.

I stare after her in anger. Curse her for her chickeny insolence.

* * *

I did see Simon one more time, come to think of it.

Back where I grew up, revisiting old haunts and old friends, I popped into my old local for a quick pint – the very same local in which we'd first met, years before. I blinked as a familiar face stared at me from behind the bar. 'Hullo!' I said in surprise.

He was exactly the same Simon. We chatted for ages in between him serving customers – not about music, strangely enough. He'd gone his way and I'd gone mine, and that was all in the past. It was great to catch up with him again.

Two pints down the line and I needed to use the gents. Standing at the urinal, my mind wandered wistfully over old times. Expressing immensely moody and serious music at the Bull and Gate, Kentish Town (Venue of Legends), was all very well and interesting and ambitious and all that – but if I was completely honest with myself, it wasn't that much *fun*. Two teenagers spending hours listening to records with each other, and putting together bands, and predicting that we would be in the *New Musical Express* and would be presented with an endless procession of women's breasts to autograph, and playing because we genuinely thought that we would rule the world – that's rock and roll. Proper rock and roll. And now I was playing bowls and keeping chickens and he was doing bar work – but it didn't matter, as we had shared our own Premier League dream together, and it's taking part that matters, not winning.

I shook my head, zipped, and turned to revisit the bar. On the back of the toilet door, a framed and mounted grid reassured:

'These toilets have been checked by a member of staff at regular intervals. Please inform us if . . .'

In the second column, to correspond with each half-hourly point during the day, line after line was scribbled a neat and prac-tised signature.

* * *

There is silence all around: no cars, no beet lorries, no unusual and inexplicable countryside noises. The world has gone to bed early.

'Do you think,' I whisper, as we lay side by side in the nestling warmth of our matrimonial bed, 'that . . .'

'What?' she whispers back.

We stick to the convention that people whisper when it's dark, despite the fact that we are both awake.

'Do you think that at my age I am a bit old to bring cuddly animals to bed?'

Every night, my side of the bed is shared by Honey Bear, Peter the Hanging Monkey and a furry-glove-like thing you're meant to wear to polish your car, called Mr Mitt.

There is a long diplomatic silence. The LTLP is clearly mulling this over carefully.

'I think,' she tentatively offers, 'that it's less the fact that they are animals, rather than the fact that they're just nice and warm to have about you on a night like this.'

Another pause.

'Right,' I affirm.

'Don't listen to her, Mr Mitt,' I hiss.

'Can I go to sleep now?'

'I'm just worried that I'm a bit . . .'

'Can't we just talk about this in the morning?'

'I just worry that I'm a bit . . . sad.'

'You *are* sad.'

'I am not.'

'Yes you are. You're sad.'

'Oh,' I say in my very small voice.

She turns over, and the conversation is closed. The five of us drift off to sleep.

TWENTY-FOUR

Tryin' to keep it real, compared to what

'You do what?' I repeat in amazement.

'I play the drums,' confirms Mike, from behind the bar. 'I've always been a drummer.'

I look from Mike to pint to Mike to pint to Mike to Chipper Barman to pint to Mike. 'I didn't know that,' I shake my head. 'Did you know that?!?' I demand of the Chipper Barman.

'I've just found out,' he replies simply.

It is bizarre. So I've been in the village pub on an almost daily basis, as a guitarist without a band. The Chipper Barman has turned out to be a bass player. And now Mike reveals that he's been a drummer all this time. Mike the Drumming Barman.

'So why didn't you . . .'

'I'm not very good,' Mike the Drumming Barman hastens. 'I haven't played for a while. The last thing I did was a tour of Europe ages back.'

If he is not very good then that probably explains things. It is not as if he has supported the Sultans of Ping, after all.

That is the thing with people in pubs. You can talk to them for years and years and still know next to nothing about them. Whereas if you find somebody in a pub that is keen to reveal their life story within the space of three pints, then your best bet is to set yourself on fire.

Instead, you put together a picture from little snippets. Like Eddie's teenage years as a Fenland mod; Len the Fish's early life abroad; John Twonil's 327-year engagement. Things that have fallen naturally into the conversation, that have revealed something more about the face at the bar.

I don't know what people think about me. I guess they know that I am a musician, although how much they know about my extensive success I can only speculate. They know that I do odd work from home and that I cook the LTLP's dinner. That I drink Wherry, or London Pride, or Adnams, or Elgood's, or Old, or Nelson's Revenge. That I had a Scooby-Doo bookcase but don't any more.

And Mike the Drumming Barman plays the drums.

Short Tony is there; he is starting to get depressed about his upcoming fortieth birthday. I can understand this – I will probably feel the same when I reach the same point in many years' time. I explain this to my neighbour, but it does not cheer him.

'Plus I've lost my karaoke tape,' he adds.

I send one eyebrow ceilingwards, a more-than-usually puzzled look crossing my face.

'I had a few drinks last night, and decided to sing some karaoke,' he explains. 'I'm surprised you didn't hear me?'

I shake my head. I have been able to hear nothing over the LTLP's snoring recently. Meteorites could have devastated Earth for all I know.

'Anyway, I usually record myself, so I can listen in the car the next day. Except that I couldn't find the tape anywhere. Then I realised – when I traded in the Jag I must have left it in the tape machine. So there's a tape of me singing Meat Loaf numbers on some garage forecourt in Norfolk somewhere.'

I look at him and shake my head sadly. 'You do realise,' I say slowly and kindly, 'that there wasn't a single word in that speech that reflected anything other than horribly badly on you?'

'I know,' he replies miserably.

As is the way, people consolidate as the pub thins out, and by the end of the evening we are all sat together, lined up on the stools at the bar. Len the Fish has long departed with his dog in tow; the Chipper Barman has an early shift the next day. The talk is once more of music.

'We need to form a band,' I insist. 'A proper band. I keep talking to the Chipper Barman about it.'

'Well I'm up for it,' agrees Mike the Drumming Barman.

'You can do vocals,' I prompt Short Tony. 'And play a bit of saxophone.'

'I'm not really sure about that,' he says. Short Tony is essentially a shy man, for somebody who regularly performs all nine minutes forty-eight seconds of 'Bat out of Hell', including all the high Cs. 'But you can use my place to rehearse.'

'When shall we do it?' asks Mike the Drumming Barman.

'How about now?' says Short Tony.

I look from face to face. 'Isn't that a bit soon?' I ask, suddenly a bit nervous.

The road that zigzags down to the cottage seems particularly zigzaggy tonight. Fortunately, Mike the Drumming Barman has been on duty, so he has his car. Short Tony and I leap in gratefully.

'Drop me at mine,' I instruct him. 'I'll pick up my guitar and amplifier, and lug it next door to Short Tony's. In the meantime, you can zip home and pick up all your gear.'

'Yeah – I don't actually have any drums though,' says Mike the Drumming Barman.

There is a short pause.

'Well I do. It's just that they're in storage,' he continues.

'Right.'

'I'll nip home and come back anyway. I've got a didgeridoo I can bring.'

The traditional four-piece line-up (guitar, bass, drums, vocals) or five-piece (the same, plus keyboards) is a relatively modern invention – a product of the rock and roll era. Some musicians have augmented the sound. Soul players, for instance, added a horn section; the folk-rock pioneers of the sixties brought in fiddles, or a banjo. It's common to have an extra guitarist, so that one plays rhythm and one plays lead, or to add extra backing vocalists or a saxophone. But the core is that classic four- or five-piece foundation.

It is true that using esoteric combinations of instruments can work in rock music. Jimi Hendrix used comb-and-paper for the riff on 'Crosstown Traffic'. 'Mr Blue Sky' contained somebody bashing a fire extinguisher. It is a shame that the synthesiser has generally stopped all this inventiveness. And I am sceptical that the guitar/didgeridoo line-up will ever catch on in the mainstream.

'I'll get some wine,' says Short Tony, grabbing some glasses from his kitchen cupboard and looking for the last known location of the corkscrew. Meanwhile, I start setting up my Massive-Cock-Extension Fender Guitar Amplifier. Unfortunately after several pints, I am a bit too pissed to work out which socket is which, and I have to disappear off to collect my smaller Size-Is-Not-Important Fisher-Price Guitar Amplifier instead.

'Are you sure this will be OK?' asks Mike the Didgeridooing Barman, as the distorted noise of a Fender Telecaster rends the air.

I explain that the LTLP is away for the night, and therefore we have no need to worry about loud noises drifting through the party wall.

'What's going on?' demands Mrs Short Tony, poking her head around the door from upstairs, and shivering in a nightie.

'Band rehearsal,' explains Short Tony.

Mrs Short Tony looks from guitar to didgeridoo to saxophone to Short Tony to Mike to me.

'The Chipper Barman can't make it,' I explain. 'And he plays bass.'

'I see.'

'I played an instrument as well,' explains Mrs Short Tony. 'When I was a kid. In the brass band.' She has dressed and joined us for a glass of wine, having established that we are unlikely to go home otherwise.

'What was that?' I ask politely, concentrating on tuning up.

'The horn,' she explains.

'What, like Motown?' I put the guitar down. Adding a horn might make up for the loss of gritty authenticity we face by temporarily missing a bass player and having a didgeridoo instead of drums.

'No – like a brass band horn. I played at the Albert Hall you know.'

'The Albert Hall? The real Albert Hall?'

'Of course. We were quite good. I've got a video somewhere of us on a Yorkshire TV show. Let me look.'

There are hasty manoeuvrings to prevent the night morphing into an amateur video showing of Mrs Short Tony's brass band playing on a Yorkshire TV show. But I am intrigued by the instrument itself.

She glides off to find it.

A lot of non-musicians get confused about the role of the record producer. The record producer is not necessarily the man who twists the knobs in order to get the recording on tape. His main role is very simple – he is the one who claps his hands and says 'Right, Dave, Roger, Rick, Nick – can you stop fucking around now and make some music? I'd like you to try the one in D minor again – the one about not needing no education. I suggest we add some singing children to the second verse.'

When bands become successful, they often decide that they would like to produce themselves. This always ends in disaster. It is all very well listening to a professional producer ordering you about and telling you to try it one more time as the outro was shit, but when the bloke who was a year below you at school tries that trick then there is liable to be a fight. To be your own producer you have to have a big ego and be very confident of your own abilities. That is not my scene at all.

That said, I have never worked with a proper producer. I have always felt able to fulfil that role myself. Steerpike recorded two tracks in the studio; the Precious Things laid down four in a council flat in St Albans. Most of Where's Johnny Christmas?'s recorded output we produced ourselves. It's a superfluous role, if you're disciplined and know what you're doing.

It is quickly apparent that the village pub band needs a producer. We flounder around, trying to work out what to play and when to play it. Short Tony gives up almost immediately. Whilst I am sure that he was very good on the saxophone in his day, it transpires that the start of 'Rat Trap' is really the only thing he knows. The only thing I can remember about 'Rat Trap' is the saxophone bit itself, so the performance is somewhat abbreviated. Instead, he goes to print off lots of songs from the internet, none of which I have heard of. Mike the Didgeridooing Barman joins in gamely, but I can tell that he is getting frustrated with the single note that he is able to didgeridoo.

'It's in E flat,' announces Mrs Short Tony, producing a tarnished horn from an old box.

'E flat?'

'That's what it's tuned to.'

I am not very good with tunings at the best of times, let alone after lots of pints of Wherry and two large glasses of red wine. As far as I can make out, however, this means that you have to use some of the black notes if you are playing along with the horn.

'What use is E flat?' I demand.

'It's just E flat.'

Mike the Didgeridooing Barman breaks off from his aerophonics. 'As this only plays one note,' he observes, 'it won't be much good if it's a note that doesn't go with E flat.'

'Well, what songs do you know?' I ask Mrs Short Tony.

She thinks about this. '"Floral Dance",' she concludes. 'We used to play "The Floral Dance" a lot.'

My shoulders sag perceptibly, like somebody has tied Terry Wogans to them.

'Go on then,' Mike prompts. 'Play it and we'll join in.'

Mrs Short Tony raises the horn to her lips.

Ommm por-por-pommm por-por-pommy-pommy-pommm;
ommm por-por-pommm; por-por-pommm pommm pommm.

We do not join in. She drifts to a halt, with questioning eyes.

'But that's just exactly the same note, over and over again,' I protest.

'Yes, but this is a tenor horn,' she replies. 'It's the higher instruments that play the melody. We just play middle notes.'

Mike the Didgeridooing Barman looks at his watch. 'I've got an early start,' he lies.

'That's me! There!'

I try to put my glass of wine down on the side table, but miss by some distance. Fortunately my hand is wise to this, and brings it back up to settle it back on my knee. It seems uncomfortable there, so my hand raises it again, to my lips. That is better. The television swirls around, across the room.

'Where?'

'You missed it! Rewind a few frames! Go on Tony – rewind.'

TWENTY-FIVE

There she goes, my beautiful wood

'Thanks for driving,' I say to Short Tony, as I lob my bowls gear into the back of his chicken-transporter truck.

'Don't worry. You're welcome,' he replies.

'I'd drive myself, but . . .' I say, trying to think of a plausible reason why I have specifically asked Short Tony to drive when it is my turn to drive and there is a perfectly good car parked outside my house — one which preferably doesn't involve 'there is a bar there'.

'It's really no problem.'

It is wonderful to have Short Tony back in the team. He has backed down, cracked, answered the call of a desperate-for-players captain, like Brian Eno going on the eighties 'Here and Now' package tour. It is good of him – he doesn't particularly want another commitment on top of his new motorbiking hobby, and I know he will be a bit nervous on picking up the woods again. We have to do everything in our power to make him feel comfortable and wanted once more.

'I offered Eddie a lift too, if that's OK?' I ask.

'Evening!' says Eddie, appearing with his bag.

'Hi Eddie,' says Short Tony.

'Have you heard from Karen?' I ask Eddie, who shakes his head.

'I'd better give her a quick call,' I mutter. 'Just in case she hasn't got a lift.'

'Eh?' blurts Mr Karen, from the other end of the phone. 'Tonight? She's in the shower, and then we were going to watch *Quantum of Solace* on DVD.'

'Ring me back,' I command. 'We need to go round to Karen's,' I tell Short Tony.

Short Tony drives us to Karen's house. My mobile phone rings as we approach – I wave it around a bit before I answer, but nobody comments.

'She'll be ready in five minutes,' says Mr Karen, wearily.

'I've forgotten my beer towel,' says Eddie.

Short Tony drives us to Eddie's house. Eddie picks up his beer towel. A thought occurs to me.

'I've forgotten my beer towel,' I admit.

Short Tony drives us to my cottage. I pick up my beer towel. My phone rings once more.

'It's my new Sony Ericsson phone!' I exclaim, but nobody says anything.

'Ready to go,' says Karen. 'Sorry – I had no idea there was a game tonight. We were going to watch *Quantum of Solace* on DVD.'

Short Tony drives us to Karen's house. We arrive at the green three minutes late, hurrying with our bags to the clubhouse whilst Short Tony fiddles with the lock on his truck.

The nights are drawing in; the dew is slowing the greens. The air is slightly chillier; next week we move to six thirty starts to beat the gathering gloom.

Fourth in the charts, and we'll get no higher than that now, no matter what the result tonight. But that's fine. Granted, it's not Led Zeppelin, but it's not Sid Owen either. I am thirty-thing years old, and I can appreciate 'We Are the Champions' as a piece of music rather than an aspiration, although I am still a bit glad that I am not a loser whom people have no time for.

We wander over to rink eleven on the wide and flat green that beholds Heacham Social Club, a fine building in the neo-Georgian style with a snooker table, Sky TV and a selection of real ales, or cokes for Short Tony. It has a brick pavilion and the holy of holies for players like us – little wheeled trolley things that you can push around and use to collect the woods, to save you from having to kick them back to the edge of the green after each end, using your deeply deeply unfashionable shoes.

We set down our stuff and wait, leaning against the railings, in almost the exact spot where TV's John Motson stood a few years back, watching us play on his way to a sporting charity dinner, giving us a taste of the new celebrity- and media-driven horizons of bowls.

The opposition arrives, bearing scoreboards and mats.

'Why don't you go second?' asks Big Andy.

'What?'

'I'll lead, you go second. You're always saying you'd like a chance to go second.'

I gape at the man. This is not quite up there with Genesis calling Phil Collins out from behind the drum kit in order to sing and front the band, but it's at least as good as offering him a bass guitar and getting him to do the 'wooo woooo's. 'Really? If you don't mind?' I reply, trying to show a bit of self-confidence. 'We can always swap back if I'm shit.'

Second! I am chuffed to bits. I 'have a good game' with extra jollity and enthusiasm. I jiggle the wood in my hand, feeling its shape, weighing up its mass and likely velocity across the surface, eager upon eager to get going. I am like a small child who has been put in charge of the monkey percolator. And there are monkeys to be percolated.

Second is where it's at. It is the dog's bollocks. It is where you go if you know your percentages, if you can make up for a disappointing lead or can build on a good start to leave the skip with some options. It is where you go if you can creep through gaps, if you can knock woods up, if you can sweep around and behind things to tiny tolerances. And, if the lead has put in two brilliant woods – two that nestle and nudge the cott and that can't possibly be bettered by anything but a show of brilliance – if you can be trusted not to fuck it up.

'Well you bowl, Alex!' exclaims Big Andy, and we exchange an awkward high ten before the skips take their turns. He is spot on – everything that I am doing is going right. I am bowling like a dream, like a natural, like a Sky Bowls Professional. And even if Alex Marshall's Premier League dream is over, dumped out in the first play-off by the very Robert Chisholm whom he had beaten in the group stages, his near-namesake (me) is lining himself up as a successor, as the next one into the Barry Hearn stable, as the first true bowler of the rock and roll generation. 'Motty, you are missing something,' I breathe quietly into the Norfolk air before taking the scorecard from my pocket in order to record our two shots up.

I cast my playing partner an affectionate glance.

'Stop playing with the trolleys,' I tell him sternly.

Looking across the rinks, we are ahead on every single one. 'Well you bowl, Tony!' I shout, as I spot Short Tony drawing in efficiently in his game that's being played on the far end of the expansive green. The whole scene fills me with pride at this nation's sporting prowess – athletes bustling between shots and crossovers, laying down mats, wicking in nicely on backhands, rolling it out, taking the cott, encouraging it to bend like a good wood should.

And I am settling down next to the cott, creeping through my gaps, knocking the right woods up and not fucking it up.

I am not fucking it up. I'm not saying that I have low aspirations, but I am not fucking it up, and it doesn't get any better than this.

* * *

If Alex Marshall fucked it up, Paul Foster is over the moon as Brian Potter, chairman of Potters Leisure Resort, presents him with a big silver trophy in the shape of some woods. He has beaten Darren Burnett in the final, and taken the title for the second year running.

I've missed Burnett's progress through the group stages. A policeman in his day job (according to the Sky people), he radiates confidence and authority – although something in his bearing suggests that an athletic criminal might have the edge in a chase on foot, especially uphill. A bowls-playing crime fighter! There is an entire TV series in that. He takes a gracious step back and applauds his opponent warmly.

As for Paul Foster, he holds the trophy aloft, his Premier League dream realised a second year running. It is a recurring Premier League dream. The camera lingers on the shot for but a couple of seconds.

As the credits immediately roll, something nags at me. It takes me a few seconds to realise – there is no analysis. There is no Alan Hansen or Mark Lawrenson figure to extend the moment, dwelling on every key episode, repeating each shot from different angles, telling you this and telling you that with the benefit of decades of expertise and hindsight. But what more can be said? No extra track that wasn't good enough the first time round, no remix crashing in after the final chord fades perfectly into the air.

That's the thing with the Sky coverage. It's got class.

* * *

'So do you reckon we should introduce the power play?' chuckles Huey, waving his lager around alarmingly to indicate the spotlights.

I am glad somebody is of the same progressive mind as me. I have taken to Huey. He appears to be a sound man who knows his bowls. 'Have you been watching it?' I ask.

'Oh, you know. When I can. It's always funny seeing them lot on the TV.'

'Them lot?'

'You must have played with a few of those?' interjects Karen.

'Played?' I repeat.

It transpires that Huey is a regular county player, who enters major bowls tournaments and who is on first name terms with the top players. I gaze at him, knocked over with awe and respect. He tells me some anecdotes about the circuit. Greg Harlow is this man's Sultans of Ping.

It has been a funny old season. From a shambolic bunch, short of players and bowling with the wrong bias, to fourth in the league table, considering spotlight introduction and recruiting a top international bowls player to our ranks (and getting Short Tony back). But that is bowls for you. Across the village, across the world, it's a sport whose time has come.

'D'yew want another pint, then?' he asks.

* * *

'I think it went pretty well,' I tell the Chipper Barman. 'Obviously it would have been better if you were there with your bass.'

I reflect on the guitar/didgeridoo combo. Bass guitar would definitely add something, as would the removal of the didgeridoo. But if Mike could get his drums back, we'd have the beginnings of a good little outfit. I'll chat to him about it at the right time – I don't want to intimidate him if all he's ever done is a tour of Europe. The Chipper Barman hands over my pint glass, but a family are waiting to order food so we do not continue the conversation. I back into the throng, clutching my beer like a small child. Snatches of conversation resound around the room; I home in towards one.

'Well you'll not need that,' I hear Eddie laugh, speaking to a person unidentified about an object unknown, 'where you're going.'

Where he is going? Where is who going? Who is going somewhere? I barge my way into the conversation to find out more.

He is talking to Mike the Drumming Barman.

Why? Why are things always so cruelly snatched from my grasp? We have only just got a band together – the first one in years – one with potential. And it has already fallen to pieces. I sip my Wherry morosely as Mike the ex-Drumming Barman talks me through his prospective backpacking route round South America.

'The idea is that I'll end up in Brazil,' he continues, oblivious.

'I hope you have a brilliant time,' I lie. I hope he gets robbed and then bitten by a poisonous snake, on the penis. It is just selfish, what he is doing. Selfish.

'I'm going to have a big leaving party,' he explains. 'You're all invited. Free food and drinks.'

That is the thing with Mike the ex-Drumming Barman. He is a fundamentally decent chap. I get some directions off him, and a date. We will miss him, but a barman has to do what a barman has to do.

'We could all play at the party,' he suggests. 'Do a gig.'

I blink at him.

'A gig?'

TWENTY-SIX

I am gonna talk about doubts and confusion

So he is off to faraway lands.

He is leaving – out of the village, out of the county, out of the country and round the world. Of his own accord, to have some fun – not running scared like a weaselly weed from Strategic HR Initiatives. I am sorry to say goodbye to Mike the ex-Drumming Barman as in the big scheme of things we have only just met. He's always been a nice chap and has made the journey from 'somebody who I'd ask for a pint from' to 'somebody who I'd buy a pint for (but could you pour it yourself whilst you're there, and get me one as well? And some crisps)'.

But it has sabotaged the village band at its very genesis. Now Mike the ex-Drumming Barman has gone all solo Phil Collins on us and we are left forlorn, like a Norfolk Tony Banks, a Fenland Mike Rutherford, wondering what we've done to deserve this abandonment.

We will never play Stoke Ferry village hall now.

I stand in the aggressively countrified kitchen at his leaving party, reflecting on our shattered dreams. Actually I am not doing that much reflection, as there is a foxy blonde lawyer lady to whom I am chatting. In fact, looking round the room, Mike the ex-Drumming

Barman seems to have a number of glamorous and urbane friends that he has never once introduced in all his time in the village. He is selfishness personified.

I can see that she is impressed by my sophistication. Despite a general stumblingness around the ladies, I can actually be very witty and urbane and, in fact, get more witty and more urbane with each glass of wine I drink, until I am so witty and so urbane that I just get overcome and have to have a lie down.

The foxy blonde lawyer laughs uproariously at one of my jokes. Actually, she laughs quite quietly and understatedly, being too classy to really roar like most people do when I say something witty. I impress her with my bowls anecdotes and her eyes dart round the room nervously, worried that she is making it too obvious that she is interested in me. I metaphorically adjust my tie. It is unusual that I find someone like me to talk to who oozes class and breeding. Short Tony and Big Andy swig beer like the Neanderthals that they are. I sip my Blossom Hill with suavity.

In the lounge, the Chipper Barman is setting up his bass guitar. This combined introductory and farewell gig – I should be excited, but there is a mounting sense of unease in my mind about it. Not only have we not quite yet got round to practising any songs, but there appears to be a complete absence of familiar and friendly faces at the party – faces that will be supportive no matter how unpolished we are. You need at least a few. Just a few. As it is, Eddie is away; there is no sign of John Twonil, or Glen, or Len the Fish; the other barmen are working or set for an early shift tomorrow. There aren't even any of the casual village pub regulars who I know by sight.

Put it out of my mind. I am being foolish. All these people here tonight – each and every one of them are good friends of the ex-Drumming Barman. And he is leaving on his long journey, and will not see them for some time. They will be nice to us, on his behalf.

I pour the foxy blonde lawyer another glass of wine. I pour myself a bigger one. There is a problem lurking in my mind. I know the problem; I have faced the problem before. I want the problem to go away. The problem does not go away. In the end I do what I have done so many times before. I take the problem, club it over the head, tie it up and gag it with a scarf, and force it, struggling and screaming, behind a small Scooby-Doo bookcase in my mind.

I have to admit that there might have been the smallest germlet of truth in the LTLP's assessment of my musical career. I have – through unfortunate circumstances beyond my control – played some shit gigs over the years. I've performed when there's been two people in the audience, when the band has taken it in turns to jump off the stage and join in the sporadic applause between songs. I've had an open packet of cheese and onion crisps thrown at me. I've played at parties where the audience has been too cool and cynical to do anything other than stand with their arms crossed, challenging us to entertain.

This was when I was younger. I was a bit stronger then.

I choke when I am under pressure. I know that from bowls. I am always rubbish on the twenty-first and final end, when the scores are level. This is like the twenty-first and final end, when the scores are level, at the World Championships at Potters Leisure Resort, the Bull and Gate, Kentish Town (Venue of Legends), of bowls. It seemed like a good idea at the time, but I haven't a clue what I'm doing here, in front of an audience that I do not know. As a three piece?!? I am a mental. I am truly, truly a mental.

A million glasses of Blossom Hill later and I find myself in the lounge. The guests are gathered round, expectantly. I fiddle with a guitar lead with some nervousness. Musicians with three-piece experience will immediately identify an issue here – viz. the onus on me as the guitar player to get the songs right. Drummers really just have to sit at the back hitting things, whilst everybody who has ever counted the strings knows that the bass is only four-sixths as difficult to play as the guitar. I am not doing down bass players or anything, but even with four strings to worry about, they only need to play one at a time, and even then only occasionally, in time with the drummer.

Beside me, the Chipper Barman, sober from rushing straight from work, tunes his bass – all four, easy, one-at-a-time strings of it. He may well be feeling as apprehensive as I am, but exudes a zen-like calm that comes from his advanced martial-arts training (and only having to play the bass). The ex-Drumming Barman adjusts a screw on his hi-hat. That is the thing with drummers. They are forever adjusting screws on their hi-hats.

I finish another glass of Blossom Hill. The problem breaks out of its bibliophiliac gaol and rushes up to hit me in the face with a hammer.

I can play the guitar and sing when I'm drunk. I have no problem in playing the guitar and singing when I'm drunk. I'm not very *good* when I'm drunk, but I can get by, as long as I'm not too ambitious about speed, and chord shapes, and dexterity etc. I realise, when I pick up the guitar, that I am drunk. Curse that Blossom Hill! I had always assumed that it was non-alcoholic. Surely with a name like 'Blossom Hill', Blossom Hill should not get you drunk? The drink-aware people should look into this. It is tantamount to marketing Rohypnol.

I can play the guitar and sing when I'm drunk. The problem is that my mind goes blank. Completely blank, like it has been drained of all thought and memory by an alien mind-draining device.

On drunk autopilot, I can do the chords to some early Leonard

Cohen. I can pick out verses to the odd Jake Thackray song. All sorts of bits and pieces – verses from this, choruses from that, snatches of words. The rhythm parts from most Pink Floyd songs. 'I Don't Like Motor Racing'. Moody, elephantine, neo-psychedelic echoey effects-laden solos. The odd simple riff.

But I don't know any songs.

The glamorous and urbane people mill about in the lounge, waiting for us to begin, clutching glasses of wine and talking about glamorous and urbane things. I have a strong suspicion that they do not want to listen to instrumental versions of the early repertoire of Leonard Cohen and nor will they appreciate a demonstration of how I can combine a delay pedal and a phaser to make my guitar sound a bit like a helicopter.

I have two get-out clauses, two pop/rock songs that I can wrestle out from my subconscious when I am drunk, two drawn from my entire repertoire of Wildebeeste, of Where's Johnny Christmas?, of Steerpike, of the Precious Things – of the hundreds upon hundreds upon hundreds of classic tracks that I have on CD and MP3, that I've spent my life loving.

They are 'Ain't No Pleasing You' by Chas 'n' Dave, and 'I'm Gonna Be (500 Miles)' by The Proclaimers.

I have never been a busker, but that is what people expect from you. If you can play the guitar then everybody assumes that means you can do the riffs from 'Brown Sugar' and 'Honky Tonk Woman', that you know the solo to 'All Right Now', that you can lead a sing-song of 'Hotel California' and 'American Pie'. You can be a lousy guitarist, but as long as you know four chords, can remember words and have the busker's instinct, then you will be all right in situations such as these. But I'm not like that – I am a creative artiste, a specialist lead bowler of the musical world. As far as I know, nobody ever asked Alfred Brendel to jam along with 'Great

Balls of Fire'. Different styles. He would be lost on the heavy rock riffs.

Chas 'n' Dave! The Proclaimers! Why? Why? Why, out of the entire popular music songbook from the last fifty years, have these artists alone etched themselves so deeply into my mind that I can strum and sing their two greatest hits whilst comatose from alcohol and stage fright? Why?

And why did we not practise?

'What are we going to play?' hisses the Chipper Barman, awaking me from – but also to – the full horror of my circumstances. Despite the brilliant lighting in the living room, he seems to have drifted backwards, the solid lines of his shape fading very slightly so that he melts into the background, which is an interesting scientific phenomenon and something that should be studied further by scientists should resources allow.

There is still nobody to cling on to in the audience. Aside from Short Tony and Big Andy, who are presumably waiting for the opportunity to throw open packets of cheese and onion crisps, they are all strangers – the beautiful circle of Mike the ex-Drumming Barman, waiting to be impressed by the small band he's put together to entertain.

And it clearly is up to him to carry this one. They are his friends, and any love in the room is for him. The Chipper Barman and me – we are but props in his own joyful farewell; just unprepared props, who have not met up beforehand to rehearse or to talk about what songs we know, which is the usual practice in the music business when playing important gigs. I try to catch the eye of the foxy blonde lawyer, now chatting to another man to pass the time until I am available again, but I have to stand on tiptoe to see past a tall person and this makes me a bit dizzy and I start to sway. Expectation blasts out, like someone is shooting me with a big expectation gun. I take another few glugs of Blossom Hill from my recharged glass, then drop my guitar pick and have to scrabble around on the carpet for it. The Chipper Barman's bass amplifier looms above me. If there were to be a loud diversion from behind then I could possibly crawl behind it and hide. No luck. Too many cables. Back on my feet. Another swig of Blossom Hill.

Mike the ex-Drumming Barman stands and works the crowd, thanking them for coming and assuring them that they are all lovely friends. All of a sudden I feel an irrational surge of confidence poking its head out from nowhere. He's a popular chap. With me and the Chipper Barman as his backing band, we could possibly carry things off. I start chopping away at a chord. Chigga Chigga. Chigga Chigga. Some applause. The room falls silent and focuses on Mike the ex-Drumming Barman, oozles of goodwill now markedly dripping from all his friends. He gives them a smile and a wink as he makes to return to his stool, and I know that we'll be all right. The first gig for years.

Chigga Chigga. Chigga Chigga.

'Phone call for Mike the ex-Drumming Barman,' announces a voice.

'Won't be a second, chaps,' he promises, and disappears from the room, all that confidence following him, watched by the faces in the crowd.

Chigga Chigga.

The crowd switches to us, heads turning in utter unison like you see on the tennis. Expectation squared, raised to the power of X thousand pounds plus one. I look out upon faces. There are faces everywhere. Faces. Faces. Some people seem to have at least eight or nine of them, all looking at me personally. Eyebrows alternately raised and lowered, and a few arms starting to cross. I exchange a glance with the Chipper Barman. He has melted back so far now that all I can see is a guitar lead attached to a vague shimmer with a goatee. I have played some bad gigs in my life, but have always got through them. But now, with the wisdom of years, I realise what is going to happen. For the first time in my life, I am facing the experience of the bum's rush.

Sometimes people talk about a dream in which they find themselves naked on a theatre stage in front of an audience of two thousand people. This moment is very much like that, aside from the fact that it is not a dream, there are six thousand people in the auditorium, and I am not entirely naked as I am sporting a bra and women's shoes.

Behind me, huge screens have been erected to project secretly obtained footage of me very carefully and methodically masturbating a hen.

I spot my mother, sitting stony-faced in the front row.

I always get stage fright. I always have, but I have been too cool to admit it. Some artistes say that having stage fright gives them the necessary adrenaline and energy for a performance. Personally, I find that it makes me frightened.

'O God of Live Performance – What Hast Thou Got Against Me?' I bellow, in my head.

Chigga Chigga.
  Chigga Chigga.
  Chig Chig Chig Chig Chig.
  I sway again slightly. 'It'll have to be the Proclaimers one,' I hiss over my shoulder. The Chipper Barman peers out from his shimmer for a moment, and gives me a look of casual pity, like he were the LTLP, cunningly disguised in a beard.
  Chig Chig Chig Chig Chig Chig Chig.

The Chipper Barman joins in on bass. Bom Bom Bom Bom.

I remember something important. 'Are there any people from Scotland here?' I mumble into the microphone.

No response. A few bemused shakes of the head. This is good. If one is going to sing a Proclaimers song, one has to affect a broad Scottish accent. It is not quite the same as blacking up to sing 'What's Going On', but the principle is broadly similar.

'Oh good,' I affirm, to the audience of lawyers, architects, accountants and marketing people.

Chig Chig Chig Cha-Cha Chig Chig Chig.

Whilst I am Chigging, I perform a sort of straining and stretching motion with my neck, in order that I can peer down the corridor into which the ex-Drumming Barman had departed. There is no sign. We have been Chigging an introduction for a good two minutes now, and there will be no miracle escape. There is nothing for it.

The mat is laid, the cott is cast. I sing the first verse of 'I'm Gonna Be (500 Miles)' by The Proclaimers.

I then sing the chorus.

Two things transpire from this, which I find interesting despite everything. Firstly, when I claim to know the song, it turns out that I kind of know the chorus and the dadilee-ada bit, and the fact that the first verse is something about waking up, but that is really the extent of my lyrical knowledge. I improvise instead.

The second thing is that the chorus really does draw its power from two magnificent Scottish voices in close harmony. In the original, that is.

I sing the dadilee-ada bit. Some people sing 'dadilee-ada' back at me, which is encouraging. I sing it again and it happens again. The first bit is over.

Chig Chig Chig Cha-Cha Chig Chig Chig.

I steal another look at the Chipper Barman, who gives me a slight shrug and melts further back into the ether of hyperspace, becoming completely invisible. Another desperate peer, and then a hint of movement over my shoulder through the window onto the lit patio. I can see the ex-Drumming Barman outside, yabbering into the cordless phone. He is clearly involved in a long conversation.

I sort of extend the bit between the verses with some more Chigs. The problem is it's not one of those songs that you can pad out. There isn't a guitar solo, or an improvisey bit, or anything like that. It's too tightly written. Three-minute, three-chord pop. If we had chosen 'Atom Heart Mother' then I'd be on far safer ground. I stare glassy-eyed into the crowd. People are clearly growing restless with my Chigs. I don't know the words to the second verse.

I sing the first verse again, followed by the chorus. Then the dadilee-ada bit. I get some dadilee-adas back. For safety reasons, I sing the dadilee-ada bit a few more times. Unfortunately dadilee-adas seem to be subject to a law of diminishing returns and before too long we are all back to the Chig Chig bits. The Chig Chig bits never really had any cachet to begin with, but they allow me to pause and collect my thoughts.

The shadow of the Chipper Barman stands there, impassive. Bom Bom Bom Ba Ba Bom Bom Bom. What I would give to have his zen calm. There is still no ex-Drumming Barman whatsoever, and his guests are starting to question the value of the entertainment on offer. The Blossom Hill has really hit me now, but the alcohol seems to bring some clarity, and I suddenly have a brainwave as to what to do next.

I sing the first verse of 'I'm Gonna Be (500 Miles)' by The Proclaimers.

Now the only noise in the room is me. The chorus, again,

goes badly until the very end – when there is a little cheer! I knew I would win them over in the end! But it is not for me. The ex-Drumming Barman has reappeared through the patio doors behind us.

Just in time for the dadilee-adas. He is such a glory boy. We finish on a crescendo and there is a smattering of applause.

'Sorry chaps,' says the ex-Drumming Barman. 'Right. Shall we do a song?'

So that is that.

Never go back. Never try to recapture.

I have my bowls, I have my important househusbanding role. Why did I ever think I could make it more? The music boat has passed – I have missed it. It is time to stop pretending. Really time, this time.

Much later, the remaining Blossom Hill and the evening's immense vats of adrenaline have got the better of me. I am slumped on the toilet, dadilee-adas echoing round my head, the nerves of earlier finally taking their toll. I have also broken the lock on the toilet door, but my attempts to mend it have been ham-fisted, and urgency has in the end taken priority.

Some footstep noises approach from outside, and at the last minute I make the connection that they must be created by some-body's feet. I make a weak effort to grab the door handle.

'Oh God, I'm really so, so sorry,' she stammers.

I gaze up at the foxy blonde lawyer uncomprehendingly, all the while rocking very slowly and subtly from side to side, wondering if there is anything that I can possibly say, my pants nestling softly and comfortably round my ankles.

She backs away and pulls the door quietly shut.

Who knows where the time goes?

The winter falls hard upon this part of Norfolk.

It is as if nature balances out the beauty and tranquillity of the summer months by unleashing a storming howling fury of weather across the village and its surrounds. Essential services, such as the windmill and the cider place, close down; the chip shop goes to emergency skeleton hours. Egg production falls to a bare minimum level as the chickens mope around in the garden, pecking away at the LTLP's struggling pot plants whilst absorbing what daylight they can.

At the bottom of the hill the snow drifts in off the fields, melts slightly and then freezes once more – making the road impassable to anybody who would not really, *really* be in trouble should they not turn up for work. Up in the loft, my canvas bag of bowls squats forlornly and near-frozen. The television sits more happily in the corner, warmed by the fire – but *Bargain Hunt* is just a distant memory. Likewise, cobwebs gather on Solitaire, or at least the specific portion of the hard disk drive on the PC that has Solitaire on it.

But then spring arrives, and the first blossom pokes through, and the birds start cheeping and Jim rings from the cider place to say that actually as I and Short Tony are such good customers he may as well start bringing crates of cider directly over to us on a trailer. And the chickens look happier, and the walk home from the village pub is marginally less cold and wet – although I don't get to go to the village pub quite as often as I used to.

It is all very confusing.

There is a message. John Twonil wants to know if I would like to play snooker. I would like to play snooker, but what makes him think that I have time for such things? I regretfully decline the snooker. I have already spent a valued morning helping Big Andy and Eddie hack back a hedge at the green – a new, cosy, nestling green on which we are hoping to play this season. A green with a cosy clubhouse, with a little raised area for spectators, with some more consistent grass.

A green with a bar.

Peck! Peck! Peck! Chicken Two – or it might be Chicken One, or indeed Chicken Three, Five or Anne Robinson – is munching away at what is probably a marguerite, or a lupin, or a geranium. It looks ever so contented, in its little chicken world. I watch it fondly through the back window.

Across the road, Big Andy's chickens are unrecognisable now. They have fattened out and grown sleek feathers – like proper, cared-for hens. Even J Lo's arse protrusion seems to be a bit less massive – and she has become the proudest chicken of all, strutting around the place like a princess around her chicken-wire castle. Her poise is such that you would not imagine that she ever inhabited a battery cage. In fact, she has developed some airs. A chicken with airs is never edifying, but who can blame her in the circumstances? She may strut around a bit now. But deep down, she is still Jenny from the Flock.

I am very pleased for Big Andy. I don't want to sound like some soft townie, but watching them blossom from scraggy, unloved, half-alive creatures to proud and beautiful fowl has been wonderful to behold. To think, I once looked down socially upon them. It has been like *My Fair Lady* except with chickens instead of Audrey Hepburn, and less singing.

They would be welcome in my coop any day.

The LTLP appears from the kitchen. 'I've cooked a bit of extra bacon rind for them,' she mentions. I smile at her, a broad, broad smile.

'I knew you loved them really,' I say.

But she is not listening to me. She is looking over my shoulder, her jaw dropping open in fury.

'Get *off*!' she screams at the closed window. 'Get off my fucking plants!'

I beat a hasty retreat. There, in the kitchen, I am greeted by a pair of wary eyes studying me intently with a mixture of interest and concern.

I look at the Baby. The Baby looks at me.

I can't help but form the impression, if I think about things very, very, very hard, that I possibly didn't use my sabbatical to the full extent envisaged by the inventors of the term. I mean, granted, I organised a cleaner, and played the piano a bit, and cooked some nice dinners with a potato. But it does seem that, given today's circumstances, I rather took for granted having some nice Time on my Hands.

Frankly, I no longer have a problem with knowing what to do with my day.

It is probably meal time, or time to do a nappy or something. As I gaze at her, I am once more overwhelmed by the situation. The LTLP will be going back to work very shortly, leaving me in sole charge. Not just of a house. Of a Baby. It is the most important role and responsibility that I have ever had in my life, ever ever.

The Baby inclines her head slightly at me, no doubt weighing up the pros and cons of passing an emergency note to Social Services in a used sleepsuit. I sit down on the bottom step of the new staircase and start biting my nails.

The Vegetable Delivery people have gone broke. I read the letter with sadness. They are a victim of the economic downturn. Woolworths, MFI, the Vegetable Delivery Service. It is like all the icons of British retailing are collapsing around our ears. I had thought that the Vegetable Delivery Service would be OK – they had always seemed busy and cheerful, and gave great customer service.

Granted, their lettuces were occasionally less crunchy than credit itself, and there was the odd inappropriate substitution: parsnips for Jerusalem artichokes; courgettes for radishes; a Vegetable Delivery Man (with a beard) for the fit Vegetable Delivery Lady. But it was a nice little business that deserved to do better. They encouraged me to eat vegetables, by the simple fact that they appeared at my door every Thursday morning. Now I will have to buy them from a shop, and let's face it, I will never bother to do that, as they are vegetables. Booooo, boooooo and triple boooooooooo.

I carry my final box indoors sadly, and wave goodbye to the Vegetable Delivery Lady. We have had some great times together, but I suppose all good things must come to an end.

* * *

I have found some old sheet music, the inside front cover of which boasts a pencil-scribbled dedication to my grandmother. There is something that I have been meaning to do for ages – call it an induction, if you like. A family induction. I gently sit the Baby in her bouncy chair and place it in the optimal position for musical appreciation.

'This is called "When the Blackbird Says Bye-Bye", I inform her. 'By Art Noel,' I add.

I don't bother going into the story of how famous he was, and how all his best songs were written on my historic restored piano, and how by playing her this tune I am linking her with a family history and connection that goes back almost a century. She is only interested in my performance. I clear my throat. At the last minute I wonder whether I should invite the chickens in to bear witness, but I decide against it.

'We've been apart for a long, long time,' I croon tunefully. The Baby stares at me in alarm. 'Honnnn-nnney don't you sigh.'

It's not a bad lyric when you come to think about it. There is more beneath the surface than you would realise. 'Just keeeep this lit-tle song in your heart . . . and the clouds will sooooon rolllll byyyy.'

It is time to hit the chorus, which I am sure that she will enjoy.

'When the blackbird says "*bye bye*", I chirp, cheerfully. 'And the blue-bird says "*hello*" . . . we'll be back together agaainnnn . . . there'll be sunbeams in the sky . . .'

The Baby bounces along, though completely off the beat. A small concern scuttles across my mind that she will not be an almost-successful musician like me. But she is still young. There will be time. At the end of the song I sign off with a big lyrical and instrumental flourish. The Baby is agog. She is part of our musical history now. It is in the genes.

I put the sheet music aside and carefully replace the banjo in its stand. One day I will learn this song on the piano.

My small alcove above the stairs that was designed for hanging a Fender Telecaster in now contains a pot. It was explained to me quite forcibly that alcoves are meant to contain pots, not guitars

– even guitar-shaped alcoves. A large pot sits in it, slightly off-centre. It's quite a nice pot, by pot standards – I can't say that I object to it overly. The guitar is filed away in the back room – I rarely get it out these days, although I sometimes wander in with a duster and have a stroke. Instead, I've been concentrating on the acoustic stuff. Just rhythm. Tunes. The things that have been missing from the whole of my life. A repertoire of tunes. Busking, if you like.

I did play one more gig – when Glen from the village pub hosted a small music festival. He had arranged for a renowned guitar player to entertain, alongside an actor from *The Archers* who would do some form of song and dance routine. In the event, neither of them was there. The replacement entertainment comprised me, Len the Fish's son and a man with a moustache who could play 'Gimme Some Loving' on the keyboards. We played that, and 'Lazing on a Sunny Afternoon' and 'Suspicious Minds' and, yes, 'All Right Now'. I told Dave and Iain about it when they got in touch via Facebook to see how I was. We contacted Simon and laughed together about old times. Iain made speculative noises about a reunion tour, but I think the moment might have passed, even though the BBC now has the motor racing rights back.

The building regulations certificate has finally come through. I have completed the last two things that the Building Inspector ordered me to do – viz., to change the hinges on the upstairs windows so that they open wide enough that you can get through them if there's a fire, and to put bars across the upstairs windows so that you can't fall out of them if you trip over. It is good to get all that sorted out. The Building Inspector wished me well and drove off into the sunset, no doubt to share a pint and some work anecdotes with the soft egg directorate.

But it is a nice cottage, suitable for modern-day living. We have done all right. Gripping the newel post at the top of the staircase, I give it an affectionate thump. It reassuringly does not collapse into a grillion pieces.

I pause at the doorway to our bedroom. It is square and chunky; it is inset in a wall eighteen inches thick and is only around five foot high – people were shorter when it was built. In fact, it's less a doorway than an opening. It aspires to doorway status. Its size and shape reminds me of something, and I wander back downstairs, pondering.

'I've got a good idea for that doorway,' I muse. 'The one into the bedroom.'

The LTLP scrutinises me, adopting the expression that she uses to deforest the ground elder. 'I can already tell,' she drawls, 'that this is going to be the most ridiculous thing that you've ever suggested in your life.'

I am stung by her barbed comment. 'That's a bit unfair,' I protest.

'Go on then. Tell me your good idea. Tell me.'

I have lost many things in my life. From big: close family and friends; to trivial: bowls games and plectrums. In between are the intangibles. Many years of friendship that I could have kept with band mates. Ham. Dreams. Hopes. Aspirations.

Scooby-Doo bookcases.

I've come to terms, I think, with the dreams and hopes stuff. But the loss of the Scooby-Doo bookcase still leaves an empty hole. A man should have a Scooby-Doo bookcase or suchlike in his life. Yes, I have an antique piano, and a Fender Telecaster guitar, and a lovely Baby, and some chickens – but they are not enough for a man who wants to flick V-signs and pull moonies at the McStarbuckisation of life. Plus there will be no interesting thing for the *Escape to the Country* people to include on their show should I ever decide to sell up and the house be viewed by the next Max who comes along.

'I was thinking about the fact that I haven't got a Scooby-Doo bookcase any more,' I explain, leaning carefully on the newel post at the base of the staircase. 'So I was thinking . . .'

'Yes . . .?' There is a glazed look in her eyes, like somebody has administered a controlled substance supplied directly from para-counsellors at Relate to take the pain away. I do love her ever so much, even if sometimes she does not understand.

'Well, if I got some wardrobe doors, I could sort of build a wardrobe-looking thing in that doorway. But it wouldn't really be a wardrobe. It would be our bedroom. So to get into our bedroom you would walk through the wardrobe.'

She gives a sharp intake of breath.

'Like in Narnia,' I add, by way of explanation.

'Then,' I continue, 'when people come to stay and we show them round, we can pretend that it is just a wardrobe. And when we go to bed they will say, "Why are you climbing into the wardrobe?" and we will say "Aha!" and they will be amazed and astonished when they discover there is a whole room beyond.

'Like in Narnia,' I add, to fill the endless silence that follows.

Notes and acknowledgements

A few names were changed, out of courtesy or for clarity. Thank you to my friends, to my neighbours and to my bowls colleagues. To Wildebeeste, to Where's Johnny Christmas?, to Steerpike, to the Precious Things. To Zoe, who sort of started the whole thing off – and to Andrew and Anna, who kept it going.

You can find some extra notes on *Sex and Bowls and Rock and Roll* at www.sexandbowlsandrockandroll.com/some-extra-notes

What's next?

Tell us the name of an author you love

| Alex Marsh | Go ▶ |

and we'll find your next great book.

book army

www.bookarmy.com